The Girl from Leam Lane

Also by Piers Dudgeon

Catherine Cookson Country (Ed.)
Enchanted Cornwall: A Memoir of Daphne du Maurier (Ed.)
Dickens' London
The Spirit of Britain
Village Voices
The English Vicarage Garden
The Country Child
In the Public Interest
The Virgin Alternative Guide to British Universities
Josephine Cox: Memories of a Northern Childhood
Breaking out of the Box: The Biography of Edward de Bono
Lifting the Veil: The Biography of Sir John Tavener
The Woman of Substance: The Life and Works
of Barbara Taylor Bradford

The Girl from Leam Lane

The Life and Writing of
CATHERINE COOKSON

PIERS DUDGEON

REVISED AND EXPANDED CENTENARY EDITION

headline

First published in 1997
by HEADLINE BOOK PUBLISHING

First published in paperback in 1998
by HEADLINE BOOK PUBLISHING

Centenary Edition first published in 2006
by HEADLINE BOOK PUBLISHING

1

Cataloguing in Publication Data is available from the British Library

ISBN 0 7553 1497 2

Set in Palatino by Avon DataSet Ltd, Bidford on Avon, Warwickshire

Printed and bound in Great Britain by
Clays Ltd, St Ives plc

Headline's policy is to use papers that are natural, renewable and recyclable
products and made from wood grown in sustainable forests. The logging
and manufacturing processes are expected to conform to the
environmental regulations of the country of origin.

HEADLINE BOOK PUBLISHING
A division of Hodder Headline
338 Euston Road
London NW1 3BH

www.headline.co.uk
www.hodderheadline.com

Contents

The map shows East Jarrow, Tyne Dock and the start of South Shields.

Catherine was born at the southwest corner of the dock on the south side of Leam Lane as it funnels out on to the Jarrow Road. See Chapter Three for full points of reference.

Travelling southwest from her place of birth Leam Lane becomes Simonside Bank and leads up to Simonside School, which she attended from four-and-a-half. 'The country began at Simonside,' Catherine recalls.

To the west of Leam Lane can be seen the New Buildings, the island community to which Catherine moved in 1912 – William Black Street (where she lived), Phillipson Street, Lancaster Street, and the posher end, Simonside Terrace, closest to the Jarrow Road. Beyond Jarrow Road to the north lies the Jarrow Slake, or Slacks (the timber pond) and the River Tyne.

Jarrow Road to the west leads to the barium chemical works and thence into Jarrow, and east under the five arches by Tyne Dock. The first arch was simply a railway bridge leading to the timber yard; the other four took railway lines on to the dock itself.

On the far side of the arches are the dock gates. Directly opposite the gates is Hudson Street, where Catherine went for Kate's beer; second left is Bede Street, where Bob Gompertz had his pawn shop. Continuing beyond Hudson Street are the railway station and Tyne Dock Church and School, which Catherine attended from 1916; then Brinkburn Street, where she would also go for the beer and later Kate lived. In the bottom righthand corner is the workhouse where Catherine was employed from 1924 until 1929.

Preface to the Centenary Edition

A few years before she died Catherine gave an interview. I believe it was to Granada Television. Certainly, they quoted from it in a documentary shown after her death, known as *The Real Catherine Cookson*. In the snippet from the interview they chose to use, Catherine says, 'Several people have tried to write my biography, and it hasn't worked. But I am doing the real facts now, in between times – have been doing for the last year or so. Not that *Our Kate* [her autobiography, published in 1969] wasn't real facts – but there were a dozen more things that happened to me. Why did I have the breakdown? *Why?*'

After she died, people went to look for the manuscript or tapes, which contained 'the real facts'. And they found nothing. The narrator on the TV said: 'Nothing was ever found of this work after Catherine's death.' Nothing was ever found because she had sent the tapes to me.

Two years earlier I had written to Catherine to ask for her co-operation on a book that would reveal the autobiographical nature of her fiction, that would show her readers how much better they knew Catherine through the novels than through the biographical material available. No one hitherto had read the whole of her *oeuvre* and analysed it biographically.

I had known Catherine for a decade or more at that stage. We first met on Wednesday 7 August 1985, at 10.30 a.m., in the study of her house at Langley in Northumberland. It was at her invitation, to discuss an idea I had for *Catherine Cookson Country*, the first illustrated book of the environment out of which she and her work grew, which would be published the following year to coincide with her eightieth birthday. Subsequently, we worked on other books – Lord Chesterfield's *Dear Boy*, an edited collection of letters by Chesterfield to his son about how to get on in the world; *The Country Child*, an anthology of biographical portraits of writers whose childhood had been a significant influence on their work; and *The Spirit of Britain*, an illustrated guide to literary Britain. These projects kept us in touch over the years, although Catherine would have been going against her nature to let anyone escape who might talk to her about books. So, when I wrote to her about this new project, the idea did not fall on stony ground. She liked it, and wanted to co-operate, even though she was bedridden by this time. The last occasion we met face to face was in a sun-filled garden room – her bedroom – at her house in Newcastle, when she was virtually blind. I sat on an upright chair clutching my briefcase on my knees, while she let rip with the usual badinage that kept every visitor on their toes, and her husband Tom knelt quietly beside the bed holding her hand.

I didn't expect to receive much help from Catherine in the state she was in, and was pleased that she had given the project her blessing. I sent Tom a list of questions, to which he replied by letter. Catherine and I spoke on the telephone occasionally, but I could tell she was not well. Then suddenly, without warning, a box arrived in the post with eleven reel-to-reel tapes, which she had been compiling all the time.

My first problem was listening to them. The machine she had used to record them was long out of production and no other machine could play them. Eventually I contacted Grundig, the original manufacturer, and they supplied me with one, telling me that although it was out of production, the machine was still so popular that there was now a user club. Perhaps, I suggested, they should ask Catherine to be their president. I don't think they did.

I realised that what she had sent me was important. At that stage, there had been three biographies, only one of which had seen the light of day. Her agent John Smith had interviewed her for one, but when she read the book she asked him not to publish it, and he complied. A close friend, Dr Manuel Anderson, had even lined up a publisher, Webb and Bower, to release his text about her, but again Catherine had asked him not to proceed. Then Cliff Goodwin's *To Be a Lady* was published, which benefited from only one session with Catherine in which he had not been allowed to take notes. She never gave the book her approval. Now, these tapes were to be the last word, the result of half a lifetime's rethinking since *Our Kate* had come out in the 1960s. Immediately, the whole nature of my book changed to accommodate them, and *The Girl from Leam Lane* was born.

The tapes were quite extraordinary. The old notion that her life had been all about becoming a lady to live up to the gentleman father she had supposed her real father to have been, was swept under the carpet. She was, for the first time, completely frank about the effect of her father's rejection of her, about why she hated her mother, about her rejection by a man eleven years older than her when she was in her early twenties, about the reasons for her nervous breakdown in 1945, and most particularly about 'the sediment of breakdown' that had lain in her subconscious ever since, so that 'an incident, a word, or even a place can stir that sediment again and there you are back full of terror . . . of what? You can't explain, except, in my case, it is aggression, deep aggression, against my early suffering, against my mother, against someone who did me a great evil that I have never written about because the result of it was I learned how to hate, to hate with such intensity that I knew that if I let it have the upper hand my future life would be ruined.'

As was her habit, Catherine compiled the tapes propped up in bed in the dead of night when her memory was best and when she believed her thoughts were most true. I could tell that some of them were recorded with her teeth in, and some with them out, which made transcribing them quite testing, but added to the eeriness and to the terrifying nature of her aggression when she started growling at someone from her past. What comes across clearly is that in order to bring herself back from the brink of insanity Catherine had had to dig deep into her psyche, and had got to know herself more completely than most people dare. So that when she laughs at herself, saying, 'I'm a nasty individual . . . really horrible in some parts of me,' she means it, because she knows the instinctual Catherine deep down below the civilised exterior. That is where she conjured some of her most terrifying fictional characters – at night, alone except for her thoughts, she breathed her life into them.

When *Leam Lane* was first published in 1997, it became a big success, the 'number one' biography of its time, with more than

100,000 hardcover copies sold in a matter of months. Catherine died the following year and was swiftly followed by Tom, which at once made it out of date. There is a great deal to address in terms of their deaths, the final weeks, Tom's swift demise after Catherine's interment, what the wills instructed, where the money went, what the Catherine Cookson Trust did with the millions left to it. And this Centenary Edition, which has been expanded by a third of its original extent, tackles these and many other controversial subjects head on.

Perhaps the best reason for its appearance, however, is that since Catherine's death on 11 June 1998, relations and associates from inside the 'inner sanctum' now feel free to 'say their piece'. In her time, Catherine was adamant that she alone should be the information source. Today there is no longer a bar on interviewing family members and associates, on people who knew Catherine at every stage of her life, even as a child, right up to the moment of her death, and to put their views together with Catherine's, so to shed light on the parts of her life that continue to hit the headlines, such as whether or not she was a lesbian and who her father really was, as well as illuminating those areas so far left untouched, such as the man, Tom Cookson, who emerges as the strength on which she drew to become one of the world's richest women and the most loved writer of the twentieth century.

Acknowledgements

In particular I would like to thank Jack and Sarah Sables, Dr Philip Brantingham, Hannorah White, Peter Hindes, Foster and Rosemary Barker, Theresa Neville, Edna Humphreys, Dr Manuel Anderson, Winnie Richardson, Irene Harding, John Atkinson, Joan Moules, Tony Weeks-Pearson, James Davidson, Steve Blower, Trevor Maxted and John Finch. My thanks, too, to Tyne Tees Television and to The Harry Edwards Spiritual Healing Sanctuary. I am also deeply indebted to Boston University for permission to quote from material in the Howard Gotlieb Archival Research Center at Boston University, to Anthony Sheil and Paul Scherer, and to Peter Chadwick of Wrigleys & Co (Leeds).

Thanks are also due to Keith Bardwell and the Local History section of the South Shields Library, and to Hastings Library, the Hastings Museum and the Newcastle Discovery Museum for access to their written records and for permission to use photographs. Similarly, I would also like to thank Vince Rea of the Bede Gallery (Jarrow), the Beamish North of England Open Air Museum, Newcastle Libraries and Information Services, The Northumberland Record Office, The Gibson Collection, Getty Images, *The Newcastle Journal*, Scottish and Newcastle Breweries, *The South Shields Gazette*. Sarah Sables, and Edna Humphreys for permission to use photographs from their collections.

Every effort has been made to trace copyright owners, and I would be grateful to hear from any that I may have failed to acknowledge.

Books by Catherine Cookson

1950   Kate Hannigan
1951   The Fifteen Streets
1953   Colour Blind
1954   Maggie Rowan
1954   A Grand Man
1956   The Lord and Mary Ann
1957   Rooney
1958   The Menagerie
1958   The Devil and Mary Ann
1959   Slinky Jane
1959   Fanny McBride
1960   Fenwick Houses
1961   Love and Mary Ann
1962   The Garment
1962   Life and Mary Ann
1963   The Blind Miller
1963   The Fen Tiger
1964   Hannah Massey
1964   Marriage and Mary Ann
1965   The Long Corridor
1965   Mary Ann's Angels
1965   Matty Doolin (children's)
1966   The Unbaited Trap
1967   Katie Mulholland
1967   Mary Ann and Bill
1968   The Round Tower
1968   Joe and the Gladiator (children's)

1969   Our Kate (memoirs)
1969   The Nice Bloke
1970   The Glass Virgin
1970   The Invitation
1970   The Nipper
1971   The Dwelling Place
1971   Feathers in the Fire
1972   Pure as the Lily
1972   Blue Baccy (Rory's Fortune; children's)
1973   The Mallen Streak
1974   The Mallen Girl
1974   The Mallen Litter
1974   Our John Willie (children's)
1975   The Invisible Cord
1975   The Gambling Man
1976   The Tide of Life
1976   Mrs Flannagan's Trumpet (children's)
1977   The Girl
1977   Go Tell it to Mrs Golightly (children's)
1978   The Cinder Path
1979   The Man Who Cried
1980   Tilly Trotter
1980   Lanky Jones (children's)
1981   Tilly Trotter Wed
1982   Tilly Trotter Widowed
1982   Nancy Nutall and the Mongrel (children's)
1983   The Whip
1983   Hamilton
1984   The Black Velvet Gown
1984   Goodbye Hamilton
1985   A Dinner of Herbs
1985   Harold
1986   The Moth
1986   Catherine Cookson Country (memoirs)
1986   Bill Bailey
1987   The Parson's Daughter
1987   Bill Bailey's Lot
1988   The Cultured Handmaiden
1988   Bill Bailey's Daughter
1988   Let Me Make Myself Plain (memoirs)
1989   The Harrogate Secret
1989   The Black Candle

Chapter One

Wednesday's Child

The night of Tuesday 19 June 1906 gave way to a warm, early-summer day on Tyneside, a light wind from the south preventing the diffuse clouds from settling into a pall over the river and keeping the temperature to a happy sixty-five degrees. Inside number 5 Leam Lane, one of a cluster of houses by the south-west corner of Tyne Dock itself, the atmosphere was anything but clement, however. For Kate's time had come.

Kate Fawcett was in her prime. She was an attractive woman in her mid-twenties, not pretty, but beautifully built: strong, with an innate feminine softness, her azure eyes, abundant brown hair and dark curving brows crowning a laughing, earthy personality, which had smitten the father of the child about to be born and warmed her to nearly everyone who came within her orbit.

At this stage in her life, one characteristic only seemed to tell another story. Kate's left foot flapped inwards slightly when she walked. It was a manner of walking which in no way detracted from her briskness of step, a barely noticeable blemish; but a kind of sad emblem, to those who knew, of the stressed and impoverished root-stock on which this singular beauty had been produced. As a child, Kate had walked the streets of Jarrow barefoot and one time had aroused such pity in a woman that she had given the girl a pair of boots.

Forty-one years later, Kate Fawcett's daughter, born that balmy day of 20 June, would recreate the goings-on in number 5 Leam Lane. In the opening pages of the manuscript of *Kate Hannigan*, her first novel, Catherine Cookson described her own birth. It was a dramatic debut performance, and a good deal more was spawned in those pages than Kate Hannigan's daughter, Ann, which is Catherine's middle name.

As the fictional Kate spreads her legs for a torturous labour the cry goes up for hot water, towels and sheets, accoutrements of the laundry with which, by the time she came to write this novel, Catherine was particularly at home. There is a doctor in attendance, Rodney Prince, but within the first few lines of dialogue we are introduced to a woman who embodies this fledgling author's talent for bouncing her female characters off the page to live for real in our imagination.

Midwife Dorrie Clarke is a fat, pugnacious, caustic, gin-soaked gossip, a busybody with a sharp tongue, and full of resentment. But she has an agile brain and a turn of phrase so tellingly true that she cannot but be real. In a matter of a few pages of Dorrie's thoughts and repartee with Dr Prince we have not only their own characters laid out before us, but those too of Kate's acquiescing mother, Sarah, her bully of a father, dark, dour Tim Hannigan, in the room downstairs, and a sense of the whole hellish, impoverished world in which they move, riddled wth religious superstition and cruelty.

It is the birth of a rare talent indeed.

Kate Fawcett's real father, William, was not in any way the model for Tim Hannigan's character. William, a Jarrow steelworker and faithful Catholic, had married Kate's mother, Rose, in the 1870s. They had produced five daughters, only three of whom – Sarah, Kate and Mary – had survived their teens. In the room downstairs at the time of Catherine's birth would have been Rose's second husband, John McMullen, whom she had married in 1890. The couple lived together first in Jarrow, then in Nelson Street, Tyne Dock, before arriving at number 5 Leam Lane.

John McMullen was the stereotypical Irish Geordie, a figure on which it is all too easy to hang the sins of every drunken Irishman since famine first drove his compatriots unwillingly to the area, formed largely in the nineteenth century by the Industrial Revolution.

Between 1860 and 1914 England's north-east coalfield

provided for the urbanisation and industrialisation of the whole of Western Europe. Its coal fuelled the iron, glassmaking, chemical and shipbuilding industries, the last of which facilitated a monstrous explosion of markets for these and other industries worldwide. The collieries on the south bank of the Tyne at Gateshead, Felling, Hebburn, Jarrow and South Shields were at the heart of an incredible urban expansion, with Jarrow's population leaping from 3,835 in 1850 to 37,719 by 1880, and South Shields from 28, 292 to 55,875 in the same period. These towns attracted workers like iron filings to a magnet. The need for labour during this period was intense, and it coincided with as desperate a need in Ireland to get out of the country and find work.

Catherine's great-grandparents, by name of McConnell, had, like many other Irish families, been driven from their homeland by the potato famine. Warnings that it was dangerous for a nation to be dependent on just one crop had been ignored and when the fungus *Phytophthora infestans* appeared Ireland was destroyed. The potato harvest failed in 1845 and 1846 and again in 1848. People were left with nothing to eat and no way to make money to support themselves. Many wandered the countryside, begging for food or work. Many starved to death. Famine took a million lives. Reports from observers make sobering reading. William Bennett's *Narrative of a Recent Journey of Six Weeks in Ireland* was published in 1847:

Many of the cabins were holes in the bog, covered with a layer of turves, and not distinguishable as human habitations from the surrounding moor, until close down upon them . . . We spent the whole morning in visiting these hovels . . . My hand trembles while I write. The scenes of human misery and degradation we witnessed still haunt my imagination, with the vividness and power of some horrid and tyrannous delusion, rather than the features of a sober reality. We entered a cabin.

Stretched in one dark corner, scarcely visible, from the smoke and rags that covered them, were three children huddled together, lying there because they were too weak to rise, pale and ghastly, their little limbs – on removing a portion of the filthy covering – perfectly emaciated, eyes sunk, voice gone, and evidently in the last stage of actual starvation. Crouched over the turf embers was another form, wild and all

3

but naked, scarcely human in appearance. It stirred not, nor noticed us.

On some straw, soddened upon the ground, moaning piteously, was a shrivelled old woman, imploring us to give her something – baring her limbs partly, to show how the skin hung loose from the bones, as soon as she attracted our attention. Above her, on something like a ledge, was a young woman, with sunken cheeks . . . who scarcely raised her eyes in answer to our enquiries, but pressed her hand upon her forehead, with a look of unutterable anguish and despair.

We entered upwards of fifty of these tenements. The scene was one and invariable, differing in little but the number of the sufferers, or of the groups, occupying the several corners within . . . It was my full impression that one-fourth of those we saw were in a dying state, beyond the reach of any relief that could now be afforded; and many more would follow.

Those who could, left Ireland in search of a better life. Tyneside was a principal destination. The McConnells had three daughters, one of whom, Rose Ann McConnell, born in Gateshead in 1858, was Catherine's grandmother. 'The family were first-generation Jarrow people,' said Peter Hindes, who is Rose's sister Margaret's grandson and still alive today, son of his father's second marriage. 'The McConnells were typical Irish Catholics. The word "journeyman" keeps coming up. Margaret's son (my father, Thomas) is referred to as a "journeyman ship-yard labourer". You went where the work was. You travelled around Tyneside, Wearside, in those days when the industrial North-East was in a boom . . . in the 1860s. A lot of people were coming in from Ireland because of the depression over there and because it was booming here.'

In *Our Kate*, Catherine, who never knew her great-grand-parents, described them as 'a respectable, highly esteemed couple, possessors of a smallholding and lavish table.' Respect-able they may well have been, but the family did not have the benefit of an education. Rose had difficulty writing and Peter's grandmother, Margaret, could neither read nor write: 'She put an X on my father's birth certificate rather than write her name,' he said. But clearly she was plucky: 'She taught herself to read and when they couldn't afford oil for a lamp indoors, she would go out into the street and read under a gas lamp. My memories of her are dim. She wore dark colours like most women in those days. Once the husband died, they seemed to be in more or less permanent mourning. All old women seemed to wear black. Her house was always dark, perhaps because it was a "downstairs house" and the back window, the window of the living room, which was in fact the kitchen, used to look out on the yard which had high walls, which made it all the darker. My impression is that she was quite severe, though Kate always said Meg had a great sense of humour.'

Catherine also described Rose as severe. 'She looked a hard woman,' said Peter. 'I think from what my mother told me she was, at least towards her.' Rose's first husband, Irishman William Tyndall Fawcett, by whom she had five daughters (including Catherine's mother, Kate), was a Jarrow steelworker, a decent man but not a lucky one. His granddaughter, Sarah, says he missed out on an inheritance because his middle name, Tyndall, was left off his birth certificate. In his early thirties he contracted TB and died.

Rose retreated with her daughters to her parents and took a job in the furnaces of the Jarrow puddling mills, where pig iron was converted into wrought iron by heating it to very high temperatures to oxidise the carbon – work there was gruelling, ill paid and reckoned to be one step away from the workhouse or an early death. She then married John McMullen, another Irish Catholic and rather less respectable than William.

John McMullen – an illiterate, belligerent Irishman – was one of triplets born into a family of fourteen brothers. Rose was almost certainly pregnant with their son, Jack, when they married in 1890. From fourteen, Jack worked with his father at Tyne Dock between Jarrow and South Shields, in sight of which Kate gave birth to Catherine in 1906.

Thus was Catherine Irish through and through. She was educated as an Irish Catholic; Lily Maguire, her best friend, really her only true friend as a child, was Irish; her great friend of the 1930s, Nan Smyth, would be an Irishwoman 'with big heart and many endearing faults'; and Catherine herself spoke with a mixture of Tyneside and Irish, while her first story, written aged thirteen, was entitled 'The Wild Irish Girl'.

John was no blood relation of Catherine, but his influence on her was considerable. He had served in the Indian Army before marrying Rose. Two of his brothers still lived in Jarrow, just west along the river from Tyne Dock, where Catherine was born. 'At that time, Jarrow seemed to be peopled with Irish,' Catherine would recall. Indeed, Jarrow became known as 'Little Ireland'. 'Palmer's Shipyard provided many of them with work, as did the smaller yards along the Tyne.'

John, who worked the ships in Tyne Dock, loading and unloading iron ore, was imbued with a set of mind-bendingly confused values. A non-practising Roman Catholic with a deeply ingrained hatred of Protestants, he exercised an irrational suspicion of sanctimonious piety in anyone who displayed it.

An ability to mesmerise people with a point of view riddled with obvious discrepancies is a not uncharacteristically Irish trait. It relies for success on an emotional conjuring trick – charm mingled with conviction giving blarney the semblance of truth. There was no sorting John out, either in conversation or in a fight. Both he and later his only son, also named John but known as Jack, born in the year of his marriage to Rose, were well known around the docks for their fighting. John did not, however, hit women. For them he reserved an inspired vocabulary of obscenities, never more imaginatively explored than when he was drunk, which was often.

The Irish were largely despised at the time for their poverty and fecklessness, but John achieved a reputation in the neighbourhood that did his countrymen's reputation no favours. 'Oooh!' screamed Irene Harding, a neighbour, six years younger than Catherine, when I asked her about him. 'He was a great big, horrible Irishman, always very loud. He would thunder at people.'

Aunt Sarah's youngest, also called Sarah (cousin Sarah), remembers: 'My mother didn't like him. He was not a nice man. When Rose married him, her parents disowned them, for the McConnells had a smallholding by that time. Even Rose would refer to him as 'a pig of a man', and his step-daughters – Sarah, Kate (Catherine's mother) and Mary – detested him. According to cousin Sarah, 'He was why they got away from home as soon as they could.' Kate returned only when she became pregnant out of wedlock, and left again, soon after the birth, to live out in service and earn the child's keep.

Catherine alone had time for him. She would call him '*Me* da', and, later, '*Me* granda', as opposed to 'My Aunt Sarah' or 'My Aunt Mary', always reserving the colloquial form for those whom she really held dear. Her relations still find it difficult to understand why she always held a candle to the old man. The answer is surely that for the first six years of her life John was

6

effectively Catherine's father. 'He was a drunken ignorant Irishman who could neither read nor write, but it was him who brought me up.'

One of his favourite songs when he came home three sheets to the wind was the Irish 'Comaylia', which he would conduct with Dennis, a two-foot-long iron poker. This same poker would also be used to knock pictures off the wall until only one remained: a portrait of Lord Roberts sitting on his horse with an Indian servant standing beside him. Whatever this archetypal British Imperial soldier, born in India, educated at Eton and Sandhurst and much decorated for his services to the Empire in India, Afghanistan and South Africa, excited in John McMullen – presumably his hatred of all that was British – he would use this image to give vent to his spleen, before standing in front of the window and letting rip with: 'Sing us an Irish Comaylia, sing us an Irish tune. For Patsie Burke has buggered his work, all by the light of the moon . . .'

His wife, Rose, suffered this, and a good deal worse besides, with remarkable fortitude. Family photographs make Rose look hard, and there is no doubt that she could be hard, particularly on her daughter Kate. But her stiff face is a sign of the stoicism which her life had bred in her. Rose kept her own counsel, but her feelings ran deep, particularly for her new granddaughter, who would open up Rose's great store of natural wisdom, comfort and love in a way that quite possibly she had never experienced before, or at least not for some time.

Whatever had been Rose's feelings for John when she married him in 1890, he had effectively rescued her children from the shame and squalor of begging on the streets (Kate remembered having to do this) and Rose from virtual slave labour at the Jarrow puddling mills. The real poor in the nineteenth and early twentieth centuries were the widows and unmarried mothers, women and girls with no men to bring in the money, when pay sufficient to keep a family was only available to men.

Marriage to John raised Rose's standard of living, but she was poorer with him than she had been with her first husband. Even so, John managed to sustain a reputation for hard work and lay the blame for any lack of it at someone else's door. In this John could justifiably call on truth as his witness. Jobs were indeed hard to come by, the problem being underemployment as much as unemployment. Today dockers are retained on a minimum wage, but until the decasualisation of the docks they got paid only when there was work for them to do. Wages were intermittent and dependent on ships coming in. There was always a pool of labour – men unpaid, and uncertain of when they would be paid – hanging around the dock offices a few minutes' walk from Leam Lane, opposite a line of public houses which stood wall to wall down the whole street.

This precariousness was at the root of John's drink problem, which in turn threatened the family's solvency further. Drink was a serious problem all over Tyneside, but was a scourge in those families, like the McMullens, that were already near the breadline. For them drink was a catastrophe if it meant that money for necessities could not be found. Nevertheless, when he was taken on, John worked hard and for a pittance of a wage. He would come home at the end of six ten-hour shifts, his moleskin trousers red and wet up to the thighs from shovelling ore, with only three shillings and fourpence in his pocket. As a result, like his mates, he felt entitled to stoke his ego at home with the northern working-class myth of male primacy, and did so for all he was worth.

The myth kept the Fathar, as he was known, firmly in charge. He was waited on hand and foot. 'In those days,' recalls Catherine, 'a man went out to work and that, in his mind, was enough; the house and all that was in it was the woman's task, and it lowered a man's prestige if he as much as lifted a cup.' Rose and her daughters would dutifully walk the three miles from Jarrow, where they lived, to the dock gates with the Fathar's bait (lunch), and back again, at times barefoot but always uncomplaining. In Catherine's memory, the Fathar's tea at home was a similar occasion for acquiescence. A scout would be posted to calculate his coming to the minute, the idea being to present him with his meal (haddock and mash or steak, eggs and chips) piping hot on the plate, and, more especially, to time – to the second – the boiling of an egg which always preceded the meal, not hard-boiled, but done to a turn so that the yoke was runny but right.

There was little or no sense of servility among the women, perhaps because they realised deep down that, as Hal says in *A Dinner of Herbs* (1985), 'Man was so made he needed a mother in some form or other until the day he died.' After all, the primary role of woman as procreator, feeder and sustainer harks back to a myth far older than that of male primacy, even to the dawn of time when man worshipped a Goddess creator of the world and

8

the idea of a male creator was patently absurd. On Tyneside men's work was non-inspirational. It was the women who provided that dimension to life – and in the kitchen, which was their sole domain, they knew as much about hard work as their menfolk, using it or the wash-house to bring in extra money from cooking or laundering, or taking in lodgers.

Kate Fawcett and her elder sister, Sarah, had both left school and started work at the age of twelve, Kate first with a butcher in Stanhope Road, east of Tyne Dock. Her job was in the wash-house, where she beat clean her employer's bloodied work clothes in a tub with a poss-stick. Her hours were from six-thirty in the morning to late at night, six days a week; her wages, half a crown.

The sisters were very different from one another. Like Sarah, Kate was a hard worker, and both were dominant women. But there the likeness ended. In those days Kate was gay, warm, large-hearted, while Sarah enjoyed none of these traits, her downright manner doing little to warm Catherine to her when she came along. By then, though, Sarah was married and had every reason to appear hard. Her story is a sad one.

'Just before I was born,' Catherine recalls, 'Kate got a letter from Sarah saying that she had fallen for this pit lad, Michael Lavelle, who was about half her size – for Sarah was a big woman – and she was distressed.' Kate wrote back to her: 'Marry him whatever you do, it doesn't matter whether you live with orange boxes for the remainder of your life, marry him . . .' Unfortunately for Sarah, Kate's words were prophetic. 'Her young husband went stone deaf early in the marriage and couldn't work, and from then on she had to bring up her growing family without aid.'

Sarah's life was one of unending toil. 'There were eight of us,' cousin Sarah told me. 'Mary, who died from TB in her teens, Rosie, Bill, Peter, twins Michael and Joseph, Kathleen and myself. My father couldn't hear. He had two falls of stone down the pit.' Said Catherine: 'When the Catholic school came out at four o'clock she had to take her youngest child with her and scrub and clean the classrooms, and cleaning meant cleaning in those days.' There were few moments of respite, and life was grim – but not as grim as Sarah seemed to make it when Catherine visited. Cousin Sarah's niece, Rosemary Barker, says that Aunt Sarah never liked Catherine, and Catherine admitted to a mutual antipathy: 'When I was staying there in my young days, she sent me to the slaughterhouse for a pint of blood to make blood puddings. The very name recalls the picture which makes me feel sick. We never got on. I didn't like her, but I admired her because of the way she worked for that family.'

Mary, the youngest Fawcett daughter, made a more promising catch, though it appears that he wriggled on her line for a while. Her husband, Alec Charlton, was a crane driver. He was a good man, but it had been a shotgun wedding, and once again Kate was involved. 'Mary knew that had she not been carrying Jack, her first son, and Alec had to marry her, he would have taken Kate because he had always liked Kate right up to the end. It should happen that years later they were both staying with Teresa, their only daughter, when Alec took ill and died, and he died in Kate's arms because Mary wasn't a woman to put up with sickness, and especially a dying man.'

Mary never liked Kate. She was jealous of her because of Alec and did her damnedest to get even, as Catherine remembers. 'In her bedroom was the latest in dressing tables; it had two swing mirrors. On a Saturday morning, as a child, I would move them from side to side, seeing my reflection in different ways. And I also went through all the little drawers in that piece of furniture and through being a nosy parker I caused a rift between the sisters that lasted for a few years. Because in one of the drawers I found a letter addressed to Kate. It was from the man she was going to marry after the 1914–18 war. He was now a prisoner in Germany . . . There was hell to pay. How Mary had come across the letter could only be surmised; perhaps she had taken it from the postman. She was a bitch of a woman, was my Aunt Mary. She was envious of anyone getting on, above her family.'

Mary had had dreams of bettering herself, and when she was married and living in East Jarrow she vented her frustration at having failed to realise them on anyone she could find lower than herself in the social pecking order – a family called Robson, for example, who lived upstairs. 'The man must have been dead for years. The youngest was a boy called Tommy. Mrs Robson had an older son who I imagine went to work and kept them meagrely.' Mary delighted in being better than the Robsons and took every opportunity to drive her advantage home. 'The day Tommy was fourteen he went down the pit, and Mary bragged to Kate that every time the poor lad was on night shift, she banged and clattered the fire irons and everything else to keep him awake. Moreover, such was Mary's temperament that days were allotted for the use of the wash-house and poor Mrs Robson had dared to light the fire under the boiler in the wash-house on a day that wasn't hers. And my dear aunt went in and raked all the burning ashes from the grate and threw them in the yard. You can't imagine such things happening, but they did.'

Always desperate to keep up appearances, Mary maintained her house better than any other in the neighbourhood. 'She had a lovely front room,' Catherine remembers. 'There was a carpet, on which there was a three-piece suite, and above all a lovely old spinet.' But the preposterous lengths Mary went to in order to protect the veneer betrayed her obsession with social status. Catherine recalls bringing her husband Tom to visit Mary, years later. 'I was carrying my first baby, it was during the second war. We came on the Friday night to see my mother and on the Sunday went to tea at Aunt Mary's. Tom couldn't believe it – she had knitted leggings for the legs of this enormous mahogany table.'

In Catherine's fiction Mrs Flannagan is the archetypal upstart. She and her daughter Sarah, something of a chip off the old block, appear in *Fanny McBride* (1959) and the Mary Ann series. Once, knowing that Catherine had had a neighbour of the same name, I asked her whether she had based the character on a particular person. 'Did I know any Mrs Flannagans? Oh, yes. In any community you'd find a Mrs Flannagan, and the Mrs Flannagan who lived opposite Fanny McBride in that book wasn't a patch on my Aunt Mary!'

Marriage was just about the only way for a girl to get on in life in those days. It was well-nigh impossible to make it on one's own; marriage was the fast track up or out. A girl might marry a striver and work with him at a small business, a shop perhaps, which could lead to bigger things – like Alice Fairbrother in Catherine's novel *The Upstart* (1996). Samuel Fairbrother was originally a cobbler, and rose to become the owner of a chain of shoemaking shops and a very rich man. Alice had made what would have been regarded by her contemporaries as an inspired choice of husband, and it is fair to assume that all three of the Fawcett sisters had at some time dreamed of such a conquest, coming as they did from so impoverished a background.

In 1901 or 1902, long before Mary was married and four or five years before Catherine was born, Mary and Kate went to work in a pub, The Ravensworth Arms in Lamesley, a village near Gateshead. Both lived in. Kate must have liked this job; she enjoyed the company of people and they enjoyed hers. Mary was a housemaid, while Kate worked in the bar. It was this division of responsibilities which handed Kate the chance of a lifetime to meet her ticket to success. For The Ravensworth Arms at Lamesley – visited, incidentally, by Robert Bradley at the start of *The Moth* (1986) – while not by any stretch of the imagination the gateway to high society (indeed, many of its patrons were pitmen), nevertheless offered a better opportunity for meeting people than grinding a tub full of clothes in a butcher's wash-house.

Kate's opportunity arose in 1903. She was serving in the saloon bar when an unusually well-dressed man appeared through the door. He wore a black coat with a collar made of astrakhan lambswool, a very choice trim. The coat alone would have been enough to cause the likes of Mary and Kate to double-take, but the effect was embroidered by a high hat, black kid gloves and a silver-mounted walking stick.

It is not difficult to imagine that after the man's first appearance the Fawcett sisters would have shared a giggle in their attic room above the pub. But his visit was repeated, and then became a regular event. Always he would take a table in the saloon bar, always Kate would serve him, and they began to strike up a rapport. The girlish giggles ceased, and Kate and her gentleman friend began a serious affair.

For Kate it was a dream come true. In Catherine's novel *Fenwick Houses* (1960) we get a glimpse of how such a man might have affected a girl from Kate's background. For Christine Winter it is his physical presence which impinges first, his bearing and the nonchalant fall of a scarf over his shoulder – and, of course, his accent. He is an alien presence, supremely self-assured but gentle with it. He is not a boy, like Christine's other male friends, and yet he is not much older than them. He has a fluency about him, an easy charm, and he is a stranger, apparently, to cynicism and self-interest. Above all, Christine's gentleman encourages Christine to be herself. It is her self that he loves. The barrier of class is not swept away, it is denied existence, dismissed as a figment of her imagination. Disarmed, Christine allows him to make love to her. She becomes pregnant. But when next she seeks him out, for the first time going to what she believes to be his home, no one has ever heard of him. The fairytale is over and the stark truth

12

is delivered by Don Dowling: 'some bugger has given her a bellyful and skedaddled.'

Kate Fawcett's affair with Alexander Davies, which is the name he gave to her, lasted for two years. It was consummated once. Like Christine, Kate became pregnant. Marriage was proposed. Plans were made in Newcastle for their new life together. Then one day Alec, as he was known, called at the McMullens' house when Kate was out. He left an address for her to contact him, but when Kate went in search of him no one there had ever heard of him. She never saw him again.

In *Fenwick Houses*, Christine's response to this desertion is fury: 'I could feel malevolence so powerful that I seemed to smell it, it was like a stench.' It was in this frame of mind that Kate had given her matrimonial advice to her sister Sarah. She ended the letter: 'Don't go through the hell that I'm going through.'

Kate's pregnancy changed her life, and her demeanour, for ever. But of course Kate wasn't alone in her 'hell'. She was pregnant with Catherine. Kate's resentment was Catherine's emotional initiation into the McMullen family. As she said to me recently, 'I must have been greatly desired, mustn't I?' And things got no better even after she was born.

Chapter Two

A Bellyful of Trouble

Catherine's baptism certificate and the formal registration document of her birth, dated a week late, bear testimony to the frantic state that Kate was in at this time. She had delayed because registration meant officially admitting that Catherine had been born out of wedlock. Today, when partners and single parents are as respectable as married parents, it is difficult to appreciate the shame Kate felt. When it came to the baptism certificate, the usual practice in South Shields was to describe the new lamb in the fold as 'bastard child of . . .', followed by the mother's name only. In fact, on Catherine's birth registration and baptism forms, the father's name was entered. When the error was discovered it seems the authorities were a bit kinder than usual. 'When someone spotted that my father was "not known", they just scratched his name out.'

The reason why Kate registered the wrong birth date of 27 June, having finally plucked up courage to go and register at all, was that 'she was afraid there'd be trouble that she was a week late in going'. The poor were so downtrodden in those days that they nurtured an inordinate fear of the police; 'they would go to extraordinary lengths to cover up the slightest misdemeanour.' Kate's fear was also a sad expression of the disgrace that was visited upon any girl in those days for mothering an illegitimate child.

Illegitimacy was of course a sin, and the Church policed society in a way it no longer does today. 'Divn't dee what I wouldn't dee unless ya want the priest after ya,' Catherine writes in *The Blind Miller* (1963), beautifully capturing a fundamental rule for all girls in Tyneside with the finger-wagging rhythms of her native idiom.

'God was a man who lived up in Newcastle, a big pot of big pots,' said Catherine of her childhood view of the Almighty. 'Someone who could order you, through the medium of the priest, to be condemned to hell. Hell was the blast furnace that illuminated the sky all over Jarrow when the residue was poured on to the slag heap. Hell was in Jarrow, administered from Newcastle . . . such were the narrow boundaries of [my] world.' How characteristic of the drama of Catherine's life that this vision should be sourced in the shadow of St Paul's Monastery at Jarrow, where between 682 and 735 AD the Venerable Bede spread the Word throughout Christendom.

In 1641 an order of Parliament asked all males over eighteen to declare their religion. No Catholics were recorded in South Shields. Two centuries later, in 1849, the first Catholic Mission opened. The Irish invaders brought Catholicism with them, but at first they failed to register as such. In 1851, according to one religious census, Tyneside had a particularly low church attendance, and Roman Catholicism was poorly represented. In 1873 the first Catholic church appeared in Whitehead Street, South Shields, sharing the Exchange Building with the Whitburn Coal Co, the Swedish Consul and a policeman. So great was the need, however, that the priest, a Father Kirwan, could drum up a congregation for three Masses a day. Then, in 1884, the first Catholic mission was set up in Tyne Dock itself, and in the summer of 1889, a chapel and a school, which Catherine would attend from 1916 on the north side of Bolden Lane, were dedicated to St Peter and St Paul. Finally, on 23 September 1905, the foundation stone was laid for a Catholic church there. It opened on 8 July 1906, one month after Catherine was born.

The Irish still constituted the main body of Catholicism, but they were far fewer than the Nonconformists and tended to live a rather separate existence, islands in a sea of Protestantism. Nevertheless, the local Catholic priest, like the local doctor, was a very real judgemental presence within the Irish community.

St Peter and Paul's first incumbent was one Father Bradley, immortalised as Father O'Malley in *Kate Hannigan, The Fifteen*

Streets, *The Blind Miller* and *Colour Blind*. He had come from St Paul's Jarrow, the church by Bede's monastery, at the end of 1899, where he had served as curate. What was needed down the road in Tyne Dock was no ordinary priest – he had a parish to create and a church to build. Clearly, Bradley was the man for the job. To raise money he would stand against the dockers on pay day, as they flooded through the dock gates, shaming them into parting with their wages before they hit the pubs on the dock bank opposite. He even arranged for contributions from Catholic miners to be deducted from their wages at source.

Bradley was tough. As his builders would record, this man of God brooked no dissent. To the children of Tyne Dock he had a mesmeric effect. Firing their imaginations with a primitive Old Testament fear of Almighty God, he was the architect of their nightmares, but he also cared for his people.

In the novels, Father O'Malley keeps his people firmly under the yoke, whether or not they actually go to Mass. He condemns Kate Hannigan's new clothes as a sign of her immorality – how else could she have afforded them? – and Dr Prince records three cases of hysteria in a month among children whose 'little heads' O'Malley has filled with fears of hell and purgatory. In *The Fifteen Streets* Christine Bracken accuses O'Malley of policing people's thinking and confirming them in their poverty and ignorance by insisting upon blind acceptance of their position in society, rather than encouraging them to think for themselves. Again, in *Kate Hannigan*, O'Malley is only there to stop people thinking; 'for, if she once started thinking, she and her like wouldn't put up with things as they were'. In *The Black Velvet Gown* (1984), set in the nineteenth century, Grandmama Diana Gullmington shows that the role of the church as social policeman is rooted in history. She scorns as absurd the idea that members of the lower classes possess reason (minds of their own), and sees the placing of human beings in a social pecking order (the great English class system) as God's work.

In Father O'Malley's world, fornication is the greatest sin of all, and in *Fenwick Houses* Father Ellis reduces Christine Winter to abasing herself on the ground before him, begging him not to inform her mother that he has come upon her fornicating with her gentleman lover. In so vengeful a religious atmosphere as this, Father Bradley of Tyne Dock church will not have turned a blind eye to Kate's sin with Alexander Davies.

Nevertheless, and perhaps on account of his intimate knowledge of Catherine's birth, Bradley made a significant impact on Catherine, which was not all bad. When in her teens he heard that she was without work, he had a word with a town councillor, William McAnany, who arranged employment for her in Harton Workhouse. That was typical of the man.

'Father Bradley was all our lives until 1945,' recalls Winnie Richardson, a neighbour of Catherine. 'He wasn't the modern type of priest at all. He was a man apart, he lived in the Presbytery and nobody went near the Presbytery. Nowadays the Presbytery is our parish rooms. He looked very austere. But Catherine was different from most people because she actually went to him and told him that she wanted to be a nun ... I wouldn't have dreamed of approaching Father Bradley about that at all! She must have had that sort of better outlook.'

Bradley died on 14 July aged 75, about the same time as Catherine was railing at the Catholic Church in the throes of mental breakdown. Years later, she paid for the heating to be installed in the church, and on her deathbed, it would be the priest of St Peter and St Paul's Tyne Dock who would give her the last rites.

A family with no father spelled poverty. Without Kate's wage the McMullens would find it difficult to survive. John was already in his fifties and his son Jack was only sixteen when Catherine was born. The family was faced with a pretty clear set of options, the first of which was to put Kate and Catherine in the workhouse.

The workhouse, the austere brick building of Harton Institution, with its tall chimneys, imposing central tower, stone-breaking yard at the back and flat-faced asylum nearby, was a fearful presence in the lives of the poor. In a case of illegitimate birth, the bastard child would be separated from its mother, and the mother would be kept in the workhouse for fourteen years, unless her people took her out.

Fear of the workhouse, like fear of the Church, had strong historical roots. In *The Dwelling Place* (1971), fifteen-year-old Cissie Brodie makes a home for her three brothers and five sisters in a cave on the fells after the death of their parents from cholera, rather than capitulate to the poor law custodian, a man called Riper. In *Our John Willie* (1974), another novel set in the nineteenth century, we have a clear sense not only of the ignominy of the workhouse, but also of the cruelty meted out there by working-class officials upon their own kind. In the McMullen household dread of the workhouse had a more immediate source: John McMullen had first-hand experience of its harsh regime, breaking stones there for a shilling a day. There was no doubt about it, Kate would have to continue in work – a decision which would cut her off from her child, for if she was to make a difference to the family finances, it would mean living out, in service.

These were some of the immediate practical consequences of Catherine's illegitimate birth. Another, no less real, was what people thought. Illegitimacy was a mark of disrepute as prominent as the dash of white hair on the heads of the illegitimate children of Thomas Mallen in *The Mallen Streak* (1973). One might think that, being near the bottom of the pile, the McMullens would have had less reason than most for embarrassment at the arrival of an illegitimate child. But that is to misread the situation. Respectability was important whatever social level you were on. In Catherine's novel *Hannah Massey* (1964), set in the 1930s, Hannah, whose main concern is to rise up the social scale, is so appalled at the thought of disgrace when it appears that her daughter, Rosie, has been living in London as a whore (which she hasn't) that she sets fire to her savings (her passport to posh Brampton Hill) and commits suicide.

Among the lower levels, indeed, respectability was often hardest fought for, as a little diversion on this theme in *Fanny McBride* suggests. Fanny is bemoaning the fact that her family has grown up and her favourite son, Jack, has moved out to get married to a 'Hallelujah' (Protestant) called Joyce Scallen, which will leave Fanny alone in the house with her other son, Phil, whom she regards suspiciously as an upstart, always making himself different with his reading and copying of fine ways, like standing up when a woman enters the room. The narrative moves forward with the arrival of Fanny's friend Mary Prout, who is suffering from 'a bad leg'. It is clear from Mary's tearful expression that she is in something of a stew, and it emerges that the doctor has laid her off work. What Mary does for a living is not immediately made clear. All that we are told is that it is largely a sit-down job, which she doesn't want to lose. Sit-down jobs are hard to find and Mary will surely lose hers if she has to take time off, for whoever replaces her won't want to hand such a peach of a job back when she's better.

Gradually it becomes clear that Mary is cautiously suggesting that Fanny take on her job for the duration. Mary can depend on her friend to play fair and relinquish the job when she is fully recovered. Moreover, it is an obvious solution to Fanny's need for a change and something to do now that Jack has left. But why Mary makes the suggestion in so roundabout a way is baffling – until Fanny twigs and explodes with a bellow of a laugh. Mary, it transpires, is responsible for taking the tickets in the ladies' public lavatory, wiping the seats and seeing that no one holds the door for a friend to save her having to put a penny in the slot.

We naturally assume that Mary has been pussy-footing around before offering Fanny the job because of the ignominy of such an occupation. That, certainly, is the kind of reaction Fanny expects from Phil when she tells him about it later. But nothing could be further from Mary Prout's mind. The problem as Mary sees it, and the reason for her stealthy approach, is how the higher-class defecators will react when they have to lower themselves before the lowest. She is concerned that Fanny doesn't dress respectably enough to take the job on! 'Not that you can't when you like, Fan. But you know what I mean, Fan. You'd have to put your corsets on.'

The whole business of class and respectability was immensely complex on Tyneside. The catch-all term 'working-class', beloved of the Labour movement as it rose to power in the twentieth century, obscured an intricate hierarchy within the workforce which was reflected in workers' families at home and turned life for some (such as Catherine's Aunt Mary) into an all-absorbing game of social snakes and ladders. Classifying all the dock workers and all the coal miners, who worked the seams of the Durham coalfield just a few miles from the docks, as working class imposed a uniformity which they certainly did not feel.

Among shipyard workers, for example, fitters, platers and boilermakers did not think of themselves as labourers. In *Kate Hannigan*, the trimmers at the dock gate stand in groups a little apart from the main workforce as they wait in the hope of being taken on. Skilled workers might earn twice or three times as much as unskilled workers, their families would have different social lives and they probably worshipped at different places. Similarly, among miners, the hewers (the coal cutters who did the hard manual work) were a very different breed from the surface workers. There were pitmen who became deputies or overmen in the collieries, and dockers who became foremen and charge hands in the shipyards. Promotion of this sort spelt job security and probably a bigger income and a corresponding rise in status in the community for their families.

Nor was there one homogeneous popular culture. On the one hand, a minority – but a very important one, with more than its fair share of influence – were devotees of church or chapel: against drinking, gambling and smoking. On the other hand, there were pub- and club-goers, who didn't go to church. So you had two sorts of divisions: the economic division, for example between the hewers and other types of mine workers, and the cultural divisions within each of these groups between drinkers and non-drinkers, chapel attenders and non-chapel-going men.

With this sort of keener focus we can begin to appreciate that there were lines of defence, positions worth protecting or improving on, at a multitude of levels within the so-called working class. There were different outlooks and expectations, too. Within each stratum there were the social climbers, who maybe went to church or chapel for no genuine religious reason but because it was 'the thing to do', or (like Aunt Mary) found other ways to appear to be on a higher level than their neighbours. Then there were those unconcerned with self-promotion, who thought perhaps that the most important thing in life was how far their racing pigeons could be made to fly. At the very lowest level, strivers – people whose one purpose in life was to keep their heads above water – existed alongside the hard cases, the no-hopers, whose daily lives were dominated by poverty and, as John McMullen's life was already and Kate Fawcett's was soon to become, by drink.

It was impossible to appreciate all these fine distinctions unless you lived among them, as Catherine did. Those who lived just outside the Fifteen Streets in her novel of that name considered people living there 'to be of one stratum, the lowest'. But the people inside this stratum knew that there were all kinds of different levels.

Most people lived in rented 'houses', either 'upstairs houses' or 'downstairs houses'. They were called houses by virtue of the fact that each housed an entire family, even though upstairs and downstairs belonged to the same building. In an 'upstairs house' there might be four rooms for habitation, in a 'downstairs house' only three. In the Fifteen Streets, the lower stratum lived 'one step from the workhouse' at the bottom end, where each 'house' had only two rooms and all were alive with bugs. These families usually arrived after they had been turfed out of a better 'house' for non-payment of rent.

Where you lived and the size of your house was a mark of your social position, and even the smallest advances were hard won. As Catherine showed in *A Grand Man* (1954), if you moved out of a house with a communal backyard, such as Mulhattans Hall, to a house which had a backyard divided into two distinct areas (one for the upstairs family and one for downstairs) you had 'a right to feel that [you] were socially on the up-grade'.

The McMullens scored badly on practically every scale: house, drink, religion, John's underemployment, his violence, his uncouth tongue, and lack of money. They were not, however, quite at the bottom of the pile. The Kanes, for example, were so poor that little Mary Ellen used to come in to borrow Kate's boots. There were still ways in which the McMullens could fall, and Kate had found one of them.

Also, when Kate came home and informed John and Rose that she was pregnant, the social disgrace was exacerbated by the unfulfilled expectation of her intended marriage up several classes, which had probably set tongues wagging in the neighbourhood. For private lives were public property. The environment in which the McMullens lived was incredibly insular – in *Pure as the Lily* (1972) Alec Walton is deemed a foreigner by workers in Wallsend a few minutes away across the Tyne. In so isolated a community, gossip thrived: neighbours 'just had to get a hold of a thread and by the time they had finished it was a hawser, iron-bound at the ends'. There were, no doubt, some within the McMullens' insular circle who capitalised on Kate's misfortune at her family's expense. There was nothing so enjoyed in a community replete with upstarts as an upstart fallen; and that was how Kate in her plight was viewed. Years later, when Catherine declared herself too good for service, a neighbour, Mrs Waller, would say, 'She's got ideas about herself, that one. She'll end up the same as big Kate!'

Whether or not Kate was subjected to violence at the hands of her stepfather when she came home and announced that she was pregnant remains unrecorded. But one night when Kate's sister Sarah had failed to return home as arranged from Newcastle, he pursued her into the backyard with a horsewhip. John, of all people, would have found the ignominy to which Kate had subjected the family hard to stomach.

Whatever happened to Kate on the fateful day when she made her announcement, once the dust had settled an arrangement was agreed with John and Rose. Not only was Kate to return to work, in service, but henceforth Rose was to be Catherine's mother and John her father. Rose was forty-eight years old at the time; John was in his fifties. Kate, at twenty-four, would see her child only on her day off. There was no bonding between Catherine and her natural mother. Indeed, one of Catherine's earliest memories is of Rose tearing her away from Kate when the young mother arrived home and gathered her daughter into her arms. Psychologists today believe mother-child bonding to be a crucial development stage for both parties. Until 1913, when Catherine turned seven, she believed Kate to be her elder sister.

Chapter Three

The Apprenticeship Years

Since the coming of the railway and the dredging of the Tyne in the 1850s, both banks of the river had changed beyond recognition. Hamlets and villages had grown into towns; fields had given way to shipyards, to iron, steel, glass and chemical works and other factories. A multiplicity of railway lines now snaked their way over four of the five slime-dripping arches at Leam Lane End on to the great dock staithes, and as little Katie lay in bed at night she could hear the horns of ships and the creaking and groaning of shunting trains. She was indeed a child of the Tyne.

But there were still reminders of the displaced agriculture of earlier days. On the north side of the Leam Lane hamlet was a blacksmith; on the south, two shops and a pub known as The Twenty-Seven, because this was where the local men docked when they had finished loading and unloading on the twenty-six staithes. The McMullens' house was next to the pub. It was divided into two apartments, numbered 4 and 5. No. 5, where Catherine was born, was the lower apartment.

Beyond lay the gasworks and then, a quarter of a mile or so higher up the bank, a few bigger houses, then the little country school at Simonside, which Catherine first attended at the age of four and a half. 'The country began at Simonside,' Catherine recalls. 'A lot of people would laugh in disbelief today, but it was open land then, mostly given over to turnips or taties. There was a pub called The Robin Hood, and nearby a stream, and it was here that courting couples would walk on a Sunday. I remember that I was sometimes used as camouflage when my Aunt Mary was courting – she was not supposed to be courting this man who became my Uncle Alec. I also have a memory of cowslips then. You don't see many cowslips in the south in the fields somehow, but there you'd see cowslips.'

Opposite the school at Simonside was a farm, from where the farmer would drive his cows past Katie's home to the slaughterhouse in South Shields. On one occasion a cow, terrified by the sound of a tram emerging from the arches at Tyne Dock, escaped from the herd and found its way up the steps to the rooms above the McMullens' home in Leam Lane occupied by a family rather appropriately called Angus. Leaning out of an upstairs window, Mrs Angus shrieked her defiance at the cow's intrusion. But the cow had the last word, quietly evacuating its bowels on the landing floor.

However unforgiving Rose was towards Kate for bearing an illegitimate child, she loved Catherine, and in the first six years of her life the little girl knew security. Rose's love may not have been a natural mother's, but it had a sound, formative influence. Gran Carter in *Hamilton* (1983), while not Rose, suggests something of what Catherine derived from her grandmother's care. She is a warm, caring figurehead, full of old-world lore, and the safety zone to which her granddaughter, Maisie, runs.

Rose would sing to Catherine the only song she knew, about the pleasure of love growing older and fading away 'like the morning dew'. She would tell her what she remembered of Tyneside back into the mid-nineteenth century and repeat other tales she had heard as a child, which took her even further back, to the roots of her culture. Even John managed fairly well to keep his oaths in check when Catherine was around, and though she would later have to contend with his drunkenness, she was never afraid of him. A clue to their relationship lies in a ritual he enacted every time he came home for his tea. The ritual turned on that egg which always preceded his meal. He would have Catherine sit beside him at the table, top the egg and give her the best of it to eat. While at the time she never understood why she wasn't given an egg of her own, years later she would thank John for his 'voiceless love'.

From her grandparents Catherine received possibly a richer

influence in the first years of her life than she would have had from her real parents had Alexander Davies had the character to take Kate on. Richer not, of course, in a pecuniary way, but in a way that few who lived in middle-class luxury in Westoe Village, well east of Tyne Dock, would know. But it did not last.

Nearly two years after she had started at Simonside School, in June 1912, the McMullens moved from Leam Lane to East Jarrow. It was a move of less than a mile that took them to an odd collection of some fifty houses, which went under the name of the New Buildings.

The New Buildings comprised three streets and two terraces – a little island on its own, with no other houses for a quarter of a mile or so. The estate was constructed in the 1880s by the Larkins, proprietors of the St Bede Chemical Works, who traded on the western flank of 'Jarrow Slake', a lazy diminutive of 'Jarrow's Lake'. Fifty years before the Larkins set to work, there stood a gibbet there, hung with a curved metal cage, iron bars welded together to hold, in the last recorded case of its use, the corpse of a local pitman, William Jobling, who had been hanged the day before for murder, even though his supposed victim, a magistrate by name of Nicholas Fairles, had exonerated him before he died. Jobling's real crime was to walk out on strike in protest over 'bonding', an employer practice one step away from slavery. As a warning to others, his body was put under military guard and left to putrefy for more than three weeks. The penalty for removing it was death. When the guard disbanded, Jobling's remains disappeared over night, taken down by the poor man's family.

Set in wasteland, surrounded by fields, the New Buildings were built in the shape of an E, the two terraces called Simonside making up the long member and looking north across the Slake, the three shorter members dropping down from them: Lancaster Street and, back-to-back, Phillipson Street and, at the east end, William Black Street.

First, the Larkins built a couple of mansions for themselves in Simonside Terrace, with a drive up to the house – 'lovely self-contained houses,' as Irene Harding recalls, 'it was the posh part'. Then came the houses in William Black Street – actually the first street to be completed. These houses were divided into two maisonettes, though each apartment was referred to as a house.

In 1913, some eighty years after Jobling was hanged, Irene

(Reny) Harding was born at number 17 William Black Street. 'My family were three brothers and a sister, and then me. Florrie was seven years older, same age as Katie McMullen [Catherine, with whom for a while she was a close friend]. My oldest brother was one year older, then ten and eight – our Bill, Jim, then Jack. My father was a trimmer on the railways at Tyne Dock. We thought ourselves fortunate because he was never out of work.'

Reny remembers the Slake's use as a tidal timber store. Great lengths of unsawn timber were lashed together into an enormous raft, secured to upright posts, awaiting the attentions of the nearby saw mill. 'There was wood all across the water,' she remembers, 'right up to the gut wall. We would walk across it, and there was a hut in the middle, where Granda Tulip was the caretaker. He looked after the Slacks, but he never chased us off. My father had his own boat, he called it *Irene*, and at one time he used to take all the children up river to see the big boats, the *Venus*, the *Queen Elizabeth*. Anyway, me father was taking a lot out and Matthew McHaffie missed the boat so he got a sculler boat from some people called Lamb and went after me father's boat and the river swelled up just as he was passing this wall and the swell caught him and he drowned. It's something to do with the tide. Me father blamed himself for that.'

Winnie Richardson, the daughter of a miner, born three years earlier than Reny in Phillipson Street, remembers that the timber pond was not itself dangerous, but the gut – outflow of the River Don – was both deep and fast, and at ebb tide could be perilous indeed. Matthew McHaffie was not the only person to be caught up in it. Winnie and Reny's neighbour, the raven-haired Irish girl called Catherine McMullen and known as Katie or Kate-Kate to distinguish her from her mother, Kate, once pushed a boy called Billy into the Slake and held his head down under the scum and driftwood and vegetable refuse. If it hadn't been for a man seeing what she was doing from the top deck of a tram, waiting nearby at the crossing opposite the old chemical works, 'wor Billy', as the victim's irate father later referred to him, might not have survived.

The houses of the New Buildings were well built. There was pride in living in them. 'The steps were always scrubbed, they were lilywhite literally,' Reny remembers, and flags not only to respectability: 'One time, during an election a woman painted her step green for the Liberal Party!'

Respectability was all, and the pressure to attain it caused not a little insecurity in some quarters. Catherine's Aunt Mary, Kate's sister, who also lived on the estate, measured her success in terms of some fine furniture, including a mahogany dining table, the one for which she knitted four matching leggings to protect it against idle scuffs and scrapes.

There was no crime to speak of; the local bobby saw to that: 'I can remember PC Mortenson who used to live in Simonside Terrace,' Reny continued. 'He would sit in his window on his day off; you had to behave yourself; he was very strict, but very good; you know, just clip you over the ears with his gloves.'

Winnie recalled the freedom the children enjoyed: 'There was nothing to stop you playing out. The houses were in the middle of cornfields and gardens. Mr Eckford used to till the gardens on one side and Mr Affleck was the farmer on the other side of the village. The Afflecks lived in Redwood Cottage opposite the saw mill [on the south-east corner of the Slake]. There was May, Cissie and Maud, three sisters. Mr Eckford ran the little shop in Phillipson Street, known as Cissie Affleck's.'

'James Eckford had three gardens on the front field, allotments,' continued Reny. 'One was a vegetable garden, so we had all fresh vegetables in the shop and the other was just a general . . . I'm not sure what that was for. The Eckfords lived in Simonside Terrace, and you know I told you about Granda Tulip, he lived in Simonside Terrace too, and his daughter they called Lily! – Lily Tulip, the flowergirl! She married a cousin of the Queen and they called her Lady Elphinstone, she became a Lady-in-Waiting.

'Oh, and I remember the Flannagans, two sons, Jerry and John and one of them married an ice-cream girl. She was a very quiet person. Then Olive Swinburn, she was about the same age as our Florrie, Beatrice Swinburn was my friend, about my age. They were a nice family, they went to live in South Shields. They called Mr Swinburn, Sep – Seppie Swinburn went to live in Seventeen Salmon Street, South Shields – see, half of me brain *is* working, my goodness!'

Reny screamed with laughter at the alliteration, but I was busy noting names she was spilling that I knew from the novels or *Our Kate*. Sep is the fellow in *The Tide of Life*, and in her teens Katie used to clean for the Flannagan family. In *A Grand Man*, Sarah Flannagan shows up Mary Ann Shaughnessy for being a liar. Olive Swinburn is the girl in *Our Kate* who flattens Katie when she challenges her to a fight. Florrie Harding, who was for a period a friend of Katie, figures in a significant 'moment' in *Our Kate* when Katie watches her walk past her window with Joan Woodcock and realises that her childhood is behind her and that henceforth she will forget the children in the New Buildings and make something of her life. I asked Reny whether she remembered Joan.

'Joan Woodcock? She married our Jim! She became my sister-in-law!' she laughed. 'I can remember when they were in their teens and were getting perhaps too keen, she was sent to her grandparents for a while.'

'There were all kinds of people in that village,' Winnie sighed, 'just the four streets, but it was such a stable community, you know. We were there a very long time and we had the same neighbours for a long time.'

Reny did the same: 'We lived there, me father died there, me son was seven when we left. I got married there . . . I lived there till the late 1940s . . .'

Winnie, being bright at school, had trained as a teacher in Sunderland (10 miles away), and then returned as a teacher to her old school (which had been Katie's too) – St Peter and Paul's Tyne Dock. She taught there all her working life.

When I interviewed her, she was still living close by. Reny married within the New Buildings, moving with her husband to Phillipson Street, just one street away. She, too, lived but a walk away nearly a century later. The girls' whole outlook remained narrow. Katie McMullen was in that sense very different from them. The world would become her oyster. Was that unique, or were there others who broke free or stood apart from the community?

'There was a university teacher in the Larkins' house on Simonside, well it was a mansion really,' Winnie recalled. 'The Douglases, the son rose to be in charge of Sunderland finances. He was an only child. He went on to further education like I did, but I don't remember anyone else did that. There were some quite well off. The people next door to us, the man worked at the saw mill and only had one child, they had wall-to-wall carpeting – in those days! Next door to that the man was manager of the Jarrow butcher's shop in Hope Street, and when he retired he bought a bungalow in Monkton! There was a big difference among the people, for there were very poor people as well, but it wasn't a slum at all.'

'There were no slums in East Jarrow,' agreed Reny with pride, before adding under her breath, 'There was only one slum, *theirs*, the McMullens, it was always full of beer bottles. There weren't any really well off either, but East Jarrow was one of those places where everybody helped everybody else – everybody except the McMullens.'

First stop for the McMullens had been an upstairs 'house' in William Black Street. Catherine remembers making the trip with their few bits of furniture, sitting on Jackie Halliday's coal cart next to the mangle, with her feet dangling over the back. (Nearly sixty years later Jackie Halliday, a man with no legs, would inspire the character of Amos in her 1971 novel *Feathers in the Fire*.) The following month they moved again, to number 10, a three-room, ground-floor 'house'; which was to be Catherine's home from the age of six until she was twenty-three. Aunt Mary lived at number 30 after she married Alec, and Great Aunt Maggie, Rose's sister, lived at number 26.

Years hence Catherine would stand on the site of number 10, which had fallen before the bulldozers, and gather up the memories of what her grandma had meant to her. It was a sad, nostalgic moment. I have a picture of Catherine on that day, standing where the kitchen had been. Confusion is written on her face, perhaps a little helplessness too. Of all the images of the old days which flooded through her mind it was that of Rose which was the most vivid. 'The tears rolled down my face and I went back to the car and wrote down the vivid impression I had got of her:

Me granny sat in a wooden chair
She had a stiff face, wrinkles and straight black hair,
But if ever I needed comfort I found it there.
Between her knees each day she'd have me stand,
And look me head for nits, and I'd play the band
Until she said, 'Here's a bullet
Mind you don't choke yourself
It'll stick in your gullet.'

That summer of 1912, Rose fell ill and Kate was recalled to run the house. It was the start of a new period in Catherine's life and it couldn't have been more different from what had gone before.

Catherine's complex feelings about her 'sister', Kate, are well suggested by two incidents, both of which are also indicative of the extraordinary nature of Catherine's awareness at this time.

The first occurred immediately after the decampment to East Jarrow. Kate was living in at her job with a baker in Chester-le-Street at the time, and no one had even bothered to tell her of the move. Perhaps the move had been very sudden; perhaps it was a sign of how estranged Kate had become, though she came home regularly, invariably bringing parcels of food from the baker with her. Now she had come to the New Buildings to find out where everybody was.

Catherine had tied a rope to a lamp-post in the street and was whirling around it, singing a song to herself, lost in a world of her own, when suddenly she caught sight of Kate coming towards her. At this instant Kate seemed utterly beautiful to her, approaching as it were out of a mist. She was a good-looking woman, as I have described, but at that moment Catherine seems to have had an insight into the depth of that beauty, into its sources that lay beyond physical attraction. I was reminded of this story when I saw that Catherine's first novel is dedicated to Kate as a woman 'who found her expression through me'.

The second incident occurred when Catherine emerged one Saturday afternoon from the Crown cinema, where she liked to see the penny matinee. (Catherine walked the streets on her own from the age of five.) Again she saw Kate coming towards her; but this time it was an altogether different vision, 'a sickening revelation'. Kate was drunk, her speech slurred, her laugh raucous, her walk unsteady. Catherine was ashamed to be seen with her. That Kate had turned to drink is the saddest comment on the manifold effects of being jilted by the father of her child because it very soon became a serious problem which would colour her relationship with Catherine to the day Kate died.

As befitted a downstairs house, the McMullens' quarters in number 10 consisted of three rooms, which were now home to Rose, John, Kate, Jack and Catherine. In the front room were six chairs, a couch, a centre-legged oval table, a desk-bed and a double brass bed set in an alcove. In the middle of the kitchen, whose window looked out on to the backyard (shared with the people upstairs), was a large table, covered with some sort of artificial material which today would appear to be plastic; a smaller oblong baking table stood in front of the window, and to the side of the black range fireplace with its steel fender was the Fathar's wooden armchair. A chest of drawers stood against the wall opposite the window and baking table, and by the wall opposite the fireplace was a six-foot wooden 'saddle' or settle, which was sometimes used as a bed. There was one bedroom, where at this stage Catherine slept with her mother.

In the yard was a tap, a staircase to the upstairs house and hen crees, which stretched the length of the side wall to a coal-house at the bottom end, where there were two dry 'ash' lavatories (one for each 'house'). These would be emptied by refuse workers or 'scavengers' using a long-handled shovel inserted beneath the pan through a hole in the back lane wall. The McMullens' washing was done in a poss-tub in a wash-house opposite the lavatories, next to the staircase.

The upstairs 'house' was occupied by a family named Romanus. Jim Romanus was a trimmer in the docks; his wife, a secret toper, drank herself to an early death. Mr Romanus used to knock her about, but no one ever intervened. Neighbourhood gossips were always ready to spread the word as to what was going on, but no one saw it as their business to interfere. So much for the myth of the supportive, close-knit working-class community; in reality it was very much everyone for themselves.

To help make ends meet, Kate took in washing, which was hung out to dry on a line in the back lane and had to be removed hurriedly when the cry went up that the coal cart was coming through. Also, though it sounds incredible in such a small 'house', she took in lodgers. This necessitated different sleeping arrangements: John and Rose in the front room, Catherine and Kate top to tail on the settle in the kitchen and all the lodgers in the bedroom with Jack. There could be as many as nine or ten people living in the three-room house at any one time, for sleeping five lodgers was not unheard-of.

In fact, there doesn't seem to have been anything unusual about these crowded conditions. In 1921 42.3 per cent of Jarrow's population lived in 'overcrowded' accommodation; two adults per room was rated normal, i.e. not overcrowded, and children didn't count in the statistics. And, as with virtually every other statistic for Tyneside at this time, the historical context put the figures in perspective. However bad things were for Catherine in William Black Street in the second decade of the twentieth century, they had been worse for her people a century earlier.

Overcrowding was a major cause of disease, and health problems on Tyneside remained among the worst anywhere in the country. When, according to the Annual Report on Jarrow in 1949, the national infant mortality rate was 32 per 1,000, the Jarrow figure was almost double that.

With normally seven – sometimes nine or ten – occupants of 10 William Black Street and only one, non-flushing lavatory in the yard, visits by the scavengers must have needed to be fairly frequent. However, the main problem for the McMullens seems to have been sheer lack of room to move about. From an early age this sparked in Catherine a particular ambition: 'We had lodgers all the time and I promised myself then that I was going to give myself a very nice, big house with plenty of space.' It is incredible to me that this child, living in so difficult a situation, should make such an apparently absurd promise to herself. For a promise it was: never just a dream. As soon as she began to earn even a small wage she started to put money by. This she added to the pennies she had saved by walking instead of taking a tram when out on messages for Kate.

Poverty bred care with money (though absolutely no interest in it for its own sake), and she stashed her hoard in a secret place in the outside lavatory. Later, with the help of these savings, she took out insurance policies which, at the age of twenty-seven, when she was earning the very good wage for a woman of three pounds, six shillings, would enable her to buy a fifteen-roomed house of her own.

The lavatory was more than her bank, however; it was the only place you could be alone, and became a kind of sanctuary for Catherine. Away from the crowded house, she could sit on the white wooden seat, which stretched the whole breadth of the lavatory and half its depth, and lose herself in her thoughts, occasionally peeling the flaking whitewash off the walls and absent-mindedly watching it fall on to the brick floor below. So precious were these moments alone, that the intrusion, without warning, by a refuse worker was especially hard to bear. Suddenly she would hear the rasp of the hatch in the back lane wall being lifted by a 'scavenger' and dart up from the seat, pressing herself, eyes closed, against the door, as the searching long-handled shovel appeared beneath the seat where, a moment before, she had been sitting. It was an assault upon her private world which filled her with such revulsion that she recalled it in her first novel, giving her memory of the desecration of her 'little square house' to Annie Hannigan to disperse the memory. Seven years after *Kate Hannigan* was published, however, she showed that she bore no grudge against refuse collectors. In *Rooney* (1957), her dustman hero is given his 'day of happiness': 'I thought, surely they are entitled to one day of love. Every working man is entitled to that!'

When Kate first came home to take over the running of the house from Rose, Catherine was a self-confident little six-year-old and the centre of attention at home. It won't have been by chance that she was selected from among her contemporaries at Simonside School to play the Faerie Queen in the Christmas concert. 'My part was the biggest and the best, and I was the prettiest bairn of the lot.' One can hear her saying it with a twinkle in her eye, but it was probably true that she was a cocky little thing at this point in her life. She wasn't spoilt – there wasn't the money to spoil her – but she was loved, and her situation as a child with parents very much older than her and no brothers and sisters to play with, no one of her own age in the house, marked her out as unusual among the children of the New Buildings.

Rose, by this time fifty-four years of age and wearied by the grind of life at subsistence level, seems to have given Catherine an unusually 'old' head on her young shoulders; a teacher at her school even referred to her as 'granny'. Remembering Rose's song about love fading away 'like the morning dew' as clearly as if she had heard it sung to her only yesterday, she remarks how clearly the words 'spoke of the disillusionment of life'. That was her grandma's mood, not striving at the beginning of adulthood but world-weary, experienced, thinking back over life as she made her way to the journey's close.

It is the classic picture of the only child, with the added dimension of much older parents. This early environment made Catherine not only more adult, but also more self-centred – she loved nothing better than to perform her leading role, recite her lines and sing and dance in the kitchen with the clippy mat rolled back and with her grandma and granda, Kate, Jack, Mary and Alec as her appreciative audience. It also made her more self-reliant, more self-motivated, and more innocent of the social conventions of play with other children, the give and take which comes naturally to brothers and sisters. And lastly, it made her more imaginative. The only child – of necessity – tends to create its own world inside. For as long as she could remember, Catherine had been able to see pictures, real live pictures, in her imagination. She was already reading too: not only comics but also her 'first real book'. This had been lent to her by the daughter of the caretaker at school and she treasured it so much that she managed somehow never to give it back. For years, whenever they passed on the street, Catherine didn't dare look the girl in the eyes lest she remember that she still had it.

Catherine wasn't a lonely child at this stage. Like other children of the New Buildings, she often went out to play in the streets after tea. She was one of the crowd; and yet she was somehow different. It is not difficult to see her having her say over what should be played or who should occupy centre stage. They would play round the street lamps or in the open space in front of the terrace or on the bank of Jarrow Slake ('the Slacks'), the huge tidal pond across the Jarrow Road from the New Buildings, running from the barium chemical works maybe a quarter of a mile to the sawmill not far from Tyne Dock.

At Christmas, like the children in *The Wingless Bird* (1990) who gaze at the sugared mice in the Conway's confectionery shop window, the kids would gather outside Cissie Affleck's shop at the corner of Phillipson Street, wondering at the festive delights they saw there. And at any time, a little group might be found huddled in the chimneypiece on the outside wall of the Richardsons' house, 'used as headquarters for deady-one by the boys', or by the girls as shelter for a game of shops, as Catherine would recall in *Maggie Rowan* (1954). In the novel it is little pieces of coloured paper which pass for currency in the imaginary shop. In reality bits of broken bottle, preferably coloured, or of china, passed as the 'boody', which represented the wonderful sweetmeats on sale in Cissie Affleck's.

One night, a little more than a year after Catherine arrived in the New Buildings, a grasping hand snitched a prize piece of green glass from her boody pile. Outraged, Catherine squared up to the culprit and accused her of the robbery. 'If you don't give me back me boody I'll go and tell me ma about you, so I will!' Whether the other girl saw an opportunity to redress the balance of power which had been upset by the advent of this cocky little girl from Leam Lane or whether she felt she had it coming to her, in one short sentence she tore Catherine's childhood world apart. The girl put her face close to hers and sneered, Catherine didn't even know who her ma was; Rose wasn't her ma, she was her grandma; Kate was her ma, and the 'old sod' she thought was her da, he was her granda. Then she drew her trump card and let fly with – 'You ain't got no da!'

With no gratuitous exaggeration this spiteful girl, on whose shoulders falls the weight of Catherine's grief, occupies a place in her story akin to that of Judas in the garden of Cedron. For the episode at the chimneypiece on the outside wall of the Richardsons' house, which climaxed in the crowd of children taking up her persecutor's chant, not only sent Catherine immediately into a spiral of uncertainty, fear and loss, but began her long nightmare voyage to nervous breakdown and afterwards to a destiny which would put her name on the lips of millions, the story of suffering and triumph which it is my purpose to tell.

Catherine's immediate reaction was not only that of a secure child suddenly informed that she is adopted; it was also a complete loss of faith in those whom she had loved and who had loved her. It was the negation of all that had been true. Then came questions about her identity which, at seven years old, she couldn't fully form, let alone understand. Worse, she bottled up her new-found knowledge. She didn't even put it to Rose or Kate, for she felt shame in her heart that the drunken woman whom she had thought of and, yes, loved, as a sister, but not revered, should be the mother of all that she, Catherine McMullen, was. Men could get drunk, even a sister could get drunk, but a ma . . . How could she even think of Kate as her ma? Kate was not a ma. Suddenly the smell of whisky on Kate's breath when she leant over her was a repulsive thing. One day, when her face came near, she pushed her away and told her repeatedly she hated her. Kate staggered back, deeply hurt.

Kate and Catherine had never bonded as mother and daughter. How could they suddenly bond now? Catherine continued to call Rose her ma until Rose died, and Kate never managed to pick up the pieces of their fractured relationship. It was a two-way passage to nowhere. In her ninety-first year, Catherine put it to me this way, with characteristic honesty and even humour: 'I think Kate rejected me from when I was born. She went through hell, having to come home to that little two-roomed house in Leam Lane where her drunken stepfather and half-brother and mother existed. I think I rejected her when I was seven and learnt that she wasn't just our Kate, a relation, she was my mother. But she was never a mother to me. She didn't know how to be a mother. For instance, she wouldn't even tell me the facts of life. When this great, terrifying incident [the onset of menstruation] happened she ran up the street to her sister Mary, who had to come down straight away and pacify me and tell me the facts of life. I was thirteen at the time. Kate was never made to be a mother, and the fact is nor did I want her to be my mother when I realised she drank. Poor little orphan of the storm, one could feel sorry for her . . .'

The episode round the chimneypiece marked the beginning of a quest by Catherine for her own identity that would take many years to complete. It began with a trip to her refuge, the lavatory. In her first novel she gives this to Annie, Kate Hannigan's illegitimate daughter, whose persecutor is named, perhaps with an ironic sidelong glance to the long-term positive elements of the affair, as Cissy Luck. Annie, like Catherine, had supposed that her grandparents, Sarah and Tim Hannigan, were her parents, and that her mother, Kate, was her sister. She flies to her sanctuary in the backyard, but there is no place that her 'queer sense of shame, inexplicable' does not penetrate.

By the time she came to write *Maggie Rowan* (published four years after *Kate Hannigan*) her illegitimate heroine, Maggie, who has been told that she is not Nellie Rowan's daughter but the offspring of Polly Harkness, a whore in Pinwinkle Street, asks, ' "Who am I?" but with a difference.' Maggie does not ask who her parents are – she knows that – but from which of them she has inherited the dominant characteristics 'of her complex self'.

When Catherine was sixteen, her Aunt Mary gave her a full description of her father as she remembered him when he used to visit Kate at The Ravensworth Arms. The picture Mary painted was so unlike anything that Catherine had imagined – Kate had never spoken of him; only once had she ever referred to him, and that only obliquely – that it quite lifted Catherine out of herself. This man, her father, she now realised, had been someone out of the ordinary, out of her class; not some docker or pitman, but a man of mystery and style, a gentleman, who was part of her. She did make some attempts to find out who he was, where he was, even promising a boyfriend, a pit lad 'who ran a betting book on the side', that she would marry him if he managed to find her father. She confesses now that she had no intention of honouring the deal, 'knowing full well that if he did find my father that boy would not see me for dust. Because my father, being the gentleman I had been given to understand he was, would take me away to his big house and have me educated . . .'

The main effect Mary's news had on Catherine, however, was to cause her, like Maggie, to look at herself differently, to consider what there was of her father in her and where it might lead. She embarked on a serious strategy of self-improvement to give whatever traits or genes she had from him the best chance of development over those of her mother, who represented her other side, the side she wanted desperately to eclipse. It was a recipe for disaster psychologically and caused her an enormous amount of grief.

Mary's story, Catherine believes, was related to her in order to hurt Kate, 'to make me more ashamed of her', in comparison with who he was. But, as we shall see, so greatly did the whole idea inspire Catherine that it did lift her out of her impoverished situation. Her absent father, she has written, 'pushed and pulled me out of the drabness of my early existence'. And who is to say whether, as she believed, her father was responsible for what marked her out as different, her 'power to convey awareness, this painful sensitivity . . . without which what I sensed in others would have remained an indescribable mass of feelings'? Who is to say what part his genetic legacy had in her talent as a writer? All that is certain is that she does have this remarkable talent, unique among her known kin.

By the time she came to write *The Glass Virgin* (1970) and *The Girl* (1977), Catherine's quest for identity had become altogether more sophisticated. The mothers of Hannah Boyle and Annabella Lagrange, both lowly creatures, trick their gentleman lovers – Matthew Thornton and Edmund Lagrange respectively – into believing that they have fathered their girls out of wedlock, giving their daughters into Matthew's and Edmund's care and an upbringing beyond their wildest dreams. In these novels Catherine's theme is the perversion of nature by so-called civilised attitudes which mark out a bastard as base and so warp human instinct that natural mothers must give their daughters away. Significantly, however, when the girls realise what has been going on they are not consumed by a desire to find their real parents, nor to establish their own identities through heredity. They are, rather, driven by a need to take responsibility for their own lives, to become free agents, free from all the perverse interferences which have so far dictated their lives, free to be themselves. That Catherine reached such a stage in her own quest enabled her, following her breakdown, to draw utterly honestly, and therefore convincingly, upon the rich, autobiographical vein which feeds her novels and transforms her work from fairy story into an exploration of human needs and endeavour, valid for all times and all people.

In the same year, 1913, that Catherine learnt who her real mother was, Kate began sending her on errands to feed the very habit that stood between them, and soon this became a daily task. There would have been plenty of other drinkers in the New Buildings, but no one other than Kate sent their child to a pub to get their beer. To begin with Catherine would be given a couple of empty bottles to fill; then, when she was eight and reckoned to be old enough to carry it, Kate gave her a gallon stone jar which would have been used originally to hold vinegar. It was so big, and so heavy when full, that Catherine would have to rest it on her hip on the return journey and pause regularly to rest it on the ground. She would have to take this Grey Hen, as it was called, as far afield as Hudson Street, a mile away, past the dock arches into South Shields, where there was an 'outdoor' beer shop.

Catherine did what she could to make Kate see what she was doing. One occasion sticks in her memory because it was the only time Kate ever mentioned her father until a few days before she died. 'I can see myself standing with my back against the wall,' she told me, 'in the corner of the kitchen and openly defying her by staring at her silently and refusing to budge. It was then she cried at me, "Don't you look at me with his eyes." It must have been at that point that the longing for a father grew in me.'

The pressure on Kate was clearly enormous. She had no life of her own to speak of. Her toil with lodgers, with laundry, with cooking and keeping the house together saw to that. She was a rat in a trap. But to inflict this humiliation, even victimisation upon Catherine as a young girl (it went far beyond sending her for the beer, as we shall see) cannot be so excused.

There were times of laughter, but they too leave a sour taste in the mouth. 'Oh yes, we laughed,' Catherine told me, 'we laughed at the most simple things. Word of mouth was the only form of communication then and Kate had sayings. But they were naughty sayings – very naughty sayings when I think of them now. And I used to say them because I thought they were funny sayings, until I was about fourteen when I realised they meant something else.'

Inevitably the drinking put an additional strain on the family's finances, leading to instances of petty crime. Along with everyone in her class, Catherine was asked by her teacher one day to bring in a length of flannelette to make a nightie. Kate did not have the money to buy it. Weeks passed and Catherine kept reminding her that the date was fast approaching when she would have to produce this flannelette at school. Finally, at the eleventh hour, Kate took her to a shop in Jarrow and, before her daughter's eyes, picked up a part bale of material, stuffed it under her coat and left smartly, with the astonished girl tripping behind. On the way home, Catherine had to ask Kate to stop while she vomited by the side of the road.

The incident shows just how close to the wind the McMullens with Kate in control were sailing. 'Necessity, through time and circumstances, made life,' Catherine wrote in *The Obsession* (1995). But necessity did not drive all the Tyneside poor to crime, as an incident Catherine related to me, which followed an injury to her hip in the playground at school, shows.

'I have never before told what I am about to say now. It had been snowing during the week and on this particular day, Kate put into my hand a ten-shilling note and a bass bag and told me to go to Tyne Dock and get three bottles of beer . . . She put the note into my hand – I cannot remember having a purse or a bag during my childhood or my early teens. I carried the money in my hand and I brought the change back in my hand. Now that day she did not give me a halfpenny for a tram to Tyne Dock, because likely she hadn't another penny in the house. So I had to walk. The terminus of the Jarrow car was about twenty feet from the actual police box that guarded the big dock gates. Here the driver would take a pole and turn the long overhead leads round to what had been the back of the car and link it to the wires above. The passengers for the return journey would be standing against the iron railings that bordered the dock shipping offices. The dock gates, the Jarrow tram and the shipping offices seemed to be a full stop between East Jarrow and Tyne Dock, and from this point Shields seemed to begin. Straight in front of the dock gates was a steep bank bordered on one side by public houses and on the other by part of the shipping offices, where the men used to line up in order to be picked for jobs on the boats. This steep bank led to the station, my school and my church. But off it led Hudson Street, where there was the outdoor beer shop and the butchers.

'On this particular day I knew that I could not walk up that bank. My leg was aching terribly and I was trailing my foot. Now, at the bottom of the bank there always stood a paper boy. And what did I do? I went up to this boy and I asked him would he go a message for me as I had a bad leg and couldn't walk up the bank. He said he would, so I placed in his hand the ten-shilling note and the bass bag. What I went through as I waited for that boy to return were ages of eternity filled with terror, knowing what Kate would do to me when I managed to get back home and tell her what I had done. That boy returned with the three bottles of beer and the change, and I gave him a penny. I recall he was poorly clad and freezing with the cold because it was a bitter, bitter day. All that I remember about him otherwise was that he kept hopping from one foot to the other, and although my situation was poor, that boy's was much worse. I never told Kate of this episode because she would have gone mad to think that I had been such a fool as to trust a paper boy.

'Over the years I have thought of that incident. A ten-shilling note would have been a fortune to that child because he was only about ten or eleven years old. He was cold and likely hungry and likely one of a large family, all in the same boat.

'That incident has grown in my mind with the years. If miracles could be handed out to honesty then there was one.'

Better she may have been than some, but Catherine never had the things that many of her contemporaries enjoyed. It became routine at Christmas to pack her stocking with vegetables, just one or two presents lying in the top. One year, to Catherine's painful disappointment, it was all vegetables.

She never had new clothes and was mortified by Kate making her wear a costume coat of thick serge material, far too big for her, with great ballooning sleeves which came in at the wrists and made her look like a bat when she raised her arms. When it was worn out, Kate replaced it with a thick blanket of a coat she'd picked up somewhere, off-white with splurges of red, pink and blue in blotches and stripes. Deeply ashamed of it, Catherine wore it only once.

Yet poverty alone cannot explain why Kate used Catherine as gofer for all her more degrading tasks, in particular for regular trips to the pawn shop.

Catherine's readers will recognise in this Katie O'Brien of *The Fifteen Streets*, to whom she gives the utter degradation of her own regular trips to Bob Gompertz, the Pawn. It wasn't until she was eleven years old that it finally came home to Catherine that the reason Kate sent her was to avoid the shame of it herself. The pawn shop, where clothes were hocked for cash, was a cheap and viable money-lending operation for families in need. But in a community where respectability was all, it was deeply humiliating for the child to be seen by women cleaning their front doorsteps (an obsession in the New Buildings as elsewhere), carrying the tell-tale parcel in her arms.

It should be emphasised that the New Buildings was a mixed community and that its isolation made it a breeding ground for affectation and snobbery. The three streets and the two blocks in Simonside Terrace housed a mixture of families ranging from the lower working class right through to lower middle class and even some middle-class people, who would probably have preferred to have lived in Harton village on the upmarket east side of Tyne Dock. There were the destitute clothes-poor, like the O'Briens in *The Fifteen Streets* or in real life the Kanes, whose daughter would borrow Kate's boots. At the other end of the scale were the Larkins, who lived in two houses at the end of Simonside Terrace (the terrace was the place to be). The Larkins were middle-class people, who at one time had a stake in the barium chemical works and sent their daughter to a boarding school. Catherine glimpsed this girl only once, as she was alighting from a taxi – 'equivalent to a guttersnipe watching the Queen pass' is how Catherine remembers it. Many years later, when this girl had grown up and moved to France, she visited England, bringing her own daughter with her, and let it be known at a banquet at Langley Castle that she had been a friend of Catherine and played with her in her youth. Word of this got back to Catherine, who was living with her husband Tom Cookson nearby, and when Catherine received her in their home the visitor again insisted on their relationship. 'Funny what fame will do.'

For the young Catherine, as messenger, the eyes of anyone on her as she carried that parcel to the pawn, whether higher or lower in social terms, spelt ignominy. As with the beer, she was the only child who was made to do it, and she came to dread Kate asking her to stay off school in the morning, sometimes pleading (when the rent was due and there was no money in the house), at other times shouting at her if she tried to refuse. Going to Bob Gompertz's pawn shop in Bede Street meant passing underneath the arches at Tyne Dock and running the gauntlet of dockers waiting to be taken on. They stood in their huddles right up Hudson Street to where the road divided. Everyone knew her as 'old John's bairn'; everyone knew what she was carrying in her arms – or Catherine had convinced herself they did. To avoid their greetings or stares, she embarked upon an elaborate strategy to throw them off the scent.

If she could, if she had a halfpenny for the fare, she would take a tram up Hudson Street, right through to the railway station, where she would disembark and emerge down the steps by the station as if she were arriving by train, then walk back down Hudson Street towards Bede Street. Fortuitously there was a back lane separating Bede Street from adjacent Nelson Street and she would duck down there, entering the pawn shop through the rear door. She would then pass right through the shop and emerge into Bede Street by means of Gompertz's front door and study his shop window as if she were there to buy. After a period of time, judged to be sufficient to have convinced her audience what she was (or wasn't) up to, she would enter the shop through the front door once more. She might even take the deception further, rummaging through the goods for sale inside.

Whether the deception was successful is hardly the point. Quite possibly her audience were totally unaware of what was going on, or if they did notice were very confused. But the pains she took in constructing this strategy give us all the insight we need into her personal agony – particularly as it was only a matter of time before Gompertz annihilated all pretence by asking what she'd got to exchange. Then her emotions were twisted still further by the need to negotiate, for Kate invariably compounded her anguish with a demand that she try to squeeze him for a little extra that week. She was rarely successful, and so the trip home was fraught with more anxiety about what Kate would say.

What Catherine dreaded perhaps even more than people looking down their noses at her was the other response she detected as these trips became regular: pity. The difference between love, compassion and pity is a theme repeatedly explored in her novels, recently in *The Obsession*. When Dr Falconer proposes marriage to the obsessive Beatrice Steele and tries to analyse his feeling for her, he realises that it isn't passion but isn't sure that it is love either. 'Was it . . . compassion perhaps? Yes. Yes, compassion. But even more than that. Pity? Well, no, no. She wasn't the kind of person you could pity. She was too strong . . .'

Starved of mother love, Catherine began to loathe being on the receiving end of its poor relation, pity, because it marked her out as weak, which she prided herself she was not. She was always fighting against her fears and anxieties, right from the age of seven. Above all, it was important to her that to the other customers in the shop she appeared quite in control of the situation. So, on the outside, whatever she was feeling inside, she played the extrovert, the consummate actress. Once, when taking her place in the pawn-shop queue, a woman stroked her rich auburn curls and said, 'Eeh! but you have bonny hair!' Catherine's response was as sharp as a dart. Lifting her full head of hair with her hand she brought the woman's attention to the darker hair at the nape of her neck. 'That's nearly black,' she said, 'Me da must have been a nigger!'

On cue, the woman had howled with laughter. But with the sobering distance of time the incident is rather less humorous than it is revealing. Catherine told me that she knew little or nothing about the racism that was rife in the area, but clearly she was well versed in the racist undertow of day-to-day conversation. What the incident reveals is an extrovert actress adept at self-effacing humour. In so many of her novels humour transforms pathos, and we can see it at work here, while she suffered inside at the ignominy of her trip to the Pawn. It is a brave, even courageous, performance for such a tortured little girl, and it wouldn't be wasted. This incident, she told me, inspired her novel *Colour Blind* (1953), and readers may fancy that they can hear the raucous laughter of the woman in the pawn shop in the mouth of Kathie McQueen, whose huge breasts and hanging stomach literally reverberate with it.

Catherine had no one with whom to share her feelings until she was in her teens, and even then she felt guilty, disloyal, doing so. Those who were moved to pity her were not moved to do anything about it. This was a community of gossips who kept trouble at arm's length. No one had any idea how Catherine felt. Her shame that they might, and her extrovert behaviour, saw to that, and Kate's widespread popularity protected her from criticism.

Winnie gave me a wholly credible description of how the other kids saw Kate: 'The mother, Kate, was a very nice person. Maybe she was always drunk, I don't know. Perhaps she was in disgrace. We didn't know about that, only that we could take tatey peelings to the door to feed her hens and she would give us a sweet, you know? She was mad, she was always cracking jokes, she made a great fuss of children. She was a nice person.'

In company, people responded to Kate's humour, her generosity, her ability to be the life and soul of the party. No one looked deep inside her, any more than they did inside Catherine – particularly not in Kate's case, because she brought to life every party, especially when there were lodgers in.

These lodgers, who might come six at a time – they'd pile in with Jack in the bedroom; Kate and Catherine would sleep in the kitchen – were often men who'd been at sea for a few months, sometimes for as long as two years. With money no object and revelry felt to be deserved, there'd be drinking and raucous sing-songs, and Kate came into her own at the centre of it all.

Catherine cringed as her mother was transformed into a slack-jawed saloon girl when she was high. Worse still, many of the men fancied their chances with her.

'Kate would flirt,' cousin Sarah confided. 'She was flirtatious, she would flirt with anything in trousers quite honestly.' On one occasion in Birtley, when a local headmaster was there, 'Kate was flirting away with him and they literally had to take her off to bed – you know, get her away or there's going to be trouble.'

There is no doubt that Kate did develop a serious drink problem. Aunt Sarah used to say that she drank methylated spirits as well, and when she arrived at the Lavelle family home in Birtley they used to have to hide the drink away. Indeed, there was a serious falling out after Kate turned up drunk to the funeral of the teenage TB victim, Mary Lavelle. The rift lasted years before the two sisters buried the hatchet: 'Kate came round the path one day,' remembers cousin Sarah, 'she came to see my mum, to put things right. Kate was very kind, very good-hearted, but my mother always said she drank to drown her sorrows.'

But it is likely, too, that Kate's biggest sorrow was the fact that she knew what her daughter felt about her. Even Catherine had been disturbed by Kate's look of utter disconsolation when she told Kate she hated her, and years later she acknowledged that she may have been too harsh. All her life she fancied she could rumble Kate when she was lying to her about whether she'd been drinking. She'd give a little laugh, a dry cough, to cover the lie up. Years later, when she was lying ill and hadn't touched a drop for months, Catherine heard that same little cough again, and felt 'a tinge of remorse'.

Perhaps repulsion at Kate's drinking was one way Catherine could justify her inability to love her mother. And it was an

Catherine with her grandma Rose McMullen in the doorway of number 10 William Black Street. At this stage, Catherine still thought Rose was her mother and that Kate was her sister.

Above: The Tyne between the mudflats of the Slake, empty of timber, past the cranes of Tyne Dock, near where Catherine was born on 20 June 1906, and South Shields, where the river flows into the North Sea. The photograph was taken after the demolition of the New Buildings estate, where Catherine lived from June 1912. The site of the estate can be seen just below the Jarrow Road, bottom right. Follow the road out of picture only a quarter of a mile and you come to number 5 Leam Lane, where Catherine was born. There is a garage now where the house stood, with a memorial plaque by the side of it.

Inset, above: Catherine's real grandfather, William Fawcett (Kate's father). When he died from TB, his five daughters were forced to beg barefoot on the streets of Jarrow.

Left: Jack McMullen stands between his parents, Rose and John, who was Catherine's step-grandfather and whom she knew as her father until she was seven. Jack, sixteen when Catherine was born, grew into a handsome docker and wanted more from his half-sister Kate (Catherine's mother) than virtue allowed. A sniper in the First World War, he was killed in action in September 1918.

John McMullen worked the ships in Tyne Dock, loading and unloading iron ore. It was hard even for the more skilled workers, like the ones pictured here. Jobs were scarce, the problem being underemployment as much as unemployment. Today dockers are retained on a minimum wage, but until the decasualisation of the docks they got paid only when there was work for them to do, and there was always a pool of labour waiting to be taken on.

The Slake, across the Jarrow Road from the New Buildings, where great lengths of unsawn timber, awaiting the attentions of the nearby saw mill, were lashed together and floated on the tide into an enormous raft, secured to upright posts. Catherine used to boast to her companions about her skill in 'playing the piano' – jumping from one timber to the other without falling in.

The inn at Lamesley, the Ravensworth Arms, where Kate worked behind the bar and met Catherine's father. It features in her novel, *The Moth*. Kate's bedroom was in the roof, on the left, behind the dormer window.

The little girl who is standing across the road from the house, number 5 Leam Lane, where Catherine was born, seems to beg identification with her.

The Tyne Dock arches, the heart of dockland between East Jarrow and South Shields. It was only yards away from Catherine's bedroom window, and she could hear the incessant creeking and groaning of the trains at night, as they made their slow way down to the docks. Later, it was here in this dark, dismal, subterranean world, where slime dribbled in rivulets of green down the brickwork walls, that the channels of Catherine's imagination were first opened.

From the age of five Catherine would wander the streets of Tyne Dock, her imagination stirred by characters she saw. 'It was what I soaked up during those years spent in and around East Jarrow, Jarrow and South Shields. Like a great sponge I'd taken it all in . . . ' she said.

Busy Tyne Dock in 1906, the year in which Catherine was born illegitimately to Kate McMullen in a tiny two-room tenement nearby.

Catherine's path to Bob Gompertz's pawn shop in Bede Street from Leam Lane meant passing underneath the Tyne Dock arches and running the gauntlet of dockers in Hudson Street waiting to be taken on. That they all knew her as 'old John's bairn' made it worse, because surely they also knew the ignominious task she was in the process of performing for Kate.

Children of the Tyne looking for treasure on the shoreline at Broad Landing in 1910, as a tug makes its way upstream to Newcastle.

On the move. Catherine remembered sitting with their few bits of furniture on the back of a flat cart for the trip (less than a mile from Leam Lane) to the New Buildings in East Jarrow, where the family moved in June 1912.

After school the streets of the New Buildings community came alive. When Catherine came to live there she was a sparky little 'only child', used to being the centre of attention. Now she had to defer to children more experienced than her in the street culture she was joining, some of whom didn't take kindly to her centre-stage ways.

absolute inability. 'It broke Katie's heart,' said Winnie with poignant insight, 'because, you know, she wanted to love her mother. And when she was at home and she was going out to work, she'd be walking along the road towards Tyne Dock and her mother would bring out a little stool and put it in the porch. She stood on the stool to give her more height and they'd be waving to each other all the way along. Katie would stop and wave to her mother, she was smiling all the time. All the time she was waving at her mother she'd be laughing at her as well. This didn't happen when she was going on holiday, this happened when she was going out to work! Katie was very fond of her mother. It was a great pity and a great heartbreak for her not to be able to love her.'

Nobody, other than Winnie, saw that.

When Catherine wrote her autobiography *Our Kate* (1969) to cleanse her own soul of the bitterness she felt towards her mother, she rewrote it at least eight times to make it palatable. Nevertheless, it remains a forceful indictment of her mother. Responses to it were widely various. Aunt Mary's daughter, Teresa (Teri), said, 'The reaction was a little bit of shock in certain places that she could talk about Kate in this way.'

If they had read the unpublished version, written eleven years earlier and more pointedly entitled *From the Seed All Sorrow*, they would have got the full taste of her bile. Yet Catherine also claimed to have received countless letters from men who had read *Our Kate* and said what a wonderful woman Kate must have been, one even expressing his regret that he had not met her, for surely they would have been married.

Perhaps people take out of a book what they want to believe. 'When I made a name for myself I made a short visit from Hastings, where I then lived, to the north to give a talk in South Shields,' Catherine told me. 'I stayed with Sarah [her Aunt Sarah's youngest daughter – cousin Sarah], and as I hadn't time to visit all the relatives, she kindly got them all together and gave a party for me. It was an awkward situation, since some of them I hadn't seen for twenty years. Sarah, I know, was so proud to have a famous cousin and she did me well with a beautiful tea. Then there we were, all in her sitting room, talking about the family and all saying how they had liked Aunt Kate. Oh wasn't Aunt Kate a joker. She was the best practical joker that ever lived (if I hated Kate for nothing else I hated her for her awful practical jokes). How merry she was. How kind she was. Always had a welcome when you went to see her. And the life and soul of any party. On and on it went, and then, quite quietly, I said, "Yes, Kate was all that, I know. But then you hadn't to live with her. You didn't know the other side." Like a shot of a gun one of the sons sprang up and said, "Don't you dare say a word about my Aunt Kate. You're not fit to wipe her shoes."

'Imagine the silence that followed. My poor cousin Sarah didn't know where to put herself . . . They knew nothing about Kate, especially he who had opened his mouth. Oh, he liked his Aunt Kate. When he left the pit (because it was too much like hard work) and he was broke, Kate was always forthcoming with a sixpence or a shilling to get a drink. Oh yes, he liked his Aunt Kate. And since then I've hated that fellow. He was the first person who had ever insulted me in public (and belonging to my family!). From that day I disowned him in my mind. I have never felt spiteful against anyone in my life, but I felt it against that man and I still do.

What Catherine didn't get a chance to share with her relations that day was that she, perhaps better than any of them, had by that time come to appreciate another side to Kate. There were times as a child, just a few, when Kate became what she might have been if her life had run differently, and I will come to them. Catherine has written, 'Kate had a depth in her that attracted me' – shades of that vision when Catherine was dancing round the lamp-post . . . If her life had been different, if she hadn't turned to drink, then I have a feeling that Catherine wouldn't have had to turn to Mary's gilded image of her father to identify what gave her the inspiration to write; nor, perhaps, would she have suffered the terrors of breakdown before she found herself capable of being a vehicle for Kate's expression, as she put it in the dedication to her first novel. Catherine not only saw, but also came to understand, this depth in Kate.

Violence is part of the rough fabric of Tyneside culture and is a fearsome aspect of Catherine's novels. 'In those days,' she once told me, 'it was not unusual for the man of the house to use a belt, often with the buckle end, on members of the family. There was violence in our household, massive rows.' John never hit Catherine, but Kate did. She would be sent to her bedroom . . . to wait for it. The last time Kate raised her hand to her daughter was when Catherine was about sixteen: she threatened to hit her back, and did. There was friction, too, between Kate and John, especially after Rose died. 'I can see Kate standing there in the doorway with the frying pan, a huge, iron pan about fourteen inches across, a big pan for an open fire. I can see her with it raised above her head. I can't remember what the row was about, but it was after that that we went up to Aunt Mary's and stayed. I remember I laid on a shaky-down on the floor and I remember thinking, wouldn't it be nice to be always here; it'd be heaven.'

Some of the most savage incidents in Catherine's novels, which arise out of the underswell of real violence and cruelty running through Catherine's formative years and which measure her rage and repulsion at all that beset her in the first two decades of her life, occur in *The Girl*, in which Hannah Boyle is whipped senseless by her 'adoptive' mother, Anne Thornton, who in turn is whipped by her husband, Matthew; in *The Whip* (1983) (a novel of sexual repression and sometimes sadistic violence to which I will return), in which Emma Molinero is bound in an attic and flailed mercilessly by Luke Yorkless; and in *A Dinner of Herbs*, in which Hal Roystan is trussed up like a chicken in a barn and left by the psychotic Mary Bannaman to die a slow death. The most masterly creation in *Fenwick Houses*, a first-person narrative – unusual for Catherine – is the character of Don Dowling, a study in repressive behaviour traceable to his extravagant, even perverse, mothering by Phyllis. We learn towards the end of the novel about the tortures to which he has subjected his brother Sam since he was a four-year-old. But the development of this psychopathic character is subtly done throughout, the first sign a rabbit nailed alive to a tree. I recall Catherine telling a story of how a woman in the neighbourhood of William Black Street chopped the tail of a puppy half off simply because it raced through her legs while she was cutting meat.

In *The Blind Miller* we have much of the coarseness which oppressed Catherine as a child, including the effect of whisky on Kate, seen here in the beleaguered Sarah Bradley. This is a powerful novel, perhaps her best in conveying a sense not only of a life of squalor, but also of the mesmerising, primitive currents which flowed beneath the surface of life. The hopeless degradation is caught in a picture that first comes to Sarah as a hallucination when she has taken an overdose of cough medicine, and thereafter comes back to her time and time again. In this image, all the inhabitants of the Fifteen Streets are wallowing and choking in a sea of mud, which we recognise as the timber pond of the Jarrow Slacks when the tide is out. So many of Catherine's early books, through which she performed an extraordinary operation of self-purification, are full of such imagery, drawing us more deeply into her subconscious than the literal connections with the environment in which she was brought up.

Then there is the anatomical imagery, which again emphasises the uncompromising physicality of life and at the same time its truth. Sarah isn't simply embarrassed when she is first introduced to the nice young man called David Hetherington. Sweat 'bursts into her oxters'. This word 'oxters' – armpits – so unusual a piece of northern dialect that it is bound to have most of her readers sit up, occurs frequently in her novels (as does 'hunkers'). What its use does here is to express the animalism of the scene, so successfully as to have us almost smelling the poor girl's sweat. Elsewhere Catherine uses the word as a wonderful leveller. In a society bursting with snobbery and prejudice, everyone has oxters, irrespective of race, caste or creed, and sweat bursts regularly in all of them. We get the feeling that our world too might be a better, more truthful place if we came to terms with our oxters and put the purveyors of deodorant out of business.

But then, besides the animalism, we have the animism, the primitive immaterial force which is all-inspiring, as when David's exciting, sensuous brother John takes Sarah racing the moon, he running wild against the wind 'like a great lolloping bear', she beside him caught fast in his iron grip. Poor, kind David will not stand a chance against this. The sexual hunger of his wife for John fairly crackles off the page. And yet what we feel is that sex is their response to the force, not the force itself.

For violence (and appalling prejudice, which is what in this novel sets Catherine up for the violence) it is difficult to imagine a more powerful scene than Pat Bradley's taking a belt to his daughter Phyllis, Sarah's sister, for going with an Arab called Ali.

'The Arabs first came to Shields in the crews of ships in the nineteenth century. Up until just before the war more than half the crew would have been Arab,' Catherine told me. 'Then what would happen is that one or two would start a boarding house and the men from the ships would stay there. In the docks, if there weren't Arabs, there were Swedes, a tremendous number of Swedes, and there were negroes and Russians, the big burly captains. There was everything there, and not once did anyone handle me, even though at that time there was a tremendous fuss about the white slave trade, girls being picked up and whisked away.' But race, like class and religion, 'was an opportunity not to be missed' by the bigots in the community, though 'there was just as much race prejudice between negroes and Arabs as there was between blacks and whites.'

Corstorphine Town was the Arab quarter in Shields. 'Despite what I said in Bob's pawn shop, I didn't know anything at that time about immigrants or how different one was from another.' But the Arab quarter did occupy a special place in Catherine's memory for another reason. 'Betty was a pet hen,' she told me. 'She was twelve years old, she had rheumatics and couldn't walk but could still lay eggs. When she died, me granda couldn't eat her, but he wasn't going to lose on her so he sold her to one of the Arab boarding houses in Corstorphine Town.'

Another Betty ends up in Corstorphine in *The Blind Miller* – Betty Fuller. Her mother empties a chamberpot over her head when she returns home after going out with an Arab, and the whole neighbourhood rises up against her. But this is nothing compared to Pat Bradley's wrath when he takes his buckled belt to his daughter, Phyllis, unleashing all the prejudice, cruelty, envy and morbid self-interest with which Catherine invests his character (morbid, for, as Sarah says, he wants his daughter Phyllis for himself). He whips her so hard that her jumper and skirt lie in shreds 'and the seat of her bloomers was all black as if she had been dragged around the yard.'

Catherine's description of this terrible act, effective as it is in the novel, draws additional power from the way it is contrasted to the love between the teenage sisters, Bradley's daughters. It is a relationship for which Catherine, the only child, longed in her increasingly alienating environment at home. Phyllis and Sarah sleep together in the same bed, they share all their secrets, they enjoy each other's company on a ferry-ride across the Tyne with an innocence otherwise hopelessly absent from a community eaten up by prejudice and fear.

In *Hamilton* a mother is guilty of even worse cruelty to her child. Maisie Carter was born of a cross-class liaison with a Rochester from Wellenmore Terrace, who left home when Maisie was two. Already disfigured physically (Maisie has one arm shorter than the other), she is beaten up so badly in her early teens by her mother, after a visit (expressly forbidden) to her warm-hearted Gran, that the girl's face is still swollen after a week, when the family doctor, Dr Kane, chances to call. While I was reading this novel, Catherine happened to telephone me. I had been wondering what the source could be for this kind of extreme fictional violence between a mother and daughter, and Catherine told me a story, which we will come to in Chapter Six, and which confirms its source as horrifically real.

There are few things more unsettling for a young child than to hear its parents row, especially when they are out of sight and the row is about sex. Violence heard through the wall can set up home in the imagination, engendering a kind of voyeuristic fear which lingers longer, for example, than abrupt chastisement. In *Fenwick Houses*, the rows Christine Winter hears through the wall between her Aunt Phyllis and Uncle Jim, who has a woman in Bog's End, form the girl's earliest impressions of sex. Likewise, in *Kate Hannigan*, little Annie hears Tim Hannigan's voice, 'low and terrible with menace', met by her grandma's pleading, 'full of something that struck the greatest terror into Annie's heart'. Both scenes arise from Catherine's own experience as a child, listening to precisely this scene between grandma and her drunken step-grandfather, as Rose struggled to fight John off.

For Kate, after Catherine's conception, sex was non-existent until she married David McDermott in 1923. Among the lodgers who came to William Black Street soon after she took up the reins of the household from Rose in 1912, one Jack Stoddart (who introduced David to Kate) was a contender for her hand, but old John would have none of it. Kate had blotted her copybook. Sex was the cause of the mess they were in. For Catherine, as she grew from a girl into a young woman, this fear and restraint sat uneasily alongside her earlier experiences of sexual menace heard through the wall, and the deviant images she picked up elsewhere. Even today she remembers vividly the occasion when she was waiting for a tram by the dock gates and, hearing raucous laughter, looked across the road to where there was a public convenience. 'To my horror I saw a woman come out of the public lavatory opposite with three men.' Then, in 1914, the year after the traumatic revelation of her illegitimacy, Catherine was sexually molested by an Irish lodger from next door, a man who had been going to marry Kate.

It was a Saturday night; Rose and John were out. Catherine was only eight, and Kate was supposed to be looking after her, but she had left her to go and fetch some beer. The man sat Catherine on his knee – she hadn't thought it strange, didn't her granda always sit her on his knee? But then he picked her up and laid her on the settle and began smothering her with kisses. It was a terrifying experience for the little girl – 'I can still hear myself screaming.'

She remembers little of what occurred until after Rose and John returned. In the ensuing fight Rose was 'knocked clean under the table . . . For me there are blocks, absolute blocks in my childhood. I have tried to get past them but I can't . . . I wasn't abused. It was what I saw and knew he intended . . . I can't remember who I told or what I said because there is a blank there. I knew that if I told anyone me granda would kill him as he would an old man in a shop who wouldn't give me the change until I kissed him. I was wise enough to know this, that there would be terrible consequences because, you know, he really loved me . . . I must have said something to me granda. The Irish lodger disappeared from the house next door the following morning.'

Childhood abuse is the subject of *The Cinder Path* (1978). The setting is Northumberland, and the novel opens around 1908–10. Charlie McFell is the fulcrum. Charlie's father, Edward, is a warped personality, damaged by his own father, William, who had bought Moor Burn Farm in 1858. Here, first Edward and then his children, Charlie and Betty, were brought up. One of Edward's earliest memories is of his father, William, sadistically throwing him down on to the rough surface of a cinder path and beating him with a birch. The pain and humiliation to which William regularly subjected Edward (and any young miscreant on the farm) are made doubly wounding by the knowledge that he had laid the path for the purpose. This strangely symbolic black strip of sharp cinders led, otherwise uselessly, from the McFells' farm to the burn which gave the farm its name. The dead-end track was never trodden; no one could possibly want to walk it. It led nowhere, other than remorselessly into the dark, obsessional reaches of William McFell's mind, and on, as the novel opens, into the mind of his son, Edward.

This time it is young 'Ginger' Slater, a workhouse boy, who gets the treatment, while Charlie and young Polly Benton look on, voyeuristically but appalled. Confirming our subliminal interpretation of William's and Edward's obsessional behaviour as sexually motivated, the event mingles with heartless

53

suggestions by Edward that it's about time young Charlie got laid, and that, apart from this, he should think about marrying Victoria Chapman of neighbouring Brooklands Farm (so that the two properties might be joined).

Polly Benton lives in a stone cottage on Moor Burn Farm with her mother, also called Polly, who has been Edward's unhappy and unwilling means of sexual release for years. Jim Benton, utterly dependent on the McFells, has been in no position to complain. Now Edward has a mind to select young Polly as similar instrument for his son, Charlie. There is a well of sickness and depravity so deep at Moor Burn Farm that any show of parental emotion towards Charlie, even by his mother, is suspect, a cause of embarrassment. For even in his mother the show of affection has a selfish source, merely fulfilling her needs. Charlie is rendered clinically bereft of feeling by his father, the vacancy in the tunnel which leads to the bottom of this well of depravity, to the place where lies the monster which, at any moment, we know will swallow Edward up.

When it does, it is young Polly's brother, Archie, who precipitates Edward's fall. Archie rigs up a rope across the path which he knows Edward will shortly ride. He means to unseat him and so save his sister. But Edward's fall from his horse breaks his neck. Again Charlie, in the position of voyeur, watches it happen. Charlie returns Archie to his sister and mother, and makes them swear a pact never to tell what has happened. Charlie has every reason to be glad that his father is dead. But when he takes his leave of them and disappears so that Edward's death may be discovered without implicating himself or the Bentons, he weeps over the 'slaughter'.

It is a strange opening, a raw and sensitive account of childhood abuse. There is compulsion and voyeurism, repression and secrecy, love and deep, deep hurt. But the literary tool Catherine uses – the image of the cinder path, her central 'device' – is itself so odd (it seems to belong to some sort of weird, sadistic public school regime) that you are left in no doubt that whatever psychological blocks Catherine has about her abuse and rank exposure to sex as a child, they are rolled aside in the novels, where her subconscious is in control.

This was never more apparent than in *Colour Blind*. After reading it, her mother Kate was astonished. She had had no idea that Catherine had been aware of her brother Jack's incestuous advances to her, which had begun when Kate moved into

William Black Street and took control of the household. Catherine herself was even more surprised, because consciously she had had no idea about Jack either.

Jack, the fourth regular member of the McMullen household, about whom little has so far been said, was a handsome, hulking docker, 'swarthy like a gypsy', and eight years Kate's junior. There appears to have been no girlfriend on the scene during his short life (he was killed in action in the First World War aged twenty-eight): Jack spoke of women, joked about them, but they never materialised. At the time of which I am writing, around 1912–13, Kate and Catherine were sleeping in the same bed. Catherine was six. One night she remembers awakening to find Jack, his face close to Kate's, whispering her name repeatedly. This scene is actually recorded in a later novel, *Fenwick Houses*, presumably after Kate had read *Colour Blind* and told Catherine what Jack had been up to that night. But in the earlier narrative, where Matt McQueen's passion for his sister Bridget drives her 'whisky-mad' and eventually destroys Bridget's relationship with the negro Jimmy Patterson, there is so true a portrayal of Jack's desire for his sister that Kate assumed Catherine must have known about it. When Catherine denied this, Kate said, 'Well, you must have taken it in as a child.'

Catherine took it all in, all the secrets, all the repressed desires and fears, but for her own sanity's sake blocked much of it out from conscious thought until, years later, it was released in the novels.

Kate had lifted a veil on Catherine's misted memories of rows between Jack and Kate that seemed to be about nothing. The truth of what lay behind this friction, never suspected on a conscious level, had been known, deep down. Like the time Kate was on her knees clearing out the ashes of the fire and Jack, close to her, was shaking his fist, before he suddenly dashed to the bedroom and, reluctantly this time, Kate had sent Catherine out for the beer.

Following the episode at the chimneypiece, Catherine's response to the revelation of her illegitimacy had been shame and fear, the fear of 'not belonging'. She countered both by immediately attempting to establish a new, more acceptable identity. She had considered pretending to her classmates that her Uncle Alec, Mary's husband, was her da. He was quite bright, good at crosswords and that kind of thing, and of course, as Mary never ceased to remind everyone at number 10, they were distinctly better off and more respectable than the McMullens. But Catherine decided to go for broke and instead to opt for Dr James McHaffie, the family doctor. There's quite a nice irony in this, for in a sense in those days doctors 'fathered' all illegitimate children, as childbirth was almost always carried out under the aegis of the family doctor at home. But the attraction of McHaffie for Catherine was that he was goodlooking, had a car and, like all doctors, was middle class. Doctors and priests were, indeed, just about the only middle-class presence in the lives of lower working-class families. So McHaffie it would be.

She regaled her classmates with stories of the big house she lived in, the servants and horses and cars, and then one day she was all set for school and McHaffie happened to be in the house visiting her granda, who had injured his leg at work. As Catherine was ready for off, so was he, and oh, the kindness of Fate, he offered her a lift in his car. When she alighted at the school gates, her classmates couldn't believe their eyes as little Catherine glided past them with a, 'There! What did I tell ya? We have got a motor.' Unfortunately her teacher called her bluff by suggesting in front of the entire class that perhaps Catherine could supply the horn for Father Christmas's sleigh from her father's motor car . . . It was an unnecessary put-down, but the story does give us the germ of an insight into Catherine's personality and her relationship with the school.

She once wrote a poem called 'My First Pair of Boots'. Boots were the basic piece of equipment for the poor. They stood between you and the cold wet road. A child called Steve is so proud to own a pair that he sticks one foot out in the aisle between the classroom desks so that his teacher will notice them as she walks past. But even when Mulligan blurts out, 'Are you ganna tyek 'em off when ya gan t'bed?' Miss Platt refuses to pay any attention to them. Such pride, such sparkle, such trusting optimism and good humour are all contained in Steve. But Miss Platt just won't play the game – until after the lesson, when Steve hangs back from the rest and, touching his sleeve, she looks down at the boots and says, 'They're grand boots, whoppers; keep 'em clean, Steve.'

Catherine was not a child you could ignore. The best of her teachers would bring her on, make something out of her eager, sparky side. Later, Miss Barrington would be one of these: she leapt at the challenge and gave Catherine something to chew on, gave her an appreciation of the beauty of words. But it is not difficult to see why mundane Miss Caulfield, full of her own self-importance, a kind of mother duck who liked her ducklings to form an orderly line behind her, would slap her down. For Miss Caulfield, Catherine's spark was not a challenge but a threat.

And so we come to Mary Ann, the heroine of a series of eight novels, published between 1954 and 1967, and the embodiment of Catherine's imaginative individuality at this time. Mary Ann has her own little world worked out inside, and she sparkles with it. *A Grand Man* opens in the school yard with her boasting about her 'great big house'. Like Catherine, Mary Ann tells tall stories about her family and their wealth and station to compensate for their poverty and her father's drinking, which has brought them to the lowest of the low, Mulhattans Hall. It wasn't lies she was telling, Mary Ann reassures herself, 'it was more in the nature of a story'. Mary Ann wants everyone to play her game, and why shouldn't they? Most other people's games look pretty silly. Hadn't she watched her own dear grannie, through a slit in the back lavatory door, as she snitched the cream from her neighbour's pint of milk before replenishing the deficit with milk from her own pint? If that was the level of life, then Mary Ann's game was without doubt better. Her tall stories and the promise of an invitation to her big house one day win her offers from her classmates of 'a stot of me ball', the loan of a 'thick skipping rope', a share in a classmate's 'bullets' (sweets). But alas for Mary Ann, as for Catherine, there were girls who had been brought up on the upstart game and were more experienced at it; in Mary Ann's case the chief among these was Sarah, the daughter of Mrs Flannagan, the most notorious upstart in the neighbourhood, who also happens to live opposite her and knows the truth of where she comes from.

Catherine's boasting may have celebrated her imaginative side, but if she thought it was going to win her friends she was sadly mistaken. In 1915, a year after she had been molested by the lodger and nearly two years after the traumatic episode at the chimneypiece, she took another big knock. She was as yet only nine years old.

One of her schoolmates, a girl from Phillipson Street, which backed on to William Black Street and shared the same back lane, was throwing a birthday party and distributed invitations to all the clan . . . except Catherine. She was sure hers would come. Why wouldn't it? They were mates, after all, weren't they?

But as the party approached and still no invitation appeared, Catherine began to feel uneasy. Reverberations of the feelings aroused by the episode at the chimneypiece stirred within. Kate knew something was up, and Catherine knew Kate knew; but no words passed between them until the day of the party. It was a Saturday, Catherine's day for the matinée at the Crown cinema. She announced to Kate that she wouldn't be going, got dressed up in a clean pinny and left by the back door, Kate's words – 'It's no use, hinny, it's no use!' – following her out. But Catherine was made of stronger stuff than Kate. She opened the backyard door into the lane and stood there watching her friends opening their backyard doors one by one and making their way across the lane to the back staircase of the upstairs house in Phillipson Street where the party was to be held. Not one of them said a word to her. Finally, when all had fallen quiet again, Catherine walked steadily up to the girl's yard door, opened it, crossed the backyard, walked up the staircase and, with extraordinary courage (or face), rapped on the back door.

In no time a group of squealing children seemed to fill the open doorway, all eyes on Catherine as she asked, could she come in? The ball was in her little hostess's court. Even taking into consideration what a cocky little show-off Catherine could be, it was surely inconceivable that she would not be let in. But the ball came back fast and low, and with a spin on it that destroyed Catherine. Her ma said she couldn't come.

Why?

Because Catherine 'ain't got no da'.

It must be nigh on a hundred per cent certain that the little girl's mother had said nothing of the sort. We are not looking here at adult prejudice against illegitimate children, we are looking at the cruelty of one child to another. Drawing back from the scene, we are looking at Catherine's alienation, her rejection at nine years of age from the world in which she moved, and, once more, a denial of the validity of her own inner world. Those fears engendered by the chimneypiece episode had been utterly confirmed.

In Catherine's response, however, we are looking at something else, the kind of mettle that would one day raise her up out of this place altogether. The experience would have crushed a lesser child, recommending to her perhaps a strategy of backtracking, of seeking humiliatingly to inveigle her way back into her friends' good books, or of retreating into herself. Catherine did none of these. She came out fighting. 'From this time the fight started within me . . . I bossed, bullied and slapped out . . . I was bent on showing them, showing the lot of them.'

In the novels, Mary Ann resorts to the same aggressive tactics towards Sarah Flannagan, and we also find this side of Catherine in another of her little fictional heroines, Mary Ellen in *A Dinner of Herbs*, who had 'a tongue that would clip clouts and a head on her that would fit her granny, the things she comes up with'. In real life, when Lottie Christopher wouldn't lend Catherine her skipping rope she dragged it off her and then, when Kate appeared off the tram, threw it at poor little Lottie so that Mrs Christopher appeared at the McMullens' front door complaining that Catherine had thrashed her with it. If anyone refused to fall in line Catherine would challenge them to a fight. Once she even pushed a boy into the Slacks. Mothers, even fathers, started calling at number 10 to complain, and inevitably it all came to a head when she tried it on with someone bigger than her, one Olive Swinburne, who put her on the floor. Henceforth Catherine thought twice about giving physical vent to her feelings.

Catherine's aggression was grounded in fear and sadness – fear not of her classmates but of not belonging; sadness at their rejection of her and at what seemed to her the only possible retort, her rejection of them – all serving to intensify the fear and love 'which combined to cause the feeling of utter sadness' in her relationship with Kate at home.

Fear, bred of a combination of apprehension and anxiety, 'was the single most important emotion of my childhood,' Catherine told me, 'and it still is, right up to this very moment. I feared Kate's drinking to an exaggerated point.' It wasn't drinking itself that got to Catherine; old John's drinking didn't have the same effect. It was the fact that it was her ma who was doing it and, more especially, that she couldn't hold her drink. It took no more than a glass or two to transform Kate into the misty-eyed, slovenly, word-stumbling caricature of herself which people who dropped in accepted without a word, but which in Catherine's eyes turned her into another person. It was bad enough when there were just the two of them together, but at family gatherings the effect on Catherine was pure shame as Kate strained to hit the top notes of 'Thora', her favourite song, 'her head well back, that slack lower lip of hers wobbling. I really longed to die on such occasions.'

Fears born in the kitchen of number 10 stayed with Catherine for many years after she had left William Black Street. Talking to me in 1985, long after suffering nervous breakdown, she recalled the period from 1945 when these fears had been joined by a whole nightmarish set of others – the fear of losing her husband, of doctors, of operations, of 'blood-spattered floors and blinding arc lights', fear of going mad. 'I turned into a solid block of fear.' The dark shadows of this time stay with her even today. 'You never get rid of a breakdown. The sediment of it lies in your sub-conscious; an incident, a word, or even a place can stir that sediment again and there you are back full of terror . . . of what? You can't explain, except, in my case, it is aggression, deep aggression, against my early suffering, against my mother, against someone who did me a great evil that I have never written about because the result of it was I learned how to hate, to hate with such intensity that I knew that if I let it have the upper hand my future life would be ruined.'

That 'someone' we will come to in Catherine's adult life, but it all started here, in the back streets of the New Buildings and in the kitchen of number 10, before she was even into her teens. In *Colour Blind* Catherine uses the cruelty of little Rose-Angela's playmates to show that human nature, even in ones so young, insists upon conformity. Being different is not allowed. Rose-Angela's difference is that she is a half-caste. She'll never go to heaven because she 'ain't white'. Rosie is special because she gives us an insight into the physical effect which Catherine's feeling of rejection had on her: Rosie's nervous system is 'like a highly tensed wire'. The fears of her own childhood produced the same state in Catherine, but with one difference: later, much later, she would use it creatively. The 'painful sensitivity' to which Catherine attributes her creativity was not appeased by her writing; I once asked her whether her writing helped her to recover from her breakdown and she replied, 'No, not in the least. My mind was still in torment, mentally and physically, fourteen hours a day at least.' But she put her painful sensitivity to work, which is the reward of the apprenticeship years.

Chapter Four

Birth of Imagination

'The feeling of aloneness I felt on the day of that birthday party was felt deep inside of me and I shall always have it. I can be jolly. I can be the life and soul of the party. But I can understand these men who are always very jolly and then go and commit suicide. I talk to everybody and people think that I am such an extrovert, Kitty is this, Kitty is that, Kitty is the other, but Kitty was born with this feeling of aloneness. I can't say that I was the first person to use this word, but what I mean by it is in contrast to loneliness. There is a great difference between the two. It is being a *thing apart*.'

To this bright little girl, rejected and possessed of this alienating feeling of aloneness, the area of Jarrow, Tyne Dock and Shields which she tramped on her 'messages' to the pawn shop or pub for Kate seemed a desolate place. It is an image which occurs many times in her books. In *The Fifteen Streets* John O'Brien, shunted into work at the docks, can't understand why he doesn't welcome the sunshine, until one day it dawns on him that the sun showed the place up for what it was. On an overcast day, 'the docks, the coal dust, the houses, the rattling trams, and the people all seemed to merge into one background'. But when the sun shone, they stood out, 'dirty, stark, tired'. Lonely and lost, he asks, 'What did it all mean, anyway? What was living for?'

The Gambling Man (1975) opens with possibly the best description of the Tyne Dock area anywhere in Catherine's fiction. It is a Sunday; everything outside is cold, silent, resting. Desolation is laid in thick layers on her canvas, her palette dispensing sounds, sensations, even moral intimations, as 'the first flat flakes of snow . . . dropped to rest in their white purity on the greasy, coal-dust, spit-smeared flags.' As Rory the rent man goes about his business he meets bootless children with snotty noses, black-shawled women with arms crossed against huge, sagging breasts, flat, down-trodden faces creasing into forced smiles of welcome and a false, chattering clannishness, aware that eviction may be only one more week away.

Almost all the messages Catherine ran for Kate would involve her walking past the sawmill and on beneath the five Tyne Dock arches, the heart of dockland which separated East Jarrow from Shields. Here, in this dark, dismal, subterranean world, where slime dribbled 'in rivulets of green' down the brickwork walls 'as black as a singed bloater', the channels of her creative imagination were opened. On one occasion, at the age of five, she was walking under the arches, alone as usual, when some-one unwelcome appeared in the distance. To avoid whoever it was she crossed over the road, put her face to the blank wall and walked sideways until they had passed. What she saw with her mind's eye when her face was up against the cold, wet bricks was a picture, a real technicolour picture as clear as day of a better life in a better place, prosperous, genteel, and with herself dead centre. She would repeat this tactic whenever the occasion required. It never failed.

The same arches were also the site of a more mysterious vision. She was walking westwards this time, on her return to East Jarrow. She had passed through the first arch nearest the dock gates and emerged into the dim light, grey, polluted, in parts defeated altogether by shade from the high dock wall and the steep bank leading up to the railway, when she noticed a beautiful boy walking towards her. He occupied the same position as her but at the other end of the tunnel of arches. They each had an arch through which to pass before they would meet. As she walked on a feeling of pure joy swept through her. It was so strong and so suffused her that she became transfixed by the image of the boy. She couldn't take her eyes off him. Then a strange light, a kind of visual equivalent of the feeling inside her, seemed to spread from the boy, a white light which grew in strength and power until it overcame the tunnel of gloom and welcomed her in. When she came to, she was emerging from the last arch, alone. Retracing her steps a pace or two, she looked back down the tunnel and saw that the boy – she knew who he was; his name was Hughie Axill – was also emerging into day at the other end.

Catherine gave this experience to Mary Walton, the heroine of *Pure as the Lily*, who, after forty years of disaster, was to recognise Hughie Amsden's eyes as those of her childhood crush, who had dissolved into white light in the same way. She describes the light as pure, 'love before it was touched by hand, or marred by life; love as pure spirit'.

It was a spiritual experience, spiritual in the true sense; illuminating of love in the novel, but in real life, to Catherine, an affirmation of a capacity, even a readiness, to achieve a state of inspiration beyond conscious control. It would be forty years before she came to realise what that meant to her as a writer. Then she would be sitting in a cold drawing room in another town, her mind a void, convinced that she would never write another word – and the whole story of *The Fifteen Streets* came to her, 'right from the opening to the very last words. Every character, every incident . . . It was all there.' And, as we shall see, she just accepted it . . .

There, beneath the rawness of everyday life, in the subterranean world of the Tyne Dock arches, the channels of creative inspiration had been opened. The conditions had been right for it to happen. Almost one hundred years earlier, the imagination of a boy, alienated, lonely and cast adrift in the city of London, had been whetted beneath the dark arches about the Adelphi. There was no white light, but his imagination had taken flight, as he recorded in his heavily autobiographical novel *David Copperfield*. There is, indeed, much to be learned about the flowering of creative imagination from a comparison of Catherine Cookson and Charles Dickens at around the same time in their lives.

Dickens, like Catherine, had a bright, sparky personality but found it difficult to mix with his contemporaries. There was something different about Dickens, something which set him apart from his fellows. He was 'a queer small boy', a poor 'Robin Crusoe' on an island of his own. Again like Catherine, he was 'a child of singular abilities: quick, eager' and sensitive, painfully sensitive – 'soon hurt mentally', as he put it. Both were also consummate actors and dogged by illness; and, significantly in terms of the development of their imaginations, both were set loose alone in their places of inspiration – London and Tyneside – at a young age, their senses sharpened by rejection and loss.

Dickens was born on 7 February 1812, and at first enjoyed a period of security, initially at Portsea and then at the family home in Chatham in Kent. But his father had fallen badly into debt, and the family had to move to a 'mean, small tenement, with a wretched little back-garden abutting onto a squalid court', at 16 Bayham Street in Camden Town, in London. By 1824 his father's financial position was so bad that he was arrested for debt and incarcerated in the Marshalsea prison. Shortly afterwards his wife and three of their children joined him there in rooms, as was the way, but left Charles, at twelve years of age, to fend for himself. There was no question of his continuing at school, and he went to work in a boot-blacking factory, 'a crazy, tumbledown old house, abutting . . . on the river, and literally overrun with rats.

'It is wonderful to me how I could have been so easily cast away at such an age,' he wrote. No one made any attempt to rescue him. He writes of 'the deep remembrance of the sense I had of being utterly neglected and hopeless, of the shame I felt in the position; of the misery it was to my young heart . . . My whole nature was so penetrated with the grief and humiliation . . . I know I do not exaggerate, unconsciously and unintentionally, the scantiness of my resources and the difficulties of my life.'

The causes of Dickens' dispossession may be different from those in Catherine's case, but the consequences – rejection, alienation, misery, humiliation, shame – are the same negative emotions, dark currents awaiting transformation into light by a child thrown upon its own resources.

To this lonely, hungry twelve-year-old boy, London, like Catherine's Tyneside, is desolate too – a 'Wilderness!' exclaims Cheeryble to Nicholas Nickleby: 'It was a wilderness to me once. I came here barefoot – I have never forgotten it. Thank God!' Dickens' solitary introduction to the streets of London came in the form of a twice-daily walk between his lodgings in North London and the factory in the Strand. Then, becoming more adventurous, he ventured out on his own into Soho and Covent Garden, wide-eyed, watching, observing . . .

Like a child lured by the hot flame of a candle he knows he

mustn't touch (but does so all the same), Dickens embraces 'wild visions of prodigies of wickedness, want and beggary'. Likewise, Catherine's imagination was stirred by characters she saw every day in Jarrow, Tyne Dock and Shields. 'It was what I soaked up during those years spent in and around East Jarrow, Jarrow and South Shields. Like a great sponge I'd taken it all in . . .'

London was a bigger, stranger and more terrifying place to Dickens than the docklands of Catherine's experience was to her, known kindly by the dockers as 'old John's bairn'. But just as Dickens came to his vision of London a lonely child, rejected and humiliated by loss, so Catherine came to hers of Tyneside with her imaginative processes similarly scored so that the spirit of the place took hold. It wasn't simply that the place was desolate but that she was peculiarly receptive to its desolation, and drawn to transform it. The novelist and biographer Peter Ackroyd wrote in the introduction to my book *Dickens' London* that the metropolis was a place of darkness, imprisonment and suffocation to the author, transformed out of necessity. The opening scene in Catherine's *Kate Hannigan* is so strong a portrayal of the spirit of Tyneside by its authorial witness that the book's eventual publisher, Murray Thompson at Macdonald, threw it on the scrap heap after reading the opening pages, believing that it would put off readers. Fortunately it was rescued by his secretary who, caught by the power of those same pages, took the manuscript home and stayed up half the night reading the rest.

The faithful autobiographical content of this first novel reveals Catherine's artistic purpose. She is exorcising her own demons. Tyneside has taken on the shape of her own fears, as London did for Dickens, and now out of necessity she must transform it. The very form of the novel, which recounts the pivotal events on successive Christmas Eves, suggests her purpose. Even among such poverty and squalor, families came together on Christmas Eve in a spirit of celebration. And yet there is no sense of a fairytale happy ending. Kate Hannigan is no Cinderella, Dr Rodney Prince no Prince Charming.

The doctor's vocational mission to Tyneside, belittled by his wife Stella, who is locked out of our sympathies by her cruel treatment of him and her inability to look beneath the surface to see what made people like Kate tick, is crucial. It has the effect of drawing him, and us, into a whole new dimension of Tyneside life, something deep in the subconscious of its people, embodied in Kate Hannigan and illuminated by her creator, who shines the 'white light' of her imagination upon it. Early on, the newcomer Rodney Prince is envious of the rapport between Dr Davidson and Kate, realising that it hinges on what has motivated him to work with the poor of Tyneside, the deep-rooted spirit of its people, something he cannot put into words. By the end of the narrative, when Rodney and Kate come together, he understands what it is, and that is what this novel is about. Catherine once described it as 'the element of their origin that comes from far back and threads the people of this particular area', something she could feel in the emotions of her characters when she was writing them down, 'their voice . . . their laughter, their humour, their sorrows and their joys'. It is the same primitive force which she divined in her mother, which is the reason why she dedicated this novel to Kate, 'who found her expression through me'.

At odd times of the year Kate Fawcett would join other women of the New Buildings, dress up in men's clothes and parade round the streets, beating tin cans and singing. Even Aunt Mary would join in. The sudden inexplicable loosening of the bonds of restraint and respectability amazed Catherine. 'There was a primitive weirdness about this, which I recall whenever I hear the Kerry Piper's song.'

Then there were the occasions when Kate, stone-cold sober, would suddenly snatch Catherine by the hand and dash off into the night with her, racing the moon along the Slack bank, running, jumping and laughing as the wind tore at her hat and the moon bathed her face in its pale, haunting light. When finally they came to rest in each other's arms, it was as if the moonlight had washed all the pressures of their lives away. It was primitive, moon-struck madness, one of those moments of release when Kate became what she might have been; its echoes in Sarah and John's escapade in the moonlight in *The Blind Miller* suggest that Kate's pregnancy may have come of this. The image of the moon in poetic mythology as fount of inspiration merges with Catherine's excitement and her unusual closeness to her mother to give us, above all, a sense of partnership in Catherine's artistic creativity. These were rare moments indeed.

By the time Catherine was eight or nine, the sometime little extrovert had acquired a talent for self-denigration that bore witness to a marked inferiority complex. But the extrovert remained all that was visible on the outside. All the negative emotions which Kate had aroused in her – the fear, the feeling of sickness born of anxiety, 'the awfulness . . . the fear and the love which combined to cause the feeling of utter sadness,' as Catherine put it in *A Grand Man* – she bottled up inside. Once, repulsed by the stench of whisky on her mother's breath as Kate leant over to kiss her, Catherine told her that she hated her. But in saying it she felt utter sadness. Every emotion was a two-sided coin: never one feeling without the other. Later she would write in her autobiography of happiness as 'the seedbed' of pain, while in her novels, which are optimistic, the reverse is true, as love is born out of bitter division. Imbibing this strange cocktail of love and hate brewed by her mother, however crippling at the time, proved to be a necessary development for the artist in her. Kate taught Catherine how to hate as well as how to love, and showed her that these emotions are inextricably intertwined. Eventually, after years of heartache and distress, Catherine would understand this fundamental principle of life – that there can be no love without hate, no good without evil, because without their antitheses, love and good are meaningless concepts. Without hate, love cannot *be*. And without such polar opposites there can be no process of transformation, no purpose in life at all.

'The law of opposites' is a phrase Catherine uses aptly as a chapter heading in *The Menagerie* (1958), and time and again in the novels she calls on it to resolve the discordant forces in her characters' lives. Later she would discover in her love for the man who was to become her husband that, 'in the channels where the intangible but real life runs', opposite poles are as one. Understanding this was critical in her life as in her art. It bred in her a sense of how the opposing principles on which the harmony of the universe depends interact and complement one another, and it is this insight which inspires the shape of all her novels.

Catherine's talent for resolving the fears and healing the fractured lives of the characters in her novels, where love and hate are at work in all kinds of social divisions within her culture, was first rehearsed in Kate's kitchen. While aggressively squaring up to her persecutors at school, she took another tack in number 10 William Black Street. Desperate to transform the bitterness inside the family, she began to use her centre-stage role to resolve the situation at home. 'I felt responsibility for the people in our kitchen,' she says. 'I could always see both sides of an argument. I could always see two sides because of what was in me. That's what I played off.'

In *A Grand Man*, little Mary Ann Shaughnessy manages to prevent the break-up of her parents' marriage and, through her manipulation of Mr Lord, a gruff, difficult old man, hopelessly unfulfilled in spite of his wealth, she rescues her family from penury. The creation of Mary Ann gave Catherine a series of eight hugely popular novels in which she expressed her growing sense of her own purpose, first enacted in the kitchen of number 10. Besides the obvious parallels between the character of Mary Ann and the innocent, sparky, extrovert side of Catherine as a little girl, the author's identification with her is spelled out in the naming of Mary Ann's grannie as Mrs McMullen. Mary Ann's love for her family, her father in particular, is her motivation, just as Catherine's deep-down love for her family and need for harmony to resolve her fears motivated her desire to transform the shambles at home.

In *The Lord and Mary Ann* (1956) we find the Shaughnessys ensconced at Mr Lord's farm. Since they arrived, her da has not resorted to drink, her ma is not just bonny but has become beautiful, her brother, Michael, is happy at his swanky new school, and in the kitchen at night great larks are had with every member of the family playing a part. This is Catherine's ideal, which she herself did taste at times, in 'short rests between battles', as she refers to them, when she would sit, curled up on the corner of the fender in front of the fire, reading a book, her granda at the table, cheating himself at patience, Jack reading the paper, Kate ironing or baking. At these times she glimpsed 'a fleeting sense of security'. But for the most part it was a dream.

So important a healing influence did Catherine become at home that soon everyone came to rely on her to deal with her drunken granda. She was the only one who could settle John when he was in drink. 'When three sheets in the wind he was manageable, but only by me.' When he came in at night Kate would rouse her from a deep sleep and say, 'Get up, hinny, and get your granda to bed!' Bleary-eyed, she would shuffle into the kitchen and coax him into his bed, peeling off his longjohns, hoping against hope that he wouldn't burst into song.

To her granda Catherine was as 'pure as the lily in the dell'. This was one of his favourite songs, usually sung when he was drunk and she wished he would just go to bed, and gave her the title and theme of her novel *Pure as the Lily*. It begins in Jarrow in 1933, and opens with one of Catherine's most evocative passages about the deep-down regenerative spring of life in Jarrow, which it is her purpose to identify. The scene is an allotment where Peter Walton and his son Alec find respite from the appalling conditions of life in the Depression. Alec has been out of work for eight years. Mary, Alec's teenage daughter, the lily of the title, comes away from her placement in service bringing a bag of fag-ends she has rescued from her mistress's ashtrays. 'They're gold flake, not Woodbines,' she tells Alec, as if she were giving him a box of Cuban cigars. Mary spreads laughter and happiness wherever she goes. Her ability to see the good in people and to shine the light of her own unaffected, delicate purity into the darkest corners is a trait visible in embryo in Peter, who laughs with every sentence he utters, and it is propagated too by Alec's voiceless love for his daughter. In stark contrast to the discontent and in-fighting among the unemployed dockers outside the allotment fences, Peter and Alec, with their hands in the soil and infected by Mary's high spirits, forget their problems and cultivate their own shared, family nature. The three of them seem to swell with laughter within the perimeter of this family plot. The passage, which includes a rendition of a poem by Peter, and his favourite song, 'I love a lassie . . . She's as pure as the lily in the dell,' is perfected by Catherine's use of the soft rhythms and inflections of the Geordie idiom.

The quality of their empathy, with its power to transform, permeates the whole novel. In *Lily*, Catherine deals with life as it is lived on the surface and the unalterable, primitive source capable of transforming it. Peter attempts to maintain his connection with this primitive source – beauty, truth – through his poetry, as does his grandson, Jimmy (Mary's brother), who in turn senses it in Lally Briggs, a spirit of the North, the archetypal northern lass: a sheer expression of natural wisdom, 'the simplicity, the truth, and the depth' which Mary describes as 'welling up out of Lally's big body'.

There is absolutely nothing idealistic about this novel, firmly rooted as it is in grim realities. Purity has nothing to do with goodness as opposed to sin, for Mary gives herself out of wed-lock to a man old enough to be her father. It is a moral purity only in the highest sense. It is truth, and a clue to what that means is given by her brother Jimmy, a school-master, who tells his talented pupil, Fenton, that truth can be 'drained' from the 'crucible' of life by great poets. Mary is pure because she has the ability to do this not in art but in life.

Catherine is dealing here with a theme altogether bigger than anything she attempted in the 'social histories', as she has referred to her early novels. She is describing the process and the purpose of her art. To achieve this she required an antithesis to Mary, which she found in her heroine's mother, Alice.

Jealousy is Alice's driving force. She will be responsible for the horrible disfigurement of Mary's lover, Ben Tollet; she will burn her daughter-in-law, Lally, alive; and she will drive her son, Jimmy, almost insane and through drink into an early grave. It is out of this crucible that Mary drains the very essence of truth: 'love as pure as the lily in the dell; love before it was touched by hand, or marred by life; love as pure spirit,' which brings us back to Catherine's 'white light' of creative imagination, first experienced underneath the arches of Tyne Dock, its purpose clearly to transform.

Up for transformation in *Fanny McBride* are Fanny's prejudices about her favourite son Jack marrying a Protestant girl and her distaste for what she sees as her least favourite son Phil's pretentious ways – the shirts he wears, his picky attitude to food and, as I have already noted, the way he gets up when a woman enters the room. The resolution of this novel posed a particular problem for Catherine. Originally she had Fanny die. 'But when I sent it to my publisher, they phoned straight back and said, "You cannot make her die. This woman is such a marvellous character. You have got to bring her back." So I had to rewrite the end.'

It is New Year's Eve and Fanny's anxieties about whether Jack will turn up for the celebrations have grown to almost psychotic proportions. Fanny and Jack have not spoken since Jack committed the cardinal sin of marrying a Hallelujah. Emotional pain and anger rush through Fanny 'like a torrent sweeping a gorge' as it dawns on her that he does not intend to come, and, at the very moment that she is raising her hand to strike Mrs Flannagan for some appalling upstart behaviour, she suffers a stroke.

We see the next scene through Fanny's eyes. Hovering midway between life and death, she seems to leave her corporeal frame and stand looking at herself laid out as dead. She has an urge to complete the transition to the spirit world and leave behind the whole fraught business of material life. But for some reason she resists it and watches instead as Phil comes down from his bedroom and falls to his knees in front of her, sobbing and burying his head in her lap. Fanny is overcome with emotion. Then the doctor arrives, and Mary Prout. And then, at last, comes Jack – but only because he has heard that Fanny is dying. Jack doesn't cry, as Phil had done.

Then St Michael arrives in Fanny's limbo-land. Rather than rewarding Fanny with a smooth pass to heaven after all the heartache she has suffered in bringing up eleven bairns, she is amazed to hear him upbraid her for a whole load of Masses she has paid Father Owen to say in memory of her late husband. It transpires that Fanny has used them to ask God to keep McBride perpetually in purgatory so that she won't have to team up with him in eternity. (Indeed, we see that the poor man is still there, suffering.) St Michael also takes her to task for the way she has brought up her family, her stubbornness and pigheadedness and bigotry and, lastly, her inability to love her children except for one. True to form, Fanny hits back, blaming God for making her like that. But St Michael will have none of it. God only gave her the patterns; 'The making up lay with you,' he says. Then he sends her back into the real world to do better – but not without first clarifying God's position vis-à-vis Mrs Flannagan. He returns Fanny to the exact position she was in before she collapsed, hand raised above the provoking upstart, ready to deliver a crushing blow.

Catherine's greatest strength is her characterisation. It flows from her ability not simply to draw her characters but also to become them. By the time she set about writing she was, as she said to me, capable of doing everything her characters do, and I can believe it. I once asked her whether Fanny McBride, possibly her most popular character, was based on someone she knew. 'Oh, my!' she replied. 'In my early days, in any poor quarter of Jarrow, you would see a woman in an old coat and slippers slinking along to the corner shop early in the morning for two ounces of tea, half a pound of sugar and a half pound of streaky bacon, or something along those lines . . . Oh, there were dozens of Fannys.'

Fanny is a big woman in every way – big heart, big booming voice, big sense of humour and big body, as we see when she swings her legs over the side of the bed and scratches 'the moist flesh under her great wobbling breasts'. Battered, battling Catholic grandmother, Fanny McBride stands like a colossus astride the Tyneside of Catherine's youth. She embodies her vision of Tyneside just as Fagin, scuttling vermin-like along the dark, dank corridors that separated the squalid slum dwellings of the old East End, embodies Dickens' Kafkaesque vision of the metropolis.

There is an operatic quality to Dickens' art, however, which is not present in Catherine's work. His is more of a performance: we see his most vibrant characters, but we don't always feel we have met them in real life in quite the same way. There is true social documentary in equal measure in both sets of novels, but after reading sixty or seventy of Catherine's in a relatively short space of time I found myself walking down the main street of a rundown seaside resort in the North-East wondering what was going on behind the vacant stares of the people I passed. Catherine reveals the lives of ordinary people, of lavatory attendants and rent collectors, of dustmen and labourers, of solicitors and businessmen, of doctors and housewives, and shows that no one is ordinary. Opening them to scrutiny displays heroic and tragic qualities, humour and pathos in every quarter. Ugliness, poverty, ignorance, beauty, wealth, intellect can no longer be taken as value indicators. She has levelled the landscape of appearances, overcome their divisive potential and redirected our interest elsewhere.

In *The Unbaited Trap* (1966) tall, flabby-fleshed, insipid-looking John Emmerson, a prosperous solicitor from the posh end of town, who also happens to be a eunuch, lives an unfulfilling life with his beautiful but cold wife, Ann. All Ann asks of him is to keep up appearances, her one fear that their desolate existence together might become public knowledge. Ann's response to John's wartime wound, which has deprived him of his sexual potency, drives him into the self that he has long come to take as his own, lonely and sad. No one knows the truth about John Emmerson. The Wilcoxes, whose daughter Val is engaged to his son, Laurie Emmerson, 'just considered him a quiet, withdrawn sort of fellow'. But, as the story unfolds, John removes 'that well-bred, cultured, ready-for-anything facade' which his wife had fashioned to conceal an intolerable truth, and when thirty-year-old, warm-hearted widow Cissie Thorpe enters his life John finds himself. Their meeting – indeed, the entire plot – hinges, rather aptly considering his wife's frigidity, on the fact that Cissie does not own a fridge.

The novel is about the way people look at others: 'How could you tell by how people looked?' Laurie wonders after he has learned the truth about his father. What most people take for granted about other people is often what sets Catherine's imagination working. 'How I come to write my books . . . Well, an incident might occur, which I don't pay much heed to at first, but it sinks into my unconscious mind, which I use a lot, and years later perhaps it pops up and gives me the formation of a story or a character on which to base the story.'

The Menagerie opens with an apparently random focus on a routine greeting between a man and a woman in the bustling High Street of Fellburn – no real place, its name a cross between Hebburn and Felling, west of Jarrow – and in this novel (set in the 1950s) typical of the hundreds of pit villages on the edge of industrial Tyneside. We begin with surface rhythms, five lines of dialogue, an apparently ordinary, salutary ritual repeated on countless streets every day of the week. But in a Catherine Cookson novel such a greeting is anything but ordinary. Just a sliver beneath the surface lie the truths about the two characters which derange it. When the man moves on, he is laughing to himself, and the butt of his ridicule, Aunt Lot, one of Catherine's genius creations, turns from him with 'the air of a fine lady' – a preposterous claim, given her 'moth-eaten' shoulder cape.

Life revolves around Aunt Lot. She is the instrument of the novel's resolution. And she literally walked into Catherine's imagination off the street. 'Aunt Lot [is] a poor young woman who is slightly off balance. It should happen one day when I was crossing the road that there before me went a figure . . . She had on a voile dress, a pair of stockings that were wrinkled round her legs, high-heel shoes that were over at the sides and made her walk in an odd way. But on her shoulders was a worn-out feather cape and on her head one of the old-fashioned straw, flower-bedecked hats which were in fashion at the beginning of the century. I never saw her face, I only saw the back of her figure, and I remember the name that came into my mind from nowhere, "Poor Aunt Lot". Why I should think that name I don't know, but she remained in my mind for some time. Who was she? Where was she from? Why dressed like that? She *was* an oddity. Now it must have been years later when I wrote *The Menagerie* that there she was all ready for me, straw hat, mouldy cape, summer dress and wobbly high heels.'

Part of her imaginative perception of ordinary people is attributable to this eye for detail, but there is much more to her

73

powers of observation than this. Early on these powers seem to have been attached to, even fostered by, her rejection and alienation from life, which brought a peculiar, creative, outsider's objectivity to her relationship with physical things. One day Catherine came home and told her mother that a neighbour called Mrs Waller had called her a 'bax . . . tard'. What did it mean? Kate had been cutting up meat for a pie on the kitchen table, and when Catherine said this Kate dropped the knife on the table in surprise. But as the knife hit the surface of the table, Catherine recalls, she at once lost interest in her own question and took no interest either in Kate's response to it. What caught her attention was that when the knife hit the table its blade tipped on to the surface and stayed there, the handle slightly raised in the air. A saying of her mother's came to her, that the blade of a good knife should never be heavier than its handle. That was the thought that filled her mind: 'This knife can't be a good knife.'

Alienation can have the psychological effect of making one look at things differently, in a detached way. In Jean-Paul Sartre's *Nausea*, a novel about alienation and the effect this has on an individual's understanding of his relationship with his environment, Antoine Roquentin, aware of an extraordinary change in his perceptions, decides to keep a diary, 'to neglect no nuances or little details . . . I must say how I see this table, the street, people, my packet of tobacco, since *these* are the things which have changed.' That Catherine remembers the incident with the knife so clearly suggests that a similar change had taken place in her. That her observation of the knife-blade on the surface of the table actually smothered her anxiety at being called a bastard suggests its potential, which in her case would be realised in her characterisation of people like Aunt Lot.

Interestingly, the feeling of aloneness that dominated her emotionally at this time, and may give a clue to her creative rapport with people and things evinced in the novels, never depressed her. 'I don't connect this aloneness with fear,' Catherine once said to me. On the contrary, it released her *from* fear. Detachment was in essence detachment from fear – though, as we shall see later in her handling of Fanny McBride, there is an intrinsic sadness to it, as if she could never quite live in our world, which she describes so well. In short, being an outsider put Catherine on a different and creative plane. As with Charles Dickens, similarly alienated and detached, Catherine's ability to focus on tiny details and invest them with significance is characteristic of her art.

In *The Fifteen Streets* the narrative builds in a little crescendo to a significant meeting between John O'Brien and Mary Llewellyn. It is, in the first place, a portentous meeting for little Katie O'Brien, who idolises Mary Llewellyn, her teacher, and hero-worships John, her twenty-two-year-old brother. Mary and John know each other only through what Katie has said to each of them about the other. For Katie, though not consciously for John and Mary, their meeting promises love on the scale of a Prince Charming for a beautiful princess in a fairytale. Katie is walking along the road hand-in-hand with her big brother when the chance convergence of their paths occurs. Mary greets Katie. 'Hallo Katie.' 'Hallo Miss Llewellyn.' Mundane. What can possibly make it live up to Katie's expectations? The inspired touch is in the observation of fine detail. 'John felt Katie's fingers opening and shutting within his palm.' The sentence says it all, to us as to John, the movement of her fingers transferring Kate's expectations to her big brother, so that when John watches Mary walking away, 'bending against the wind, the coat pressed against her legs . . . he saw that she wore shoes and that her ankles were thin,' and we know that the meeting has been important for him too, that his awareness of Mary is already acute and augurs more than passing interest. Nothing is said to suggest that they will fall in love. But it is there, our little secret, Katie's and Catherine's, and now her readers' and John's too.

Reading was not a common pastime for children in the New Buildings. Catherine's appetite had been whetted by the book which the school caretaker at Simonside had lent her, and she read comics too – once she even stole one from a shop, which led to a crisis of conscience. There was the *Chatterbox* annual, the weekly *Rainbow Comic* and *Tiger Tim's Weekly*; and during those fleeting moments of security Kate would read aloud from *Handy Andy*, *Wee McGregor* and *Tales of an Irish County Court*, and to old John during the war extracts from Sir Philip Gibbs' despatches from France. But more significant to her imaginative development, Catherine's love for words was encouraged by two mistresses at school.

In the course of four years, Catherine attended four different schools. She had been moved from Simonside early in 1913. Catherine recalls overhearing a conversation between Kate and the headmistress in which Kate said something about her being a Catholic, and as Simonside was a Protestant school this would appear to have been the reason for the move. But in fact the next school she attended, The Meases in East Jarrow, was also Protestant; and it is worth noting that Catherine also heard Kate say to the Simonside headmistress something about her real name being not McMullen but Fawcett.

Was Kate telling her that Catherine was illegitimate, and if so, why? Perhaps there was already (six months or so before the chimneypiece episode) trouble brewing with Catherine's classmates there. Later that same year, 1913, Catherine was moved from The Meases to St Bede's Infants' School in Jarrow, which was a Catholic School. Her third move, to St Peter and St Paul's Tyne Dock, came in 1916, not long after she was cruelly rejected by her friends from that birthday party. St Peter and St Paul's was also a Roman Catholic school. Stern Father Bradley, whom we have met in the guise of Father O'Malley, and kind Father O'Keefe, who is portrayed in the same novels as Father Bailey, lived in the school grounds.

These moves, one after the other, cover the period between 1913 and 1916 when Catherine's trauma took root. During this period she began her 'messages' for Kate, to the pub and to the pawn shop. During this period, too, she was molested by Kate's intended, and received the two significant rejections by her friends on the pretext of her illegitimacy. If the school moves were not occasioned by Catherine's increasing difficulties in relating to her contemporaries, the three upheavals in so short a time will certainly have done nothing to settle her emotional state. She remembers that there were frequent rows about her not wanting to go to school. She would even pretend to be ill, and was capable of making herself physically sick to support the pretence.

Almost immediately at St Peter and St Paul's there was a tussle over Catherine's rich, wavy auburn hair. The headmistress, Miss Caulfield, insisted that she plait it. Kate insisted that it remain flowing and free. Catherine was in the middle. She would arrive at school with her hair loose and return home with it plaited. The issue is recreated in *Colour Blind*, where half-caste Rosie is thrashed on her hand with a cane because one of her 'jet-black' plaits has come undone. Miss Caulfield had a cane four feet long and used it frequently on Catherine for being late and for lying to her about attending Mass on Sundays. She became terrified of the woman and suffered her more telling sarcasm badly. It was Miss Caulfield who taunted her with the nickname of 'granny'.

There were, however, three Miss Caulfields at Tyne Dock school, and while the one nearest the headmistress in age was a terror too, the Miss Caulfield who taught Catherine on the first rung of the educational ladder had earlier taught her at St Bede's, and there was a rapport between them. She, and later Miss Barrington – 'big Miss Barrington, kind Miss Barrington' – recognised that Catherine had a way with poetry. During this period she imbibed Wordsworth, Tennyson and Shakespeare. She was quick to learn and recited with a natural sympathy for rhythm. This fed Catherine's self-image, but, equally importantly, 'I learned the beauty of words, words I couldn't spell, or even understand. But there was the sound of them, the lilt of them, the pictures they conjured up in my mind.' Longfellow was a favourite poet, and it is not difficult to see why. The rhythms of his 'Song of Hiawatha' are a perfect vehicle for communicating the sense of his magical narrative incantation, and in Catherine's novels, especially the earlier ones, 'poetic' rhythms provide a similar dimension to her prose. Incidentally, the title of her novel *The Blind Miller* pays tribute to Longfellow – 'Though the mills of God grind slowly, yet they grind exceeding small.' The same quotation had been rehearsed by Christine Winter three years earlier in *Fenwick Houses*.

The rhythmic quality, the lilt, is an important element of Catherine's prose. At the start of *Maggie Rowan*, where Catherine is among coal miners, dialect is delivered phonetically and is richly evocative of her characters' 'brotherhood' culture. Accent, rhythm and intonation capture 'the element of their origin' as poetry can capture truth. When the miners go down the pit, the Geordie becomes thicker and the usually neutral-accented pit deputy speaks in the same idiom as his men. Above ground, at home, the warmer cadences and the boisterous interchange of impudent humour (from the men) and mock-serious moralising (from the women) are revealing both of Maggie (remember, she is different and cannot understand why) and of the pitmen, their jocularity seeming manfully to conceal their plight in the pit – 'the lilliputian halls of a living hell' – and at the same time revealing their strength of character in overcoming it.

Generally in her novels, however, Catherine is sparing in her use of dialect. She writes within the Geordie idiom – she 'skelps the hunger off' her characters, she rescues their dinner lest it be 'kissened up to cork', and she has even been known to 'bugger me eyes to hell's flames' – but it is rare that she lets dialect flow. She was alive to the fact that many readers outside the North would have difficulty in understanding it. Thomas Hardy, like Catherine a writer inspired by the spirit of a culture, made the same decision. 'If a writer attempts to exhibit on paper the precise accents of a rustic speaker,' he once wrote, 'he disturbs the proper balance of a true representation by unduly insisting upon the grotesque element: thus directing attention to a point of inferior interest, and diverting it from the speaker's meaning.' Catherine gave a rather pithier explanation in the Author's Note to her first novel: 'Owing to difficulty in comprehension by the uninitiated, the Tyneside dialect has not been adhered to.' Hardy's friend, the poet William Barnes, took no such decision. Many of his greatest poems, such as 'The Geäte a-Vallen to' (The Gate a-Falling to) are written in Dorset dialect and spelled phonetically, which captures beautifully the spirit of his culture, but not a very wide audience.

As we shall see, in her upstart years, which continued from her late teens through her thirties, Catherine did all she could to rid herself of the habits of a culture which had weighed her down. Even today, though her voice has 'a lilt or inflection, an inheritance from the North that adds to its charm, at least for me,' as her husband Tom has described it, she is not over-fond of the accent. I suspect this was also the case with Hardy, whose father was a builder and mother a maidservant. He rose socially and enjoyed living in his rather clinically middle-class, spick-and-span house, Max Gate, where he wrote much of his best work. It was a long way, though not geographically, from the humble thatched cottage of his birth in Upper Bockhampton. 'Never mind that his acute shyness, his increasing fame, the need to placate his snobbish first wife and other intellectual and emotional factors all led him to disassociate himself outwardly from his real past and family circumstances,' the novelist John Fowles wrote in his introduction to *Thomas Hardy's England*; 'public disassociation is not suppression'.

St Peter and St Paul's Tyne Dock had another significant impact on Catherine, relevant to her imaginative growth. At the hands of Father Bradley indoctrination in the Roman Catholic faith began in earnest. She had been introduced to Catholicism at St Bede's, which had also given a high priority to religious instruction. But at Tyne Dock Father Bradley's stern approach acquired a sharp, Jesuit edge from visiting 'missioners', as Catherine refers to them. She cannot remember to which orders these troubleshooters from head office belonged, but it was they who brought fear and guilt on to the religious agenda, and they who invariably heard her confession. In their mouths the flames of hell were a reality, everlasting fire a destiny which could be met surprisingly easily, for example by pocketing change given in error by the beer lady or by not going to church (both of which exercise Catherine's conscience to an inordinate degree).

'Sunday was God's day. He made that for himself. And on that day you must worship him. You could miss out on Monday, Tuesday, Wednesday, Thursday, Friday, Saturday, but Sunday was a must. You must worship him by going to seven, nine or eleven o'clock Mass. The penalty for disobeying was eternal hell. Hell was achieved through mortal sin and it was a mortal sin to miss Mass on a Sunday.' The eldest Miss Caulfield, who appears to have been something of a lay equivalent to these missionaries, would like nothing better than to trap Catherine into admitting that she hadn't attended Sunday Mass and wouldn't think twice about relieving the Devil of his obligation to chastise her by beating Catherine with her cane. But this was as nothing to the guilt engendered by the climax of the Mass itself, when bread, according to the doctrine of transubstantiation, literally becomes the body of Christ.

'I recall one Sunday morning, which was the only time I remember Kate or my granny going to Mass. We walked up the long freezing road to St Bede's in Jarrow, where I had my first communion. I had a coat on. Kate had a coat on. My granny was wearing a bead cape and a bead bonnet. But the worshippers at that seven o'clock Mass in Jarrow were made up of poorly shawled women and thinly clad men, but they were saving their souls and that was all that mattered. Then there was Communion. I *hated* the taste of God on my tongue. From an early age my imagination went to work. I had a picture of thousands of nuns all over the world and all those bakeries turning out God by the billion. I knew by this thought that I was committing a mortal sin and would have to go to the priests [she actually confessed this sin to a missionary, who was suitably appalled] and put up with a penalty imposed on me to get out of purgatory.

'It was unthinkable that you should eat or drink for hours before God was placed on your tongue. I myself went out every

Friday morning, which was the school's day for taking the Eucharist, cold, hungry and thirsty, longing for the time when I could take the lid off a can of tea and gollop my slice of bread and dripping. To miss this occasion was not only a mortal sin, but to come under the thunder and exposure of the dreaded headmistress. I am angry when I think of the millions of children like myself, who suffered in the same way, not in the last century or in the Dark Ages, but in this century!

This recollection, in my case, goes far back, close to 1915, and the mental torture went on for years and years after that. The fear of hell's flames was ever constant. I married when I was thirty-three, and up to that time I still remained a Catholic, but fighting against the terrors of religion all the time. I didn't want to leave the fold, but my reason was at work, and the battle went on inside me.'

Hell was a serious threat for Catherine. Around the time that she was introduced to the confessional, Mrs Romanus from upstairs gave her a copy of *Grimm's Fairy Tales*. She lapped them up, reading the book not once but dozens of times. It was an imaginative period in which anything was possible, especially the gridirons of hell.

'From the time of my first confession I had nightmares. I dropped down through layers of blackness, groping for light, and woke up screaming.' Another imaginative, highly strung child, who would also become one of our greatest storytellers, experienced similar religious terrors, but from a Protestant quarter. Robert Louis Stevenson was introduced to Calvinism by his nurse and had 'an extraordinary terror of hell implanted in me'. He too suffered the most hideous nightmares, from which he woke screaming in a frenzy of terror. His experience inspired the message of *Jekyll and Hyde*, namely that the hard law of religion is 'one of the most plentiful springs of distress', as Stevenson put it, driving the devil underground, better to do his work. Similarly, Roman Catholicism, which became one of the most repressive influences in Catherine's life, inspired themes in many of her novels.

From the strict disciplines of Catholicism flowed misery for the 'fallen', as we have seen, and mixed marriages (Protestant to Roman Catholic) were regarded as sinful. Catherine would experience spiritual whiplash from both, and explored the latter to particular effect in *Colour Blind*, where Father O'Malley is against the marriage of Bridget McQueen, a white Roman

Catholic, and Jimmy Patterson, a black Protestant. The crossing of boundary lines in marriage, be they sectarian or repressive demarcations of race or class, is a major theme in all her novels, the inner strife of the protagonists resolved spiritually by an appeal to truth over bigotry and prejudice – though often there is no happy ending in this world.

Historically, religion was as powerful as class in dividing the community and generating cruelty and hypocrisy. Catherine's first taste of this came when, in the presence of her granda, she praised the Salvation Army for not being afraid to declare their religion openly – and for not getting drunk. Kate had to drag her out to the yard for her own safety. To show how firm a grip religion had on the community, even on those of its members who did not go to church, Catherine takes us back in time and, as with all her major themes, identifies a powerful hereditary thread which bound her people.

In *Tilly Trotter* (1980), set in the nineteenth century, Catherine digs for the roots of the religious obsessions which inspired the irrational prejudices of people like her granda and finds them festering in a bed of primitive superstition. A century later, such superstition was still rife in number 10. Knives crossed on the table or when washing up were a bad omen, and the cutting of nails on a Friday was expressly forbidden. The word 'pig' carried a risk far worse than walking underneath a ladder (though there was a ban on that too), and readers of the recently published *The Obsession* may remember that Catherine, in an ironic side-swipe at this irrational fear, refers to the animal as a 'grunter', the name given it to avoid disaster at home when she was a child. A picture dropping from a wall or the sound of a cricket (or 'death beetle', as it was called) on the hearth spelled trouble, even tragedy. Extra care would be taken when such things occurred, and if, even months later, some disaster befell the household a finger would be pointed in all seriousness at some careless or chance transgression of superstitious lore.

Catherine identifies the sophistry and ignorance which mesmerises Tilly's people in the nineteenth century with those of her own people, spellbound by the psychomancy of Roman Catholicism three-quarters of a century later. Burning witches at the stake may already be a thing of the past by Tilly's time, but ignorance and fear, fertile breeding grounds for superstition, remain, and are used by Hal McGrath to pursue Tilly in the most horrifying manner. He nets her, stocks her (reclaiming the old village stocks from Tillson's barn for the purpose), fires her cottage, and finally attempts to throttle her, all with the bulk of the village behind him, convinced by McGrath that the teenager Tilly is a witch.

Evidence revolves around Pete Gladwish's dog. Used as a ratter down the pit, it is shown kindness by Tilly and that night, unaccustomed to such attentions, it displays none of its usual desire to perform. Pete beats the living daylights out of it and the dog disappears. The finger is pointed at Tilly and slanderous gossip swells in the small village community when it is revealed that Tilly is herself attached by a hereditary thread down the female side of the Trotter family to Cissy Clacket, the last witch to be buried in the parish, one hundred years earlier. Then there is the evidence of Andy Fairweather's own eyes. Hadn't he seen Tilly kicking her legs up in the vestry with Ellen Ross, the vicar's wife, 'like a pair of whores on the waterfront at Shields'? Ellen was in fact giving Tilly a quick dancing lesson. She is eventually drummed out of the village with her husband George when she saves Tilly from her persecutors by plunging a peg from the stocks into the neck of Burk Laudimer, and only narrowly escapes conviction on a charge of manslaughter.

That this same primitive sense of the supernatural was exploited by Catholicism comes across beautifully in a story Catherine tells of the first time she realised the power of prayer. The dreaded Miss Caulfield fell ill. Catherine prayed that she would die. She did – of cancer. Catherine couldn't believe it. Far from relieving her daily torture, the event threw her into a paroxysm of guilt, and she knew that her terrible sin would have to be absolved in the confessional. Her Father Confessor was so staggered that he wondered Catherine wasn't already in hell's fire, burning. 'I became a very good Catholic after that.'

Like many other people, and even as a young woman, Catherine was unable or unwilling to allow her reason to distinguish the stories Father Bradley told her from what lay beneath them. There would appear to be a touch of irony in a writer who, through the power of her narratives, slips truths about the human condition to her readers, often without their realising it, not being able to suspend disbelief in the matter of religious stories. But the point is that more was demanded of a Roman Catholic in those days than the mere suspension of disbelief. A literal acceptance not just of the story, but also of the

Roman Catholic dogma attached to it, which excluded all Protestants from joy, was fundamental. Questioning heaven and hell, as a lodger once did in the kitchen at William Black Street, was not healthy. The man earned a place in *Colour Blind* for Ted Grant, who questions 'this Adam and Garden of Eden business' and says that life in the first place was nothing but slime; and in *Fenwick Houses*, Ronnie Winter tells his mother that he's heard there's no such thing as the Garden of Eden and that we all come from apes. But these were borrowed opinions of learned men. For people like the McMullens or indeed Christine Winter, 'too busy' to read books, blind faith was the order – literally – of the day.

I spoke to Catherine about this a year or so before her eightieth birthday, after the Anglican Bishop of Durham had publicly questioned the literal truth of certain fundamental tenets of Christian dogma, and she angrily refused the Church any back-tracking in the business which had alienated her from it. 'Of course I believe everything that the Bishop is saying,' she told me. 'I was saying the same fifty years ago. It was a wonder they didn't excommunicate me. I could not accept the transubstantiation and of course that caused the priest to have a heart attack. Today they let Protestants come into the Catholic Church . . . but at one time it was a sin for a Catholic to enter a Protestant church, a mortal sin. All these little frills on the outside make you think that everything has changed, but it hasn't. I agree with the Bishop of Durham, things he said about the resurrection, but of course he should never have been a bishop, he should never have been a priest.' A little more than a decade later, she said to me, 'One type of person I do hate and that is a turncoat, and when men . . . God becomes a turncoat, well, you can look no further.'

For all the guilt and fear they aroused, the priests at St Peter and St Paul's did at least encourage a spiritual dimension in Catherine's life, fuelling her lifelong quest for an answer to the question: Why? More than forty years later, this seeking would lead to her discovery of 'a spirit that was an individual thing, not connected with any doctrine'. Today she is not so presumptuous as to declare herself an atheist: 'I am an agnostic. I still search, but having done so I have lost the fear of the after-life in which I lived for years.' This search became bound up with her creativity as a writer and produced some of her best work. But from the years of her life when, as 'a good Catholic', she was swept up in religion, came one of her most enchanting fictional relationships.

In the Mary Ann series, we have a delicious treatment of a child's matter-of-fact acceptance of the sanctity of the Holy Family. Mary Ann is in league with the Virgin Mary, Joseph and the infant Jesus, dashing into church, kneeling before the statuary and apologising that she can only stay a minute because she has to catch a bus, and then rabbiting on about Mrs McBride, her da and her brother, Michael. In *The Devil and Mary Ann* (1958), we even have a humorous approach to the divisions within the Church. A Protestant couple, Mr and Mrs Wilson, meet Mary Ann on a train when, for the first time, she is travelling to the Convent of the Holy Child of Bethlehem, a boarding school paid for by the Shaughnessys' benefactor, Peter Lord. Mr Wilson is alarmed at the prospect of the little girl being subjected to the terrors of hellfire by nuns, and draws an awesome picture of what will befall her, before his kindly wife stills him. Later, Mary Ann will fly to the Wilsons, demanding that they help her escape the convent because she has caught wind of things not being right at home: a Mrs Polanski is attempting to seduce her da. As in all the novels, Mary Ann is at centre stage, resolving, transforming; but in this one her time in the convent has some special delights, such as the gay-minded Sisters Alvis and Monica, and Sister Agnes Mary, who has a voice like a man's and who, to Mary Ann's astonishment, tells Sister Catherine to 'stow it!' when her colleague reprimands her.

When Mary Ann, as supplicant, seeks a special favour from the Holy Family she sometimes observes a change of expression in the sculpted faces of Virgin and child which makes their view clear. The development of this enchanting relationship calls to mind Giovanni Guareschi's humorous series of novels about Don Camillo, the Italian parish priest with his simple but certain faith. As with Don Camillo, who conducts down-to-earth and humorously telling conversations with Christ, so with Mary Ann a deal done with the Virgin Mary invariably precipitates the action. Both narratives give ultimate credibility to the make-believe elements in ecclesiastical doctrine. Both became best-sellers. And while in reality Catherine had already renounced her faith in Christianity when she wrote these books, it is not her main purpose to reveal that here, although the reason why she did so is implicit.

Mary Ann tells stories and lives in a make-believe world upon which everyone around her depends for their salvation. The key to the art of storytelling is in making your audience believe. Mary Ann has this skill to a high degree. The Christian story, in its simplicity and spiritual depth, has proved itself one of the most convincing stories of all time. In her teens Catherine believed it wholeheartedly; she became a devout Catholic and remained true to her faith into her early thirties. It was the Church itself which shook her out of it when it insisted on blind adherence to its own special dogma – about transubstantiation, about mixed marriages, about the literal acceptance of hell and so on – which it attached to the simple story, and then faced her with an all-or-nothing choice. But no storyteller can get away with insisting on what its audience should believe. Storytelling is a far more magical process than that, as Mary Ann knows so well.

All storytellers deal in myth, clothing naked truth in such a manner as to lead their audience to it, but along their own path. Mary Ann carries her people with her on the wings of her art, and they find solutions to their problems in their own way. Catherine, perhaps because she was so devastated by the response of the Church to her, a believer (particularly when she married a Protestant), is determined in the Mary Ann series to point up the fabrication involved in telling a story, deliberately drawing attention to it with exaggerated, C.S. Lewis-style religious symbolism, for example in naming Mary Ann's saviour 'Mr Lord'. She does the same sort of thing in many of her novels, for instance in her use of the fictional village of Fellburn, with its simplistic, geographically regulated class system: Bog's End for the workers, Brampton Hill for the nobs. And even the names of her characters are often encoded; you just know that anyone called Donald is going to be nasty, anyone called Bailey is a goodie, and so on. Mary Ann, the fibber with a twinkle in her eye, is behind this, too, for she is the pure storyteller part of the writer – didn't old John once say to his granddaughter that her talent for fibbing would get her into the clink or into the money? Once, at the end of *The Lord and Mary Ann*, the author actually comes out into the open and challenges our acceptance of what has been laid before us to believe. After all the ends of her narrative have been neatly tied in a bow, she asks if we 'believe all about everything now? You don't? Well, it'll serve you right if nothing nice ever happens to you!' It is charming, disarming, but there is also the gentlest satirical nudge.

Mary Ann, the arch-storyteller, understands that lying is not just saying what isn't true but can be saying more than is true. Fabrication is an essential part of storytelling, but, as Catherine shows in much of her other work, it is not the essential part; in the end, the story is merely a vehicle. This, her missionaries could never accept.

The Mary Ann novels, published at intervals, which lent balance to her less humorous early work, offer an insight into the side of Catherine from which all her stories naturally flow. But by the time she came to write them, Mary Ann was only one part of this complex woman.

Chapter Five

The Road Out

At the end of 1917 Rose died. Catherine was sleeping in the room where she passed her final moments. Dreamily she was aware of other people in the room attending her grandma, then she heard her being sick and the death rattle as she expired. No one had thought to remove the child to another bed. In the morning Catherine discovered that her gran had been laid out on the table. Rose lay there for three days, Kate occasionally putting a fresh bowl underneath to catch the blood and fluids which seeped out of her and would otherwise have messed the floor.

Rose's passing was a turning point. From this time Catherine began her 'scribbles', as she calls them. Indeed, there ensued a succession of events associated with artistic endeavour. First came the piano.

At eleven going on twelve, as the errands to the pub and the Pawn continued, she determined to do something about Kate using her. She had been sent to get a half-bottle of whisky from a pub in Jarrow, where Kate had taken part-time work. Plucking up her courage, Catherine begged the publican and his wife to refuse to serve her. They were sympathetic. A week later, Kate lost her job. She never knew why. The piano appeared, against all reason, shortly afterwards. Was it the publican who gave Kate a reference for the hire-purchase agreement? It was no ordinary instrument. When it arrived and was eased into the already overcrowded front room of number 10, Catherine discovered that it had cost Kate £100. This was a huge amount of money for Kate to get tied up with on the never-never. Catherine has said that Kate bought the piano 'to show off to the neighbours'; a Mrs Tyler had one, and of course Aunt Mary had her beautiful spinet. At any rate, the piano arrived, and rather endearingly Bob the Pawn found Catherine a teacher. She took her first examination and passed with honours. But then reality dawned. Kate didn't keep up the payments and the piano went back.

The significance of the piano is that it gave Catherine something of her own to get wrapped up in. I doubt that at this early stage it was imaginatively rewarding, but there was always the promise that it would be. The piano answered a need. She was upset when it went back, but the experience took her forward. Having identified this need, she found an alternative means to fulfil it. 'It was after the loss of the piano I went in for words.'

She had already discerned beauty in words through her poetry class, and now as in school her interest focused on their imaginative, associative properties which stemmed not from their literal meaning but from their sense. Words had fascinated Catherine from the start. As a very young child unusual words didn't pass over her. For example, 'imposition' was a word she first heard in the script of the 'Faerie Queen' concert at school (she would have been six). There was no reason for Catherine to store it in memory, but she did. Perhaps it sounded interesting; most likely her attention was caught by the intonation which the character (a housewife) used to articulate its sense – 'a thorough im-po-sition!' – in this case about the outrageous price of a duck. Financial hardship being central to the McMullens' anxieties at home, this may have struck a chord. Perhaps, as the housewife in the play is so disdainful of the duck seller, the hook might have been this disdain, an emotion prevalent enough in her experience at the lower end of the social spectrum. Years later a neighbour used the word, again disdainfully, after Kate had insisted Catherine charge her three shillings and sixpence for processing a particularly large load of laundry. Her mind turned at once to the Faerie Queen.

On one level, her keen interest in words was simply part of Catherine's eagerness to learn. But our ability to draw sense from words beyond their literal meaning – their power to seduce by appealing to the imagination as well as to reason – is what first led her, at eleven or twelve years of age, to cook up stories of her own. She would get an *idea* from a word which would then set her mind whirling with a story as she walked to the pub with the Grey Hen.

In *The Menagerie*, when Larry Broadhurst kisses Pam Turnbull, long after she had jilted him almost at the altar, Larry's mind turns, of all things, to the word 'penumbra'. Pam had used it once during their earlier life together. It had bothered Larry then: he hadn't known what it meant, but didn't let on for fear that upstart Pam would think him bovine. In effect, the word signified the gaping cultural gulf between them, and now, at the moment of their reconciliation, he remembers it again because he fears (and is right to fear) that their reunion won't last.

The novel is about upstart Pam's inability to connect with her roots. That Larry remembers the word has nothing to do with its meaning, everything to do with the idea that it represents in his mind of their irreconcilable differences. And we shouldn't feel sad for Larry, for his sense of the word is what matters; what it triggers serves him well. At the end, he is urged by Jessie, who is everything Pam is not, to write a novel 'about Aunt Lot and everything . . . it's a way of life'. We have no doubt that he will.

This period of Catherine's life, when her imagination was growing, coincided with the First World War. After Rose died and Jack was killed in action in September 1918, there were just three McMullens left at number 10: old John, Kate and Catherine. By this time the chores of going for the beer and to the pawn shop had been added to. Kate was washing for a woman in Croft Terrace, a quiet, 'swanky' part of Jarrow, and Catherine was the gofer. So heavy were the loads of laundry that she could manage only a few paces at a time before having to put her burden down on the pavement and take a breather. Anyone could have seen that all these trips were taking their toll on the girl.

In addition, on Saturdays, Catherine was 'doing' for their neighbours the Flannagans, scrubbing out their scullery and washing down their stairs. Then there was the daily trip to Tyne Dock, a mile each way, to and from school; and she had begun to take it on herself to go to the piles of used cinders by the tram sheds to the west of the New Buildings to search with real destitutes for usable pieces of coal for the fire. Kate had never asked her to do this, and old John would not have been seen dead doing it, though occasionally he would help her back with her pickings. That Catherine chose to go scavenging in this way was sign enough that she was now part of the whole depressing ethos, and it was exhausting her.

She had first experienced the odd, tired feeling, not just tired but 'funny tired', around the age of nine when at St Bede's. Now it was her regular companion. But Kate, despite her sympathy for Uncle Alec when he was ill, had no time for Catherine's infirmity. Kate worked hard and drank hard. Frailty had no place in her vocabulary. The integrity of the poor was bound up with this ethic. You worked until you dropped. Stamina, or gumption, was prized; sensitivity was a luxury no one in Kate's position could afford. She put the pains in Catherine's limbs down to growing up. She may have thought her daughter was malingering; or, since it was below Kate to go to the Pawn, it may have been that she didn't want to face having to take on this particular chore. Whichever way she looked at it, there was nothing to be gained by cossetting Catherine in sympathy.

In 1919, after Catherine had turned thirteen, there came the fourth major upset in her young life. She fell in the school playground and injured her hip. She was brought home and put to bed. But she didn't get up. Kate insisted she must. The accident had occurred towards the end of the year, and in Christmas week Kate sent her on a 'message' for three bottles of beer from the pub – this is the occasion, which I have already described, when Catherine pressed Kate's ten-shilling note in the hand of the paper boy and fortunately he returned with the beer and Kate's change. Catherine had protested that her leg was hurting. Kate would have none of it: 'You went out to play snowballs yesterday. Well, if you go out to play snowballs you can go a message. Get yourself away.' The pain was what caused her to enlist the paper boy's help. 'That I wasn't shamming about my leg was demonstrated early in the next year,' Catherine told me. 'Again it was snowing heavily. But she would have none of my pleas that my leg was painful. I could hardly walk. I was going to school and that was about it. To walk to school generally took me about fifteen minutes, that is if I hurried. This morning it must have taken well over an hour. I remember opening the door of the classroom, going in and that was that, I had passed out. That was my last day at school. I was carried back to a strange doctor, who said I must be taken home and my leg kept up. I lay on the saddle in the kitchen.

'That night I must have become unconscious again because I remember hearing my granda's voice, "If she gets past three o'clock she'll survive." Then I was conscious of Kate's face above me and I turned mine away from the smell of whisky. I must have woken some time later in this blackness, there was no light in the kitchen. I was shivering, and I was in awful pain, when I cried out. My cry must have disturbed her drunken sleep because she came to the foot of the saddle and she said, "Stop that and get yourself to sleep." That incident kept as alive in my mind as that with the paper boy, but this with bitterness. I was to learn that hate and bitterness were two emotions that can wipe out love.'

Catherine did not begin to recover until the spring of 1920. She remembers the day she got out of bed with extraordinary clarity, as she does all the critical moments in her imaginative development. Her first steps took her to the kitchen window. Looking out, she saw the yard door on to the back lane was open. As she stood there, two of her playmates, Florrie Harding and Janie Robson, happened to pass by the open doorway. It was as if she was looking at her life from another world. She knew that she would never play with them again. Something had happened inside her. There was a complete cut-off. Her rejection by and of her friends had earlier led to the feeling of aloneness which I have described. But now, at this moment, aloneness became complete detachment, a kind of disinterested neutrality, a simultaneously depressing and enlightening transition, 'an all-knowing, desolate life, a negative life that told me there was nothing of value, nothing worth striving for'.

At the start of *Fanny McBride* there is a clue to part of what Catherine felt. Fanny is alone, deserted by her family. She lies in bed looking at the ceiling, calculating the passage of time by the position of a shaft of light from the sun in relation to a dis-coloured patch above her on the ceiling, reputed to be a blood-stain left after the murder of a woman upstairs. The stain is her sundial, fixed, stationary, redolent only of what has been. There is a future, but only outside, in the movement of the sun. Fanny lies still, like a prisoner in a cell, as if her story has come to an end on the very first page of the novel.

There is something of Fanny's mood in the depressive aspect of Catherine's own 'cut-off' in 1920, but there was also a mature understanding which translated it into a 'moment of realisation'. This didn't defeat her bleak moods, but it did play a large part in her subsequent momentous decision not to return to school. Catherine had at last decided to take control. For the first time, *she* would take responsibility for her own life and be accountable only to herself.

She told herself that she knew how to do only two things: she could write and she could do housework. First she took a job as a daily for a woman in Simonside Terrace and developed a classic crush, 'a girlish passion' as she called it, for the woman's eldest son. Fortunately, the fellow didn't take to his role in the classic serving-girl romance, and before long Catherine left and turned to an occupation more suited to her new spirit of self-motivation.

She took one sixpenny lesson in pen-painting and discovered that she had a talent. She began painting decorative motifs on cushions, tray-cloths and mantel borders, and set up a club to market her wares. 'I sat at a table under the window in the kitchen for eight to ten hours a day filling in a pattern of a basket of flowers on a satin cushion cover with oil paints applied with the nib of a pen, five days a week. Saturday was given over to collecting the club money for the said cushions; part of the Sunday I would spend making the articles.' There were clubs for everything in those days; they worked on the principle that people could afford small amounts from the weekly wage to put towards little luxuries. The enterprise was a success and with it came her first taste of self-respect. One result was that she began to sort out her life at home. She informed Kate that she would no longer be taking the Grey Hen for the beer, and it was during this period – 1920 to 1923 – that she first faced up to her mother when Kate went to strike her once again on the ear.

This new spirit took her life in another direction too. 'From when I was about fifteen [in 1921], I was courted, as the word was, by three pit lads, and may I state emphatically they were all gentlemen!' These innocent relationships were sometimes conducted within the St Peter and St Paul's church social scene, which revolved around dances on a Saturday night. 'Me first lad,' Catherine once confided, 'a fellow called Micky Moran, was a pitman who spent all his spare time decorating the church, you know these stencils that go round the church – all the crosses, all the way round . . . Granda used to call him "the spare priest". I was about sixteen at the time. We'd go to dances in the school-room after we had played whist [today it would be called a youth club]. Then there was Kit Gannon, he was also a miner, and Todd Lawson, he became one of the leading footballers – a Newcastle footballer! They were all miners from mining families. Although there were very few miners in the New Buildings – they were mostly working in the shipyards or on the trams and things like that – in my teens my friends were from mining families. That is how I know so much about what went on in their homes.'

What Catherine found in their homes was warmth, something quite other than the fleeting moments of security between battles in her own home. She portrays such a scene in *Tilly Trotter*. Tilly, alone and with no place to live after the Trotter cottage has been burned down, finds work in the Sopwith mine and a roof over her head with the Drew family, who are everything Catherine would have liked her family to be – warm, caring, rich in spirit in spite of their poverty. What Tilly saw in the sea of faces before her when she first visited for Sunday tea was a revelation. Sunday, with the mine closed, was the one day on which Biddy Drew could count on her whole family to be round her in the kitchen. There was laughter, but behind it a real closeness, a happiness which Tilly sees comes from deep within. It answers a crying need in Tilly, not for sex with boy or man, but for someone to be kind to her.

Catherine was changing, blossoming. The little illegitimate child, Annie Hannigan, persecuted by her friends and driven into her lavatory sanctuary in the backyard because she had no da, was on the wane, and the sparky little fibber Mary Ann, cutting deals with the Virgin Mary to make things right at home, was retreating into the shadows of her psyche. Neither would ever completely leave her – they are as much part of her complex make-up today as all her autobiographically inspired fictional creations – but from Catherine's teens other aspects come to the fore.

There was something different about Tilly Trotter, just as everyone said there was something different about Catherine. A few who met Tilly – like farmer Brentwood and young Steve McGrath – see promise in that difference; others, a threat or challenge. Tilly is a beanpole of a girl, 'like a yard of pump water, as straight as a die', but the difference told in her eyes, 'the strangest eyes . . . so clear and deep', and she was a girl who could 'read and write as good as the parson hisself'. Sex is available, but Tilly isn't. She is just not interested. What she needs is warmth. Steve, a year younger than her at sixteen, a lad to whom she owes more for her survival to date than anyone, is put off by Tilly time and again. As it happens, Steve, whose extraordinary act of faith transports his affections across three books – the entire Tilly Trotter trilogy – will, in the very final pages of *Tilly Trotter Widowed* (1982), be rewarded for his patience.

There is something of the teenager Mary Walton of *Pure as the Lily* about her, too; and something of Alec Walton, Mary's father, in the way John McMullen enjoyed this period of Catherine's innocent teens. Catherine was coming into her own; the pen-painting and her new social life were positive developments. John was proud of the way she was going, and deep down felt the same love for her as Alec did for Mary.

Fifteen-year-old Christine Winter of *Fenwick Houses* reflects another facet of Catherine at this time, particularly in her relationships with boys. Don Dowling informs Christine that she is going to be his girl, they'll get married when she's older. Christine says she 'ain't', he's more like a brother to her. She is carefree, and wants nothing earnest to impinge on her life. She likes to be told by her friend Molly that she is pretty, but doesn't want a lad getting serious over her. Molly is a tonic, a real friend, with a laughing, down-to-earth personality. Even her out-rageous bad language sparks laughter in Christine and binds them more tightly together. It was during this period that Catherine too found a friend and confidante in Lily Maguire, the first real girl friend of her own age that she ever had. They would go off together on their bikes into the countryside. There were no bad times with Lily Maguire any more than when Christine and Molly were together; only plans for the future and laughter.

Christine's friend Molly is part of Fellburn, an embodied spirit of the place. She will probably stay there and marry a pitman, though she has plans to do better than that. When Christine finally agrees to go to the church social with Don (in the company of her brother, Ronnie), she insists that the two boys forget their differences. Then all three of them are like kids again, and Christine doesn't mind when both take her by the hand and run down the hill towards the bridge and the schoolroom, where the dance is to be held. All is innocence, all is fun. That is what Christine wants. 'Enjoy yersel' when you're young,' says neighbour Mr Patterson, lolling by the wall as he watches them going down . . . 'Life flees. We're nowt but feathers in the fire.'

And yet, in spite of their common determination not to get

seriously involved with a man, each of these three girls – Tilly, Mary and Christine – is hurt when a man gets under her skin. For Tilly it is farmer Simon Brentwood, an older man. For as long as Tilly can remember there has been a spark between the two of them, and she idolises Simon – until the day she comes across him with Lady Agnes in a barn, their limbs working like windmills in a storm. For Mary Walton it is also an older man: Ben Tollet, a shopkeeper for whom Mary works. He takes advantage of her, although Mary had already fallen for him, and she becomes pregnant. Mary's father, Alec, feeling much the same about Ben's advances as old John did when a shopkeeper once demanded a kiss from Catherine in exchange for her purchase, beats Ben up. For Christine in *Fenwick Houses*, it is her gentleman friend, Martin. Martin comes from outside Christine's class, just as Catherine's father came from outside Kate's. He may be only middle class, but he is a world away from any of the boys Christine knows. Christine's progression from schoolroom dances with pitmen to Martin, and his subsequent using of her, which tore Christine apart, bears some comparison with Catherine's experience.

In her teens Catherine yearned for her real father and needed what no young pitman could give her emotionally. 'From the time I was fourteen I had sat every Sunday at the eleven o'clock Mass behind a tall, handsome, very well-dressed man, and, as a child, I longed that such a man could be my father . . . Anyway, this man never spoke to me. He came out of church before me and walked straight away, passing little groups of people chatting together, of which I'd be one.

'Then one Sunday he stopped and spoke to me. He said, "We walk part of the same way home." I was dumb. We walked to the Tyne Dock gates. He went one way to Eldon Street, where he lived nearby, I went the other way through the famous Tyne Dock arches, past the little street where I'd been born, up the Jarrow Road, on to the open stretch of the Jarrow slacks, where the tide lapped the bank and the seasoning timbers bobbed up and down. And so into the kitchen of 10 William Black Street. And I hadn't touched the ground. I had been borne on the white light of wings. *He* had spoken to me! After all these years I had admired this wonderful being, and he had spoken to me.'

The man, Jim Dailey, was eleven years older than Catherine. The story of their ensuing relationship, which Catherine spoke about for the first time in conversation with me, so hurt her that it precipitated her departure from the North, and we will return to it a year or so into the affair, when she is twenty and he is thirty-one.

As Catherine says, her teens were marked by a strong desire to find her father – 'It was the beginning of a period when I began secretly to search for him, first of all by asking questions of my Aunt Mary, because Kate only once ever brought him to the fore until she was in the last years of her life.' Aunt Mary gave Catherine what she wanted to hear, and it couldn't have come at a worse moment.

Catherine was galvanising her strengths. It was a positive, if, with the pen-painting, an exhausting period in which Mary chose to tell Catherine that her father had been a well-spoken, well-dressed man of distinction, with his kid gloves, top hat and silver-mounted walking stick. This revelation threw Catherine completely off course, adding just the kind of vanity to her mounting self-confidence – 'a false sense of superiority', as she has put it – that would immediately distance her from her new-found friends. Years later Lily Maguire, her first close female friend, would recall that the moment in their friendship that stuck most vividly in her mind was Catherine telling her that, as she saw it, Lily would end up marrying a miner, while she would marry a rich man from a better class.

What Aunt Mary had done was to catch Catherine at the most susceptible moment in her swing from utter depression to self-belief. Suddenly everything seemed to fall into place. Her father must be the reason why she had had such difficulty fitting in. She wasn't like the rest of her friends in the New Buildings. She was better than them. This did her inferiority complex a power of good; unfortunately, like everything else that Mary promoted, it amounted to a veneer which, whether true or false, would do little to help Catherine find the warmth and acceptance she so desperately desired.

Then, a year later, in 1923, Kate married David McDermott, the seaman lodger who had been introduced to her by Jack Stoddart all those years before. He was a quiet man, and Catherine seems to have got on well with him. He liked a drink, but was away at sea for months at a time. Kate probably felt that the timing was right for marriage: she was forty-one, and Catherine at seventeen was making her own way. But it was another upset in the status quo at home which exacerbated Catherine's feelings of aloneness.

Tensions were certainly running high in number 10 and Kate now had a drinking partner when David was at home. One day the atmosphere became so highly charged that Catherine screamed at her mother that she was getting out once and for all. The strain of Catherine's long days pen-painting, nose to paper, day in, day out in front of the kitchen window, unrelieved by any great show of profit, was, after more than three years, beginning to tell, and when one day she found herself too weak to contest Kate in some raging argument, Dr McHaffie was summoned. He diagnosed her exhaustion as a symptom of anaemia caused by lead poisoning from the paints she was using. Anaemia, a lack of red cells in the bloodstream, is also a symptom of hereditary haemorrhagic telangiectasia; but at this time there was no reason for Dr McHaffie to suspect that Catherine had contracted so rare a vascular disease.

Catherine wound up the club and registered with an employment agency, which found her a job as a companion–maid in a big house in swanky Harton Village. Psychologically it was a bad move. Having been elevated in her own mind by Mary's revelations, she now found herself below stairs, at someone else's beck and call. She discovered that 'companion–maid' was a euphemism for servant. Washing, cleaning, cooking and serving, she worked from six in the morning until nine at night, when she flopped exhausted into bed. She stood this for only a fortnight.

It was around this time that Catherine met Councillor Bill McAnany at one of the regular whist drives and dances at Tyne Dock schoolrooms. Behind the scenes Father Bradley had asked McAnany whether he might not be able to do something for her, and on 22 October 1924, at eighteen years of age, Catherine began working as a laundry checker . . . in South Shields workhouse.

At first things went well. The matron in charge was a bit of a tartar, but very good at her job, and Catherine threw herself into work, her own situation put into perspective by the real destitutes, 'the weeping women and grim-faced men [who] had watched their last sticks of furniture being carried out by the bums,' as she wrote in *Colour Blind*.

From her late teens she had become increasingly aware of the depths of degradation unemployment could bring to a town. 'All about me were men standing in groups, thin men, lost men, men who sat on smouldering tips, picking cinders all night in order to fill a barrow to be pushed to either Shields or Jarrow, hoping to sell the contents for a shilling. Men who had lost hope.' Now, in the workhouse, when on part duty in the evenings, she was admitting families – 'the men to one side, the women to the other, the children to the nurses' home or the nursery, or an old couple knowing they'd have to spend the rest of their lives in the workhouse. Shields workhouse in those days was not far removed from the Dickensian era.' Individuals like Mrs Henagen – the woman's name and the pain and degradations of this place whisper to us across the years through Catherine's novels – aroused her compassion. Confined in a wheelchair, in the foul-smelling atmosphere of the infirm ward – the stench of urine particularly repulsed Catherine – Mrs Henagen was only thirty years old but looked twice that, prematurely aged by despair.

Catherine arrived at the workhouse a strong Catholic, regularly stopping off at St Peter and St Paul's on her way to visit her family, drawing comfort from the peace and quiet of the darkened church, lit only by the red Sanctuary light. She believed that being a checker in the workhouse laundry was what God intended for her at this point, but none the less felt driven by ambition, an urge to move forward, although at this stage she could not identify a goal or purpose to aim for.

She knew she could write. She had started her scribblings at the age of eleven, and in 1922, at sixteen, she had written a 16,000-word story about God entering the world as Christ on the second floor of a tenement building. She called it 'On the Second Floor'. She even managed to persuade Lily Maguire's sister, Maisie, to copy it out in calligraphic text for the grand sum of two shillings and sixpence, before submitting it to the *South Shields Gazette*. Not for one moment did she think that 16,000 words might be a little too long for inclusion in a newspaper, and she was mortified when it was returned, obviously unread, by the next post.

Rejection was no stranger to her, but now, at the workhouse, 'I definitely found out what it meant.' Among the staff, who ranged through all the social levels from the bottom rung up to lower middle class, there was an acute awareness of who was who and of the place of each in the pecking order. Here Catherine's upstart pretensions, her commitment to attain the 'norm' that her father represented, were never going to win her friends. 'There were eighteen staff in my department and within no time they knew of my history and of the drunken family from which I came, and there I was in the workhouse nursery with a whole lot of illegitimate children.'

Catherine's selective image of herself as vested with genes from her father which set her apart from the hoi polloi might have militated against compassion or seen her disdainfully marking time at the workhouse, but in fact the opposite was true. She proved her commitment to rising above her situation through sheer hard work, drawing on just the kind of gumption which enabled one of her best-known heroines, Katie Mulholland, against all odds to establish an empire barely a stone's throw away. In her relationships with the other staff she set the same high, indeed perfectionist, standard which marked her attitude to work, and this did little to warm her fellow workers to her. On one occasion when a female member of staff was talking smuttily at the dinner table, Catherine reprimanded her in front of everyone, even threatening to report the woman to matron. It was not the best way for the new girl to settle in. But Catherine wasn't playing at her part, nor was it primness which inspired the reprimand but her increasingly ruthless integrity.

'She is quite just, and she can be awfully kind, but she looks to the end of things and doesn't care a rush for any one, but sticks to what she wants herself. I tell you, 'Tild, I used to hate her, but I don't now; I respect Katherine, she is so perfectly *true*.' The quotation is one that Catherine may recognise, but it is unlikely that many readers will. It comes from a novel by Elinor Glyn called *The Career of Katherine Bush*, which she read around this time, and it gives a good idea of what drove the real Catherine, if not quite so true a record of how this new persona was received by her colleagues.

Her outburst at table earned her the nickname of 'bloody St Catherine' and began a long period of persecution at her colleagues' hands. She was made an outcast – or rather, she had made herself one and was unable to retrieve the situation. Whenever she came into a room, all talking and laughing would be suppressed. She'd return to her bedroom to find that the others had stripped it or made her an apple-pie bed, folding the bottom sheet up midway down the bed so her feet were caught up in it when she got in.

The campaign against her drove her back inside herself and she began once more to put pen to paper. She sent a play she had written about rivalry between the house and hospital sides of the workhouse to a writers' correspondence school, only to receive another rejection note strongly advising her not to take up a literary career. Rejection was coming from all sides; but it served only to steel her resolve. She had been bred on strife; later she would write that strife became 'a kind of yeast' which led to an awareness of an extraordinary strength within her.

Determined to move forward, she got hold of a copy of *The Naval Book*, a book on nursing for naval trainees, and became intrigued by the anatomy of the human body. Father Bradley had told her that she wasn't sufficiently well educated to become a nurse. This was her response. She also took to reading *T. P. and Cassell's Weekly*, a new literary periodical (it was founded in 1923), always taking care to hide it from her colleagues lest they thought she was overreaching herself.

Quite distinct from and far more significant than these attempts to educate herself was what she describes as her cultural ambition: 'I did not think of the word "education", the word prominent in my mind being "culture". I knew that ladies had to have culture, and culture had something to do with the arts.' She was giving herself the finishing school which, if she had been born a Larkin – like the little girl in the New Buildings who went to boarding school and thence to France – would have been her due. She bought a second-hand violin and took lessons at a shilling a time. But soon she and those within earshot (her playing inspired matron's dog to a regular howling accompaniment) agreed that it wasn't for her. Next she took lessons in French, but her accent failed to come up to her tutor's expectations. So, 'in some despair I took up physical culture [martial arts – she actually learned how to wield Indian clubs], this with the hope of getting rid of my puppy fat and of developing a beautiful body'.

All this was fertile ground for her colleagues' derision, and rather than be defeated by it she decided to play the clown to their provocation. For example, she deliberately acted up one day when she heard her persecutors sniggering from behind closed doors as she practised her clubs, making a fool of herself in the hope that it would defuse their antagonism. We are reminded of the incident in the pawn shop when she poked fun at herself at being the daughter of 'a nigger'. There's the same self-effacement, the same attempt to transform pathos with humour. Here it shows us just how much she would have loved to gain acceptance by her persecutors.

Catherine will have been aware that in her society, with its many different social gradations and subtly defined sub-levels, anyone who attempted to cross a social demarcation line would very likely be vilified as an upstart. But though her alienation depressed her she would not give up her attempts to improve herself. This remained her central goal. In any case, Catherine could see nothing intrinsically wrong with what she was doing. In her experience, everyone, if not actually trying to rise in the world, would have liked to. Even old John McMullen, who professed to mistrust anyone who, by work or learning, had risen in the world – they had sided with the enemy! – was deeply chuffed when Arne Fuller, an old friend of his who had made good, invited him for a drink. He didn't go, but he bored everyone with the story for months afterwards, truly proud that Arne had asked him.

Among Catherine's detractors were those who, like her Aunt Mary, enjoyed the social infighting and posturing for its own sake and made constant attempts at 'refeenment'. They, and others like Kate, who despised the two Richardson girls in the New Buildings for their posh accent but would have liked to talk that way herself, were slaves to Mrs Malaprop. To Catherine these were the real upstarts. She would lampoon them in *A Grand Man*, where Mrs Flannagan sends a note to school saying that her daughter, Sarah, cannot attend because she has an 'illustrated' throat.

Weren't such half-hearted attempts at social superiority worse than her honest and open commitment to making a better life for herself? Upstarts and snobs litter Catherine's fiction, but the snobs generally come off worse. An upstart may be a snob too and, like Aunt Mary, behave condescendingly to those on a lower social level. But not all upstarts were snobs and Catherine certainly wasn't. Her self-improvement strategy was something she was doing for herself. Catherine had made a mistake in publicly reprimanding the woman at the dining table for her smutty talk, but this wasn't snobbish behaviour.

Anne Thornton in *The Girl* is a snob and, like most snobs, cruel with it. The novel's title reflects her snobbery, for she insists on calling Hannah Boyle, her ward and the daughter of a Newcastle whore, 'the girl'. In *The Wingless Bird*, Charles Farrier's mother is a snob, aghast when her son indicates his intention to marry shop-girl Agnes Conway. When she and her husband refuse to attend their wedding, Catherine kills them off in a road accident.

In *The Devil and Mary Ann*, Beatrice, the merciless convent girl who mocks Jarrow and Mary Ann's ma and da, calls Mary Ann a sow's ear and forges a rude piece of poetry about Sister Alvis in Mary Ann's handwriting, is also a snob.

Snobs exist at all levels of society other than the lowest. Upstarts exist at all levels of society except the highest, though they may rise to the highest level by being an upstart. There have always been snobs, but upstarts have only existed since money replaced heredity as a measure of class. Snobbery aside, upstarts were simply people rising in a world that was changing in the direction of accommodating them, people availing themselves of the new and still slim opportunities that for centuries had been denied them. The word is meaningless to Americans, who do not have our social history, and it is interesting that Catherine, whose novels turn to a high degree on the anachronisms of the English class system, found it difficult at first to conquer that market.

The Golden Age of Agriculture, when labourers knew their place and lived largely off the land, was long gone. The world had already changed dramatically over the past half-century, and it was still changing. Now that money was part of the equation, the old loyalties between labourer and hereditary landowner, which had existed for centuries, had been eroded. Since the Industrial Revolution the money men in the City of London had taken control of working men's lives. The working-class myth, which attached pride and dignity to the position of the workers (and suggested that rising out of it was a betrayal), suited the money men, for it fostered company loyalty, but they were not about to succour it at their own expense. Nor did it seem to Catherine that there was much real working-class solidarity in any case. In fact, the only example reflected in industrial action came during ten days in the middle of May 1926, with the General Strike. Through inter-union conflict and squabbles over demarcation lines (between boilermakers and shipwrights, for example) the unions failed consistently to present a unified front, or to convince the majority of workers to join them. In the words of Mr Hetherington to Katie's brother Joe in *Katie Mulholland* (1967), 'it's every man jack for himself'. Catherine's persecutors were deluded if they saw her efforts to rise above her class as betrayal, because in reality the values they felt had been betrayed belonged to a world which had long gone.

In *Tilly Trotter* and *Katie Mulholland* we see the great change from an agricultural to an industrial society taking place, and along with it an increased freedom of movement – for the mercantile and commercial classes, at least.

Coal provided the fuel of revolution, and the various industries returned the favour in their own ways, the railways by decreasing the cost of moving it, iron and steel by shaping the ships that carried it to foreign lands, glass by using otherwise unsaleable coal in its manufacturing process and the chemical industry by its use of brine, a nuisance in the pits but invaluable in the manufacture of alkali; and in its turn the chemical industry provided essential ingredients for the manufacture of pottery, paper, soap and textiles. If you were an entrepreneurial spirit and wanted to get on, you tried to get into coal.

When we meet George Rosier in *Tilly Trotter* in the 1830s he is merely a mine manager of the Sopwith Coal Mine, owned by landowner Mark Sopwith. Sopwith, like all the other hereditary landowners in a region once noted for its agricultural strength, is now concentrating on mining the mineral that lies beneath his land. Rosier, as any other entrepreneurial spirit would have done, seeks a share in a mine. When he appears in *Katie Mulholland* he has clawed his way into the industry and begun to cement a profitable relationship with Palmer's shipyard in Jarrow, which was at the epicentre of the industrial revolution. Rosier's son Bernard is eighteen when, on a June day in 1852, he stands with his father in Palmer's and watches the launching of the *John Bowes*. This ship, the first profitable iron collier, could do in five days what 'would have taken two sailing colliers a month to accomplish'. It was a turning point in the revolution – and, incidentally, the reason why our Queen Mother, a Bowes-Lyon, had such close links with Tyneside and was one of Catherine's foremost fans.

Others of Catherine's new gentry, such as the Mallens and Edmund Lagrange in *The Glass Virgin*, also rose from the merchant classes. By the mid-nineteenth century the remarkable surge of economic activity in a variety of industries had changed the power structure of Britain completely and set in motion a social revolution in which, as a woman, Catherine was a pioneering participant. In *The Upstart*, she shows one aspect of the social confusion which resulted from this great change, when the old values still existed alongside the new.

By 1898, when the novel opens, money has long been the

principal measure of class, and there is utter confusion when the *nouveau riche* tradesman-turned-businessman Samuel Fairbrother comes into contact with a below-stairs set-up which hasn't changed for a hundred years. Butler Roger Maitland is appalled when his new master, the owner of a chain of shoemaking shops, associates him with the kitchen staff. Loudmouthed Fairbrother has bought his thirty-four-roomed house, stone, mortar, servants, lock, stock and barrel, the last owner having fallen on hard times. His ethic is work, work, work, and, having never had a favour offered him on a plate, he cannot see why life for his servants should be any different. He and Maitland look at each other across a gaping cultural divide.

At the outset, both are uneasy, and Fairbrother and his wife Alice show signs of being totally at sea in their new environment. Maitland offers his resignation, but is persuaded to stay. It is inconceivable that the house can be run without his experience. But there is no easy solution, and the Fairbrothers (they have eight children) display all the symptoms of the discomfort that goes with rising from one social level to another – recrimination, anger, hypocrisy – which erupt into family feuds. We watch Maitland, a quiet catalyst in this extraordinary experiment, tactfully educate Fairbrother in his new role as master, while maintaining a kind of classless integrity behind his butler's mask which will, in the course of the novel, put him firmly in control.

When Catherine searched history for the reasons behind the anachronisms, hypocrisies and absurdities of the English class system from which she, and all her people, suffered, she found confusion, envy and exploitation at their roots. In the end she prefers a kind of existential solution to the class problem. It is the characters who take responsibility for their own lives and eschew or overcome the pettifogging prejudices and hypocrisies of society who achieve fulfilment. Her novels cover a period of change from the rise of the mercantile class at the expense of the landed gentry in the eighteenth and nineteenth centuries, when money replaced heredity as the means to position in society (e.g. *Katie Mulholland*, *The Glass Virgin*), through the 1930s, when financial disaster brought a desperate call for workers' rights (*The Blind Miller*), to modern days, when class problems are borne in the psyche of her people, however deeply they may be buried in history, and a psychological adjustment is required to overcome them. The best novel in these terms in undoubtedly

The Round Tower (1968), which won the Winifred Holtby Memorial Prize from the Royal Society of Literature.

It is set in the late 1960s and early 1970s in Fellburn, with its posh Brampton Hill and its Bog's End slum, this time focusing us on Affleck and Tate's engineering works. The chairman of the company, Jonathan Ratcliffe, one of the *nouveaux riches*, lives in Bower House on Brampton Hill. The drawing office of Affleck and Tate is managed by Arthur Brett, who lives next door at The Larches and is a man with a good deal less ambition than his boss. Ratcliffe's one irritation is that Brett owns six acres of land leading down to the river which he has never cultivated. It is a beautiful spot, but it takes Brett every last penny simply to maintain. Ratcliffe, hungry to enhance his own property, has tried in vain to get Brett to part with the land. But to Brett it is worth more than money; it is a symbol of something which Ratcliffe, for all his new-found wealth, will never have.

They are very different men. The Larches is brimming with antiques, many of them inherited by Brett from his grandfather, who set up home there in 1892. There is continuity in Brett's life, even a hint of breeding, and he fancies that he has an aesthetic appreciation. But for all this, Brett is a mouse of a man. He has none of Ratcliffe's guts, and his wife Irene sees eye to eye with him about very little. Yet, in his weakness, Brett needs Irene, while at the same time hating himself for 'visiting the corpse long after love is dead', as he puts it indelicately. When a thing of true beauty (Ratcliffe's daughter, Vanessa) falls into his hands, Brett shows his true colours by devouring and then rejecting her in favour of the sick, safe world he knows. Afterwards, faced with the truth about himself, Brett realises that there is only one course left open to him. But even his suicide is not courageous.

In welcome contrast to the Ratcliffes and the Bretts are the Cottons who live on Ryder's Row, a short row of houses among the goods sheds at the foot of the railway embankment, fronting on to the main Newcastle Road. The Cottons are attached to the Ratcliffes through Emily, who has served them for years when no one else would suffer their regime. Emily is worked to a standstill. She has a son, Angus, and a daughter, Rose. Angus is a balanced young man, hardworking, open, kind. He and Vanessa have grown up in parallel worlds which would never have touched had it not been for Emily's position in the Ratcliffe household. Seen through the innocent eyes of Angus and Vanessa, as children, the social gulf between the families does not seem so wide. But when they grow up, Brett's wife Irene, who shares Jonathan and Jane Ratcliffe's snobbishness, is in turn suspicious of and disgusted by their friendship, which continues harmlessly enough up to the point when Brett makes Vanessa pregnant and Angus stands accused.

This is the cultural stew in which Catherine brews her novel. Class attitudes and envies are skilfully played of course, but if readers expect a romantic resolution they will be disappointed, even though Angus and Vanessa do come together. Angus is in love with Van, as he calls her – he always has been – but the closer they become as adults, the more unsure is Van. On one occasion she is even repulsed by Angus's ignorance and crudity, which she sees as deeply ingrained in him, as deeply as his loyalty to his mother Emily, which binds the family together but which Van suspects runs deeper than his love for her can ever go.

On the one hand, Catherine gives us the Cotton family, homogenous, caring; on the other, the veneer of the Ratcliffes. But she repels any facile judgement between the two. For a moment even the closeness of the Cotton family, the very core of the working-class myth, seems to tip over into claustrophobia, as Emily's favourite bit of poetry (from Longfellow, of course) suggests:

> *I have you fast in my fortress,*
> *And will not let you depart,*
> *But put you down into the dungeon*
> *In the round tower of my heart.*
>
> *And there will I keep you for ever,*
> *Yes, for ever and a day,*
> *Till the walls shall crumble to ruin,*
> *And moulder in dust away.*

Catherine is engaged in drawing a realistic picture. Van, for all her rejection of her snobbish family, realises that she *is* coming to the Cottons from a foreign place, emotionally as well as materi-ally, intellectually as well as socially.

When Van takes up residence on Ryder's Row, she descends into a deep depression. Like the ribbons round the maypole, her thoughts become entangled and her nerves wrought up. She is incapable of sorting out what she feels from what she thinks, and though she doesn't in fact commit suicide, she discovers, as Catherine was to do, that thirty aspirins in a glass of water take a long time to dissolve.

Angus's success in his haulage business does nothing to help the situation, particularly as he uses his money to buy The Larches – Brett's old house, where he raped Vanessa – on Brampton Hill. What Angus won't realise is that dressing for the part is not enough. Money cannot solve social problems which have become psychological problems.

Casting off the inherited ideology of an English class system which has become part of the nation's psyche is an ideal to which it is easy to assent, but as difficult for Angus and Van to achieve in their case as it will be for Catherine in her own. Angus and Van will not find peace of mind until they build a house of their own, within, and the walls which confine them in their separate worlds 'crumble to ruin, and moulder in dust away'.

Catherine's escape from the fortress which confined her took colossal inner strength, more even than it took Katie Mulholland to carve out her empire, though the source of their strength is, of course, the same. 'My characters are strong,' Catherine once said to me, 'they always come through. But that is because they are me . . . I am capable of anything. Doubt is the only obstacle. But I had to have something to cling on to.' Ironically, it was Catherine's persecutors who supplied her with it.

She was reading large quantities of books at this time. 'I was twenty and a reader of novels, particularly those of Ethel M. Dell, Charles Garvis, Warwick Deeping, Ouida, Arnold Bennett and such like.' These are storytellers, writers with the power of getting their readers to turn pages. Ouida was the pseudonym of Marie Louise de la Ramée, who lived from 1839 to 1908. Her mother was English, but her father, Louis Ramée, was a teacher of French, his mother tongue. Ouida wrote forty-five novels, her popularity achieved from flamboyant, emotionally charged narratives, as in *Under Two Flags* and *Moths*. Warwick Deeping was another immensely popular, prolific novelist, whose best-known work, *Sorrell and Son*, was published a year after Catherine entered the workhouse. It turned, significantly in the context of Catherine's own life, on a father's determination to provide his son with a private education which would protect him from class prejudice.

Arnold Bennett was an even more significant figure for Catherine. The son of a potter and pawnshop owner from near

Hanley, since 1910 part of the Borough of Stoke-on-Trent, Bennett, at twenty-two (in 1889) had escaped his working-class environment, where there was 'an atmosphere of grim sticking to it, of never being beaten by circumstance', and went on to make his name by writing about it.

Then came Elinor Glyn, though not by Catherine's choice. Glyn was a novelist forbidden to Catherine by the Catholic Church. 'Well, what could you expect when she wrote about naked women lying on bear skins?' Catherine chided her colleagues for reading Glyn, which was why one day she found a copy of *The Career of Katherine Bush* placed in her room by her persecutors. It was a masterly temptation, for the novel tells of a secretary girl's determination to rise in the world. Catherine took it up and couldn't put it down. They had read her right, but they could have had no idea just what effect it would have. 'I read this book,' she recalls, 'and I can say it was from this time that my life changed, and utterly.'

Elinor Glyn lived from 1864 until 1943, and many of her works – often sensationally romantic – were adapted for the big screen in the silent film era. The scene for which she became infamous, and to which Catherine refers – a scene of great passion (in fact on a tiger not a bear skin) – was featured in Glyn's most sensational novel of all. *Three Weeks* was published in 1907 and described as a *succès de scandale*.

The Career of Katherine Bush tells the tale of a girl who becomes secretary to Lady Garribardine, who has a friend who discovers that Katherine is highly intelligent and falls in love with her. At first Katherine's mistress is incensed, because the girl is common and this man belongs to the aristocracy; but then, rather than spoiling the match, Lady Garribardine decides to educate Katherine in the ways of the world, and directs her to Lord Chesterfield's *Letters to his Son*.

Catherine told me how, on reading this, she simply flew down to the South Shields library and devoured the first volume of Chesterfield's *Letters*. 'Over the years I have come to think that Elinor Glyn was put on this earth mainly to write that book in order to show an ignorant North Country girl the path she must take.' In Chesterfield Catherine found 'a mentor, a friend; and the fact that I was in the same boat as his son drew me closer to him.' She had found her 'something to cling on to'. For it was Chesterfield who showed her a way forward and gave her the confidence to take it.

Philip Dormer Stanhope, the Fourth Earl of Chesterfield, was born on 22 September 1694 to a man ruined by privilege. As Catherine put it, 'Chesterfield's father, the Third Earl, was a rake, a kind of man who apparently never grew up'. He shunned his wife, who died when she was thirty-three after bearing him nine sons (of whom Philip was the second), and went off to France. Their son, the Fourth Earl, Catherine's mentor, was brought up by his grandmother, Gertrude Pierrepont, the Marchioness of Halifax, and she set him on the path to success. She saw to it that he had a good education, certainly, but equally importantly she taught him what in those days were known as the 'graces' and might today be called social skills or style. He went to Cambridge University and by nineteen was learned, witty, a great orator, a gambler known for his 'high play', and, in spite of a fairly hideous appearance, popular with the ladies.

Chesterfield entered Parliament in 1715 but after a highly successful maiden speech was challenged by a member of the Opposition, who pointed out that he was not yet twenty-one and therefore too young to represent his constituency. Chesterfield stepped down until he came of age, whiling away the time as Gentleman of the Bed Chamber to the Prince of Wales. When in due course he became an active politician he did well, although he might have done better had he not delighted in putting down those who were at one time or another favourites of the King or Queen. He became Ambassador to The Hague, then Lord Lieutenant of Ireland, where, through tact and good judgement, he achieved much in a very short space of time. Finally, he became Secretary of State at the Foreign Office, before retiring at fifty-three with rheumatic gout and increasing deafness.

During his time as Ambassador to The Hague, Chesterfield conceived a son with a woman called Madelena Elizabeth du Bouchet. The boy, also named Philip, was born in 1732. Chesterfield saw to it that he was well educated. He sent him to Westminster School, thence to the universities of Lausanne and Leipsig, and finally on the extended European tour to France, Germany, Switzerland and Italy under the protection of a full-time tutor and with introductions to the best society in all the European capitals.

The *Letters* written by the Fourth Earl to his illegitimate son began when Philip was seven – the age at which Catherine was told of her illegitimacy by her playmate. They continued during the boy's Grand Tour – he nearly always addressed him 'Dear

Boy' – and through his political career (he was twice elected to Parliament) and his diplomatic appointments in Hamburg, Ratisbon and Dresden, until his untimely death at the age of thirty-six. In a symbolic sense, these letters – patronly, sometimes avuncular in tone, and full of advice – affirm a connection between father and son that Philip's illegitimacy called into question. They are an attempt by Chesterfield to rest a finger on the roulette wheel of fate, which had spun the boy a poor return at birth. They concern education in the narrow sense very little, though they do show how to go about getting it. Indeed, they are at their best when Chesterfield seeks to supplement Philip's academic education with wise words from a man of the world.

When they first appeared in book form in 1774, one year after Lord Chesterfield's death, they were an instant success: five editions appeared before the end of the year. This initial enthusiasm was due not to Chesterfield's reputation as a man of deep genius (which he was not) or to his political success, but rather to the public perception of him as a man of social ingenuity and wit, and to his 'perfect knowledge of mankind'. For historians, the letters offer an extraordinary insight into the habits of the day, the temper of the Age of Reason. Their interest for Catherine, however, was that they provided her with a step-by-step strategy for rising in the world. Nevertheless, the traditional English prejudice against success found a harsh voice in some critics of the eighteenth and nineteenth centuries, who seized upon Chesterfield's philosophy of self-interest and the frankness with which he expressed it. Echoes of this dissent call into question how Catherine could deliver herself up to a tutor who has been described as having 'the mien of a posture-maker, the skin-deep graciousness of a French Maréchal . . . a calculating adventurer who cuts unpretentious worthies to toady to society magnates, who affects the supercilious air of a shallow dandy and cherishes the heart of a frog'.

'In my young days,' admits Lady Garribardine in Elinor Glyn's novel, '[the *Letters*] were considered highly immoral and pernicious by most of the canting Victorian hypocrites – when, of course, every one of the world knew that Chesterfield's advice on all points was the most sensible and sagacious that could be given, but hypocrisy had risen to a colossal height in the 'sixties and 'seventies.'

What Lady Garribardine is suggesting is that Chesterfield's

ate Fawcett, Catherine's real mother. When Catherine first saw Kate drunk, her speech slurred, her ugh raucous, her walk unsteady, she was ashamed to be seen with her and the child never did ccept Kate as her mother.

The New Buildings allotments, where James Eckford had three gardens and supplied the whole island community with fresh vegetables. The Eckfords lived in Simonside Terrace and were neighbours of Lily Tulip, the flower girl. Catherine shows in the opening pages of one of her best novels, *Pure as the Lily*, what sweet pleasure having an allotment gave to a working man.

In the autumn of 1913, when Catherine was seven, she learned that she was illegitimate from a spiteful little girl who was playing shops with her in the street, as here using broken bits of coloured glass for 'boody' to make their pretend transactions. The revelation shattered Catherine beyond redemption.

Boys chasing a hay cart, trundling along the Jarrow Road past Simonside Terrace at the north end of the New Buildings in 1910, just before Catherine arrived on the estate. Although in the heart of industrial Tyneside, the countryside was less than a mile away.

Inset: The Alkali pub on the Jarrow Road, one of those to which Kate sent Catherine to fetch beer. There was a rota depending on where she could get tick. It is still there today.

Unlike this little girl, Catherine had to fetch the beer in a stone jar called the Grey Hen, made for holding vinegar. It was so large and heavy when full that she had to rest it on her hip while walking, sometimes 'even as far as Brinkburn Street or Stanhope Road,' maybe two miles there and back to the New Buildings.

The Jarrow tram approaches, having followed the river past the New Buildings, then Leam Lane and through the arches to the terminus at Tyne Dock. The dock gates are on the right of the picture. The road to the left is Hudson Street, leading past the dock offices to the pawn shop. Just visible on the left is the public lavatory where Catherine was shocked to hear laughter as a woman emerged arm in arm with some men.

The classroom of a Tyneside school at the time Catherine moved through four schools in as many years, the last of which, St Peter and St Paul's Tyne Dock, acquainted her with the beauty of words and the terrors of hell's fire.

The Crown cinema on Hudson Street, Tyne Dock, showed a Saturday matinée and was the only venue available to couples 'walking out'. The building is still the Crown today.

Catherine as a teenager grew to become as tall and graceful as a river reed, 'if rather flat, like a boy, immature still,' as she wrote about her fictional counterpart in *Tilly Trotter*.

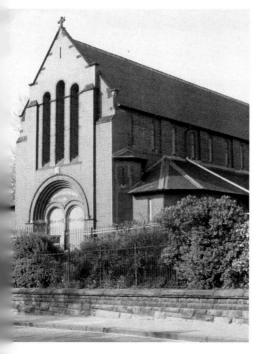

t Peter and St Paul's Tyne Dock, founded in
ie year of Catherine's birth. She attended the
djacent school from 1916. Here she met stern
ather Bradley and kind Father O'Keefe, both
whom find their way into the novels. As a
enager she would enjoy the quiet of the church
id beseech a particular statue of the Holy
imily to intercede in her life, like Mary Ann
aughnessy in *A Grand Man*.

Catherine can be seen centre stage (second row) in a rare picture of the New Buildings community. Kate is standing in the same row, three in from the left.

The laundry at Harton Workhouse, where Catherine worked from 22 October 1924. The checker whose position she filled is the furthest left of the four women wearing Sunday uniforms.

The grim exterior of Harton Workhouse, where once her step-grandfather, John McMullen, was reduced to breaking stone for a shilling a day. The asylum was to the right, the stone breaking yard to the rear. It is now South Tyneside Hospital.

Female inmates of the workhouse in the Infirm Ward. Families were split up at the door, men to one side, women to the other, and their children were taken from them. Catherine couldn't believe the suffering she saw.

Catherine aged about twenty, when she was in love with a man eleven years her senior, and had been advised by a writers' correspondence school 'not to take up writing as a career'.

detractors are as out of touch with the ways of the world as Catherine's colleagues at the workhouse were – or preferred to be seen to be. Yet there is a certain cynicism in Chesterfield which does seem at odds with Catherine's deep moral sense. He urged his son to 'pry into the recesses of others' hearts and heads', to 'bait your hook to catch them,' to 'flatter people behind their backs, in the presence of those who will not fail to repeat, or even amplify, the praise to the party concerned,' to 'preserve the *appearances* of Religion and Morality'; he states that 'without some dissimulation no business can be carried on at all,' and holds that 'a man of the world must, like the chameleon, be able to take every different hue'.

But Chesterfield answered Catherine's needs in various ways. To begin with, his son was illegitimate and it was as if he were speaking to Catherine directly. Then there was her belief that her real father was, like Philip's, a gentleman, and her need, in her increasing isolation, for a father figure to advise her. The main key to her allegiance, however, is that he appeased her nagging sense of inferiority. And the self-denigration process which had begun in the back streets of East Jarrow by the Richardsons' chimneypiece required appeasement. Chesterfield describes his servants as 'my equals in nature . . . only my inferiors in fortune'. Catherine uses this quotation more than once in her novels, and on many occasions her characters benefit from patrons who espouse the idea it expresses. For example, in *The Black Velvet Gown* Percival Miller, when educating the children of miner's widow Riah Millican, brings Chesterfield on to the syllabus and quotes him exactly on class equality. In *The Devil and Mary Ann*, when Mary Ann has begun her schooling, paid for by Mr Lord, he writes to her as if he were Chesterfield. His letters begin 'My dear child' and are couched in exactly the same style as Chesterfield's. To her father, Mike, he says of Mary Ann that at times he finds her 'more than my equal, even my superior'.

Contrary to what Chesterfield's critics said of him – most famously Samuel Johnson, who declared that Chesterfield taught 'the morals of a whore and the manners of a dancing master' – moral virtue is in fact a key concept in the *Letters*. 'For God's sake,' he writes to his son, 'be scrupulously jealous of the purity of your moral character,' and while he recommends dissimulation in business – 'not straightway laying all your trump cards on the table' – he distinguishes it from simulation, which is deceit.

Chesterfield's advice always flows from first-hand personal experience. He is ethically scrupulous simply because he has learned that deceit doesn't work: 'If in negotiations you are looked upon as a liar, and a trickster, no confidence will be placed in you, nothing will be communicated to you, and you will be in the situation of a man who has been burnt in the cheek; and who, from that mark, cannot afterwards get an honest livelihood if he would, but must continue a thief.'

He recommends the chameleon as model for the aspiring diplomat – 'to adapt your conversation to the people you are conversing with' – as common sense. 'Baiting your hook' may be a provocative expression, but it turns on a realistic assessment of the political jungle which his son intended to explore, not on an espousal of slyness or cunning. It is not Chesterfield's purpose to train his son in the role of reformer, but rather to encourage him to derive his morality from experience: 'We must take things as they are, we cannot make them what we would, nor often what they should be.' How near that comes to Catherine's 'Necessity, through time and circumstance, made life.'

What emerges from the *Letters* is that while moral rectitude is essential, it is justified as indisputably by how things actually go on in the world as by any precepts of religion: 'There is nothing so delicate as your moral character, and nothing which it is your interest so much to preserve pure. Should you be suspected of injustice, malignity, perfidy, lying, etc., all the parts and knowledge in the world will never procure you esteem, friendship or respect.'

In short, Chesterfield proves moral values at the altar of reason, not religion. On this reading, Chesterfield's eighteenth-century critics – devotees of reason to a man – failed to grasp the nettle of their age and were stung by their own hypocrisy. For Catherine, dire warnings of hellfire from the Catholic Church had engendered only fear and guilt. Here was a man who understood the world and gave morality new roots in wisdom derived from experience. What was there to fear in that?

Nevertheless, useful as he was at this stage in Catherine's life in getting her up and out of her situation, Chesterfield could not divert her from the path to breakdown. Indeed, it could be said that he encouraged her along it. 'Chesterfield is often spoken of as "artificial",' wrote Roger Coxon, 'and in the broadest sense that he scorned the primitive.' Since Freud, we tend to think of 'natural' as meaning an absence of phoniness, but Chesterfield, writing long before Freud, believed that artifice could be so completely absorbed that it *became* natural. At the workhouse Catherine went along with this view, but 'when the mirror of breakdown was held up to me [and] I saw myself as I really was . . . a fugitive from my ain folk,' she threw off the 'pseudo-lady covering the real me, and I knew if I was ever going to write a word that anybody would want to read, I'd have to strip her off and be myself.'

In her novels Catherine digs far deeper than her mentor and with great insight embraces the primitive. She puts humanity on the slab and wields her scalpel to cut away man's pseudo-self, in particular his hypocrisies over class, race and religion. There is no joy for the upstart who leaves his true self behind, or for the bigoted in society; they are society's prisoners and gaolers.

In *A Dinner of Herbs*, Willy Harding is a cowhand on the Roystan farm. His benevolent master, Sir Reginald, who could have been a disciple of Chesterfield, takes it upon himself to open up 'a new world' for Willy. But it is only because Willy refuses to let his 'education' at Sir Reginald's hands uproot him out of his true nature that he finds fulfilment. In *The Menagerie*, when Pam Turnbull is considering whether to return to her home-town boyfriend, Larry Broadhurst, her rich husband Ron tells her that she will miss not only the material things he can give her, but the social and intellectual bonuses too. Pam admits to Larry that if she had been left to herself, 'to grow up being myself,' she and Larry could have been happy. Part of her wants 'to live ordinary, and part of me never can now'. She, unlike Willy Harding, does not remain true to her nature, and Larry, pushed and pulled out of his own true nature by his love for Pam, narrowly escapes the mental breakdown which befell Catherine.

The Invitation (1970) is a wonderfully comic illustration of what happens to upstarts who lose sight of their true selves. Set in fictional Fellburn, with Brampton Hill and Bog's End mapping its social topography, this is a novel about the way social mountaineering frays the ropes which, at bottom, connect us to our nature. Maggie Gallacher is another of the rumbustious, half-comic characters at which Catherine excels. She and her husband have risen in the world, not just to Brampton Hill, but to the very pinnacle of respectability in a supra-district known appropriately as The Rise. Just how far they have come is shown on the first page of the novel, when they receive an invitation from the Duke of Moorshire, described as 'the mountain peak' of their striving.

Unlike her husband, Maggie still has her feet firmly on the ground, as firmly at least as the painful corn on one of her feet will allow. She has enjoyed their rise but, much to her husband's chagrin, is still capable of delivering a 'body-shaking, mouth-stretching' brand of laughter that is more characteristic of a slum dweller in Bog's End. It is Rodney who has changed.

Maggie's excitement over the four weeks leading up to the party, a musical evening, is tangible. Her preparations have been exhaustive, right down to rehearsing for the high point of the evening, shaking hands with the Duke. Come the day, Maggie stuffs her ample form into a blue velvet gown and yields her corn, still raw from last night's encounter with a safety razor, to the heel of a pink slipper.

Maggie's corn becomes a symbol of her situation. She has managed to shave off only its hard-skinned exterior, though she knows only too well that it (like Maggie herself, if she is to succeed in her new social environment) must be pulled up by the roots. Rodney, however, takes in her fine appearance with a comment about what money can buy, and slips into his dinner jacket with minimum fuss, as if partying with the Duke were a weekly occurrence.

Catherine's description of the party is a triumph of comic affectation seen through Maggie's eyes, the response of her corn to the heel of her slipper reflecting precisely the misery which she suffers at the hands of Rodney, who is clearly embarrassed by her every word and deed. Only once during the evening does Maggie find a soul-mate: a man called Bailey, who agrees with her that the music is awful. Rodney ensures that the association is short-lived.

The real party piece is Maggie's determination to meet the Duke. He hadn't been on hand when they arrived – his brother had been taken ill and he had had to excuse himself. And when he does arrive and starts mingling with his guests, Maggie seems always to be just out of reach. Rodney, of course, manages to have an audience with him when he is off getting Maggie a plate of food (lest her sweet sherry go to her head and crown his embarrassment). Then, at last, at the end of the party, guests line up in couples to shake hands with the Duke, and it seems inevitable that Maggie will achieve her heart's desire. Gradually she and Rodney shuffle towards the great man until there is only one couple between the Gallachers and him – whereupon, against all precedent, the Duke wheels around the couple he is receiving and walks them away down the steps towards the sunken garden. Maggie lets out a ripple of indignation and when a woman standing nearby admonishes her, she rocks back on her heels and lets all pretence go with a loud 'BUGGER THE DUKE!' As all eyes turn towards her and the head of the Duke stops bobbing down the steps and turns, Rodney whisks her away to the car.

In September 1927 Catherine was promoted to assistant laundress at the workhouse, but four months later when the position of laundress fell vacant and she applied for it, she was passed over. It was not quite the final rejection, but, added to the rest, it led her, armed with Chesterfield, to the single biggest decision in her life to date.

'My answer to the question why I left the North is there were many reasons, all tangled and representing one word – rejection. I had been rejected by the man who had fathered me. I think Kate rejected me from when I was born because she went through hell . . . I think I rejected her when I was seven and learned that she wasn't just Our Kate, a relation, she was my mother. I knew I was different from the time I ever began to think because I was illegitimate, a bastard. When I was eighteen and went into the workhouse as a laundry checker I definitely found out what rejection meant . . . There I was, this tall, good-looking girl, who dared to act the lady and was aiming to educate herself by learning the fiddle, taking French lessons and studying anatomy and physiology because she intended to be a nurse. Who did she think she was?! And then the great surprise, just look who she was courting now!'

Jim Dailey, the handsome, well-dressed man, eleven years her senior, whom she had idolised as a girl of fourteen, wishing he could have been her father, had finally, five years later, walked her part way home from church.

'From then on, every Saturday night he would take me to the pictures. On a Sunday morning we would go to eleven o'clock Mass. Sometimes he would walk part of the way up the Jarrow Road with me. That was added wonder. In the evening we went to Benediction and after we walked up into the country, and this pattern went on for a whole year, and never once did that man kiss me, and never once did he accept an invitation to be my partner at any of the three staff dances, headed by the master and matron, which were great events in our life. And my heart did not question. It was too full of adoration. I may say that only once did he ever take me into a public place except for a coffee after the pictures. And this was to a dance in Shields. That was before he got to know my history and that of my family.

'One night he was waiting with me for the Jarrow tram. It was sleeting badly and we had taken shelter, of all places, round the corner of this little street where I had been born, next to a public house. (Oh, I had to be born next to a public house! And within ten yards of the actual dock wall.) And as he stood waiting for a tram he bent and kissed me. I was down with wonder. And then he told me why he had been so reticent. He had been getting over a love affair. He had discovered, just before he was about to marry, that his future wife was subject to epileptic fits . . .'

Catherine felt more than a bit used – 'he knew I was deeply in love with him, but I was sympathetic, and I thought things would change from that. He would now accept the invitations, not only to the dances, but to other functions. But no. Not once during the following year did he ever deem to accompany me to a public place.'

They had arrived at this watershed in their relationship at the very site of her lowly birth, which, directly or indirectly, had dogged her ever since. And now she became convinced that it was all happening again. 'The excuses were many and of all kinds. And what I suffered from the main part of the staff was unimaginable . . . their laughter, their covert remarks and sneers, their even betting on when he would turn up this time. Yet he took me to the gates of the workhouse every Sunday night and he stood for a few minutes like a number of other couples around us. During those two years I never had a partner at all the dances and functions. But I danced because there was a tall young fellow who worked as a mental assistant and he was a very good Charleston dancer and I was grateful to him because he would always ask me to dance.

'How many nights I cried my eyes out, asking the question: Why? Why?' Then, somehow – whether it was Catherine's doing or Dailey's is not clear – plans were laid for a holiday together in Cumbria. To preserve appearances, she was to go on ahead. Catherine had never been so far away before and excitedly made friends with other tourists before he arrived. She was on form and proved very popular in the pub where they stayed, but her performance made Dailey feel almost superfluous. Now no

longer in the driving seat of their relationship, he became poss-
essive and his nose was really put out of joint when Catherine
accepted an invitation to travel to Scotland, with Dailey tagging
on morosely behind.

Back home Catherine's workhouse colleagues assumed that
the holiday had gone rather better than in fact it had. A 'violet
ray installation' had been purchased to treat, state the Workhouse Minutes, diseases like 'rickets, malnutrition, surgical
tuberculosis and tubercular glands . . . also lupus,' and staff
were offered a free course. As Catherine sat awaiting her turn,
dressed only in bra and knickers, a superior noticed a spot on
her waist and had her subjected to a rigorous examination
during which a doctor's free-ranging hands made certain
confirmation that her hymen was still intact. At a time when
sexual disease was rife, her holiday with Dailey had led to
suspicions that she may have contracted syphilis. Apparently
nothing could have been further from the truth.

'Then came the climax. It was my twenty-first birthday. Kate
couldn't give me a party in our kitchen. But my Aunt Mary at the
top of the street had made her three rooms into a very nice
comfortable home and her front room was well furnished. It
even had a spinet piano in it. I invited eight of my associates,
four of them real friends, they all brought their boyfriends. Mary
had a very nice tea set out and we waited – and we waited – and
we waited – and the main guest never turned up. Oh, there was
some laughter and gossip . . . Well, the next week a letter said he
was sorry, but he had been taking the money to pay an insurance
claim and had lost it and he was very upset. He thought our
friendship should stop because he would have to save up to
repay the money that had been lost.

'There had been one time when we had talked of marriage. He
was being moved to Durham. But he said it was too much to ask
of me to leave my post and also my home – my home! – at any
rate, yet.

'Not being a fool, my eyes had been opening slowly and I
realised the character of this "gentleman" with a beautiful face,
marred by a very small mouth.

'Coming to my real self at last I wrote him a letter that should
have burnt his fingers as he held it. I was due for my holidays
and decided to go to Ireland to see my stepfather's sister, who
was blind. Kate sent me a letter from him and it was to say that
he had been to a priest and told him that he had made use of me

over the past two years, not sexually, oh no, but as a salve to ease his hurt feelings. And the priest had said that he had done me a great wrong and he had to ask my forgiveness.

'After I read the letter I took up one sheet of paper and I wrote across it three words – I wrote not in a straight line, but right across the page three words, GO TO HELL! I did not see him for many months after, and it was coming out of the pictures. He begged me to become friends with him again because he missed me so much. I laughed in his face. But he kept on and I lost the last bus home. There was only now what they called the drunk bus – the 207 from Shields market to Jarrow. This was always full of men who had just come off the ferry. The pubs in South Shields closed half an hour earlier than those in North Shields, and the men still able to stand on their feet got on the ferry, went over the river for a last drink, came back and got on the bus. And it was into this bus that I had to be pulled by them – on to the platform – while my late suitor was still begging me to write to him. The bus started and he walked along with it for a while and there I stood with those drunken arms around me, looking down at him, the man who had rejected me. And I felt in a way that I had won, but only in a way.

'The drunks were very merry and they kept shouting to each other, "She's not going to write to the lad!" And different voices, "Why isn't she going to write to the lad?" "The poor fellow's bad!" "The poor fellow's sick!"

'The bus stopped at the bottom of William Black Street. I got off to the cries of the merry drunks, saying, "You be a good lass and write to the fella. Now go on now!" I walked up the dark street to the house that had always been my home and as I did so, the smile left my face and from deep within me there came a cry and it said, "I'll show him! I'll show him!"

'Of course, I knew that I had been rejected not only for myself but because I was illegitimate, I came from a notorious family. It wouldn't do him any good in the insurance business to be linked up with such people.

'That was the end of my courting days, so to speak. The fellow from the mental block began to ask me out. This caused a great furore, a different kind of furore, in the mess-room. The staff came back to me in a horde. Didn't I know he was engaged to be married? No, I didn't. So the next time he asked me I put the question to him. No, of course he wasn't. Not any more. He had once been engaged to this girl but that was broken off ages ago.

One Sunday dinner I was home for the weekend and was drying up the dishes with Kate in the scullery and there was a knock at the door.

'It was my dancing partner. He had come, he had actually come to ask me to marry him, with a special licence. I laughed. He was the last person on God's earth I would have married. The most intelligent part about him was his feet. When I went back into the scullery and told Kate we leant together for a moment. It was a rare moment, we laughed again. And then I went back into the front room and he asked me if I would write a letter for him. He wanted to get into the Halifax police. I did this for him and he went away, very disappointed. A week passed and then the staff were in their glory, most of them, with the exception of my few friends, they were in their glory! My boss even came to me and slapped down on to my desk a newspaper cutting. It was to say that a wedding had taken place on Saturday last and that his wife had given birth on the Sunday. I couldn't believe it. But it was true. And the staff had the time of their lives. The Great Lady had had a second rejection. I knew that I could stand no more of this and so I began looking up employment in my line as far away from the North as I could possibly find . . . And I was away from the North. The last I remembered of it was standing up in the train as it came out of the tunnel at Tyne Dock, making for Newcastle on my journey south, where I was to remain for forty-six years. And I said that day . . . on looking out of the window, I saw in the distance the little church in Simonside, the school where I had gone until I was nearly eight, and farther beyond, the outline of East Jarrow and 10 William Black Street, and I cried to it, "I am never, never coming back!"'

Chapter Six

Girl from the North Country

On the day that Catherine left the North, John McMullen walked her to the tram, the tears running down his stubble, for he shaved only about once a week. 'As his white moustache pressed into my cheek, I felt an overwhelming love surge through my being. After all he had been the only da I knew, and he had treated me not according to his lights, but far exceeding them. I was on my way.'

Notwithstanding the 'deviant exultation' that Catherine said she felt 'at cutting adrift from the North and all it stood for,' there was also real apprehension at what she was doing. Fourteen months earlier, she had applied for the newly vacant post of Laundress at Harton Workhouse, and been turned down. In the wake of this rejection, and still smarting from the business with Dailey, she had answered an advertisement in the *Poor Law Journal* and been accepted for the position of Laundress at Tendring Workhouse near Clacton-on-Sea in Essex. So it was that, in March 1929, she had made her momentous decision, and two months later found herself on the train going south.

The day that Catherine left the North to make her way in the world was riven with emotion and self-doubt. She knew that

121

Kate would be blubbing her eyes out in the kitchen. She sensed that when her granda kissed her as she stepped on the tram it was likely the last time she would feel his tear-drenched stubble against her cheek. At that moment, she'd been broken hearted, 'but that didn't soften me,' she said years later. Once the train was on its way she looked out at the brick-built, back-to-back communities that passed her by and told herself she was glad to be leaving – 'I was leaving this place and I was never coming back'.

For weeks she had been repeating to herself a poem called 'Believe This', which she had found in *The Happy Magazine*. The first two lines were:

> *I will succeed I simply cannot fail,*
> *The only obstacle is doubt . . .*

And later –

> *The moment that 'I can't' is said,*
> *You slam a door right in your face . . .*

The four lines had been concentrated into a five-word mantra in her mind, which the twenty-two-year-old repeated to herself as the train clattered rhythmically out of Tyne Dock station:

> *I can, and I will! I can and I will! I can . . .*

Such was the measure of her determination to reject the North, which she felt had rejected her. Such was the measure of her ambition to make something of herself on her own terms. Along with the cutting from the magazine, she carried in her suitcase a few sheets of notes and quotations from her beloved Lord Chesterfield. She must have felt like Chesterfield's own bastard son, for whom the famous letters were written to help him make his way in the world almost 200 years earlier.

Uprooting from a town, a county, a region was unusual in those days, and took courage, particularly for a young woman from the North-East, where ties are traditionally strongest. The measure of Catherine's courage was ten times that of Chesterfield's son, who, though illegitimate too, had the backing of his father and was male. Catherine had been born during the reign of Edward VII, five years after Queen Victoria died and eight years before the First World War began, into an unfair, masculine society.

'Ambition' was a meaningless word for most women. 'Even if I had been ambitious there weren't the openings,' said Gladys Morris, who was born six years before Catherine and, in 1915, looked to the newly created Women's Institute movement for support. This movement arose as part of a general groundswell of change, championed in the political arena by the suffragettes. Indeed, Catherine's rise should be seen against this background. On the day she was born (20 June 1906), her local South Shields paper, the *Shields Gazette*, published a story about a group of suffragists (less militant than the suffragettes), who confronted Asquith (shortly to become Prime Minister) in his London home. They were foiled by a stylish butler and a speedy 'motor brougham', which swept Asquith away.

Catherine's particular route out of the male-dominated society into which she was born, which exercised control through the class system and an educational system that kept the workers down, and women in particular in higher education, was to progress within a field (the Workhouse movement) which needed to employ women, then to educate herself and make her way in a profession as a writer in which her lowly birth was a positive advantage.

In the example of her life and that of her indomitable fictional female heroines, who put into practice her slogan 'I can and I will', she can lay claim to have contributed to the big change of the twentieth century, namely the coming of women into their own. Her own rise was an outstanding achievement. Catherine was self-sufficient at just twenty-three. She had a responsible, managerial position overseeing people much older than herself at a salary of £130 a year. She depended on no one.

Meanwhile, over the next seven years, the Great Depression ate away at her people. Between 1929 and 1934 unemployment rose from 32 per cent to 75 per cent. In October 1929, Wall Street had crashed and sent tremors throughout the world. Unemployment rose from 2 million to 12 million between 1920 and 1933 in America, by 1931 nearly six million were out of work in Germany. On Tyneside numbers seeking 'relief' in Harton Workhouse alone soared to over 40,000. In 1936, Ellen Wilkinson would lead 200 unemployed workers from Jarrow on a march to London to plead their case. The Depression was on, and the world ground inexorably to war.

Yet, in the same period, Catherine rose to become middle class, the owner of a 15-room house, the first in her family ever to own a house. It was an incredible achievement, due largely to her assiduous care with money, careful investment and her demonstration that courage did not, after all, exist only in the domain of males. But she did not find it easy.

At Tendring real loneliness set in. Only the fact that no one knew that she was illegitimate gave her pleasure. 'When I left the North my first job was in a workhouse in Essex, not far from Manningtree. I was stuck there for nine months and I realised that I hated the country. Suddenly this girl who had come from this industrial area, where even at night time you heard the horns of the ships and the background noises of the goods trains, found herself in the midst of desolate countryside. In fact it wasn't desolate, I was. The land was mainly farmland; it was like a different country and I was so lonely.'

The Tendring Peninsula supports an oyster industry and three resorts, Clacton, Frinton and Walton. Tendring village is five miles inland. The workhouse was built in 1835 in the midst of thousands of acres of farmland, facing west down a long, tree-lined drive to a road. Visitors were met by a single-storey entrance block, beyond which lay a courtyard and the wings of a large, three-storey building, the hub of the site. Clacton-on-Sea, the nearest town, is ten miles away. To Catherine, the place seemed like a great, silent vacuum. The peace nearly drove her mad, and this twenty-three-year-old, who had only twice before spent time away from home, began to feel deeply depressed.

One Sunday morning she took a bus to Mass at the Lady of Light Roman Catholic church in Caernarvon Road, and afterwards asked the priest for an entre to a Catholic family. He told her that she would find plenty of people to meet in the town. By the time she caught the bus back late that afternoon, she had met no one and was exhausted, lonely and very angry.

On a subsequent Saturday she travelled again into Clacton and sat sadly on the beach, looking out to sea. Suddenly her nose began to bleed. This nosebleeding had become a tiresome, regular event, first experienced when she was eighteen. She had devised various ways to stem the flow and now applied them, but the bleeding was unusually free and nothing could stop it, so she went in search of a chemist.

Concerned passers-by offered her hankies to sop up the blood, one a scarf even. By the time she found a chemist, she was desperate; the flow was, if anything, getting worse. She was given some wadding and told she must see a doctor. Off she set to find one. 'Then all of a sudden I came to a stop with an odd sensation in my head. The only way I can describe it is as if someone was pulling a sausage out of its skin. I felt the blood moving across the vein in my head and the clot of blood then like a thick rope fell.' Mercifully, the bleeding then stopped.

Her nosebleeds were always worse when she was under pressure, and Catherine realised she had to do something to brighten her life in Tendring. She decided to invite a friend down from the North and contacted Elsie Chisholm, a hairdresser from North Shields whom she'd first met during the holiday with Jim Dailey in Cumbria. Elsie agreed to come and they spent happy times together that first summer of her independence, but it was only ever a holiday and soon came to an end.

Catherine was not settling well. It is clear, also, that the manner of her management of the laundry staff was causing a few problems. She had convinced herself that she'd been passed over for the position of Laundress at Harton on the grounds that they hadn't been up to her strong personality. Matron, she argued, had feared the consequences of giving such a person-ality as hers the reins of power. Years later she weighed the argument in her novel *Maggie Rowan*, where Maggie is given only a measure of responsibility in Mrs Thornton's laundry for the same reason. Maggie is efficient, punctilious, a dedicated Assistant Laundress, but is fundamentally flawed, bitter about life, and, as a result, not much good as a people manager, or indeed as a suitor for men. Mrs Thornton sees the latter as a positive advantage – there is little prospect of Maggie leaving to get married – but she is adamant that on no account must Maggie be given a position of power, she must never be made Head Laundress, for 'once Maggie felt power she would be like the beggar on horseback . . . she'd ride to hell'.

Maggie Rowan is but a fiction, but she is the result of some hard self-analysis on the part of her creator, who, by the time she gave the character life, accepted that there was a fault in the bedrock of her own character, to do with bitterness, aggression, hate and lack of love, which prime Maggie to ruthlessness, even cruelty, once she finds herself in a position of control.

Catherine threw herself into her first managerial job as Head Laundress at Tendring, but before long some of the older workers under her resented the way she hurled her authority at them. Like Mrs Thornton in the novel, however, the workhouse Matron applauded Catherine's efforts, boosting her brittle self-image, and when a vacancy for a job came up, she asked whether there were any more hardworking girls like her up North.

The person Catherine chose to contact – one Annie Joyce, a former colleague at Harton – was not in fact a particular friend, but she had once expressed a desire to work away from home. Soon after she arrived, Catherine realised what a mistake she had made. Annie was not on her wavelength, but, more to the point, Annie brought with her a direct line into Catherine's past, and some of those who resented Catherine's position over them now made it their business to use Annie to dig for some dirt on this slave driver of a Head Laundress.

Inevitably, Annie told them of Catherine's secret. In papers at the Catherine Cookson archive at Boston University, Catherine records that when Matron was told of her illegitimacy she was not happy. There was a row, which led to her looking for employment elsewhere. In those days, when sex outside marriage was a sin, people looked down on illegitimates as base born. Many of them ended up in workhouses as inmates. It was unusual to find one working openly in a managerial position, because such a stigma undermined authority. Whether Annie's revelation was in fact sufficient to bring matters to a head, or whether it merely served Matron's purposes to record it as such in a context of growing unrest between Catherine and her staff, cannot be said for sure. All that we know is that Catherine began to make preparations for another move.

In December 1929, just eight months after she had arrived in Tendring, she answered another advertisement in the *Poor Law Journal*, this time for Head Laundress at Hastings Workhouse in Sussex. A letter came back giving a date for interview. Catherine, by this time, was desperate to get out of Tendring, and put her mind to how best to ensure that she got the job. There were three others in the running – a shortlist of four – and she was worried what Matron would say to the Hastings people when asked for a reference. She selected her clothes carefully, paying particular attention to her coat and choosing a Henry Heath hat to complete the picture.

On the 19th she travelled by train to the south-coast resort and, with the other interviewees, was shown around the workhouse by Matron Silverlock, wife of the workhouse Master. She was then interviewed by the Board of Guardians. By now she could draw on five years' experience and speak knowledgeably about the workings of a workhouse laundry. Moreover, the tour had convinced her that there was plenty of room for improvement. So, she lost no time in giving the Board not only her opinion but also a list of things to put right.

The strategy worked. Even when her Matron at Tendring wrote to say that she thought Catherine too young for the job, she got it and, as she told me, 'I arrived there on the twenty-ninth of January 1930, with the enormous wage of three pounds six shillings a week – and in 1930 that was indeed an enormous wage, especially for a woman.'

It was, indeed, much more than she would have been paid as Head Laundress at Harton. To put it in perspective, in 1930 the dole was £1 for a single man and thirty shillings for a family-man, woman and child. Best butter was a shilling a pound, bacon threepence for flank, fourpence halfpenny for side, five-pence or sixpence for ham; two dozen eggs (small) were a shilling; margarine fourpence; and one pound of steak and rabbit was a shilling. There were, of course, twenty shillings to a pound.

Catherine started work on 3 February, having found lodgings in Clifton Road on the east side of town, around the corner from Cookson Gardens. Catherine immediately focused hard on the job in hand. After the debacle at Tendring she wanted, needed, to work hard, and she had not forgotten the promise of a big house of her own, made to herself all those years before. Her weekly earnings at the Institution came to her as three pounds by way of salary and six shillings dinner money. Virtually starving herself, she lived on the six shillings, spent eight shillings and sixpence on her flat rental and put most of the rest into an endowment policy with Sun Life of Canada.

Throwing herself into work, she set in motion a project to pave a sorting area in order to minimise the spread of dirt in the laundry; she instituted an efficient regime for her staff and began to campaign for better conditions for inmates – large grass plots were provided for the older inmates to enjoy picnics in pleasant surroundings, and Catherine organised the picnics herself.

When the Portress fell ill, she volunteered to take over her duties in addition to her own and moved into quarters in the workhouse, as a resident officer. Later she also acted as Assistant

Matron in the absence of the regular officer who was ill. In short, Catherine put herself out. She knew that this time she had to make it work.

She was known among her staff as a slave driver and by some of them as something much worse. But this time Catherine did her best to win round both the other officers and the inmates, one of whom proved particularly difficult. An asylum case called Jessie came at her with an iron bar used for lifting the door off the coke-heated flat-iron stove. 'I called to some of the women to get her from behind, but for once they turned a deaf ear to an excuse to stop work, and those who could disappeared into the sorting room. So, talking to this woman and holding my hand out for the iron bar, I backed her up towards the stove, and when she was inches from it, I threatened to push her on to it if she didn't hand over the implement. The heat was too much for her, she flung the bar down on to the hearth and I, taking her gently by the hand, led her to the job that she had refused to do, helping to fold some sheets. She grinned at me and I managed to grin at her. We understood each other. In the nine years that followed I never had any more trouble with Jessie, except that she became terribly jealous if I gave my attentions to any other inmates.'

Catherine was just beginning to feel settled, when, on Maundy Thursday, 18 April 1930, two months after she arrived, John McMullen died. The only sadness Catherine conceded over leaving the North had been John's farewell. His 'voiceless love', as she described it, meant a great deal to her even in her final years. But his death had not come at a good time. The one thing she didn't want was for the North and all it held for her to impinge upon her new life in Hastings. She didn't go to his funeral. Her beloved granda was, after all, already gone . . . Instead, she sent Kate twenty pounds to cover the cost. Later she learned that the funeral director had received half of this sum; the rest, Catherine assumed, had been spent by Kate on drink.

She cared nothing for Kate or the North any more, and she could not have chosen any place in England more unlike Tyneside than Hastings in 1930. 'The South was always more genteel,' observed cousin Teri. 'The poverty was still there, but you didn't exactly see it the way it was up North.' Catherine herself noted that 'the workhouse inmates could be considered to be on a picnic compared to those in Harton'. Other than the salt-laden wind from the sea, there was nothing about the town that bore the slightest resemblance to Catherine's homeland.

'The finest, purest sea breeze on the coast – acknowledged to be so – excellent bathing – fine hard sand – deep water ten yards from the shore – no mud – no weeds – no slimy rocks. Never was there a place more palpably designed by Nature for the retreat of the invalid – the very spot which thousands seemed in need of.'

Mr Parker's enthusiasm for this southern coastline in Jane Austen's novel *Sanditon*, written more than a century earlier, characterises the Sussex shoreline perfectly, Sanditon itself believed to have been influenced by a plan to extend Hastings west along the coast into what became St Leonards. By the time Catherine arrived, Mr Parker's dream of a fashionable resort and retirement retreat, with clean stone terraces and crescents of fine houses and hotels, had long been realised. This middle-class recreational resort and rest home for the genteel and elderly was a million miles away from the Tyne Dock arches dripping slime in 'rivulets of green' and its sea of mud, the Jarrow Slacks, polluted with chemicals from the barium works, and its sad groups of unemployed workers waiting at the dock gates to be taken on.

As she recalled for the *Sunday Telegraph Magazine* in July 1988: 'Hastings was another world, in which everything moved at an easy-going pace and no one looked poor or even drab.' And she was very happy in particular that the Hastings people were different from her people. It was here that she first encountered the English middle-classes. 'A sweet little gentlewoman' took her under her wing and gave her a tour of the area, explaining first the history and then the crucial difference between 'the ladies of St Leonards and the women of Hastings (especially those of the old town)'. When asked how to recognise them, the woman tittered, 'The ladies of St Leonards always clean their teeth after meals.' The distinction would inform the social character of Fellburn, the fictitious town in which so many of Catherine's novels are set, with Brampton Hill being St Leonards, where the middle-class ladies lived, and Bog's End deriving its class order from working-class Hastings Old Town.

At the time, Catherine would have been happy to be one of those ladies. Meanwhile, she lived and breathed workhouse life, and there was growing respect for this laundress who tirelessly devised strategies to improve efficiency. Matron Silverlock was very pleased, commenting in the Minutes of the Guardians that Miss McMullen alone was capable of taking on the extra duties of Portress and Assistant Matron when these officers fell ill. Soon, she would be able to increase the value of her insurance policy with Sun Life of Canada to £1000, still without any concrete plans to do anything with it.

But there was no respite from her work, and no friends outside the workhouse, particularly as now she had to sleep over in the Workhouse Lodge to relieve the Portress. On her day off, when she would repair to her flat, the aloneness that had so often crept up inside her since childhood found a welcome home once more. Seaside resorts off season have a way of seeking out loneliness in one and in the winter of 1930–1 the plaintive cry of the gulls and the incessant ebb and flow of the surf through the shale caught Catherine's mood to challenge the point of it all.

One weekend her landlady was away and there was no one else in the house. Catherine went to the cinema to see *Bulldog Drummond*. In the middle of the film she felt loneliness descend upon her like a pall, and when she came out she fought back the tears until getting home, where she flung herself on the bed and wept. The emotion brought on a nosebleed so strong that the thought came to her that she might bleed to death, and worse, 'So what if I did?' It was the first time she had asked herself the question, but it would not be the last.

A few days later, she forced herself to get in among company and attended a staff workhouse dance, asking Master and Matron Silverlock to escort her. A smart young man came over to their table, introduced himself, mistaking the Silverlocks for Catherine's parents, and asked her to dance. Later, he asked Catherine out and they dated for the next six months, mainly going to concerts at White Rock Pavilion in the town. Catherine referred to the man in biographical notes, which never found their way into her autobiography, as Keith.

Keith was very fond of music. Unfortunately, Catherine came to the conclusion that she wasn't at all musically minded, 'except for something with a tune'. However, she enjoyed the man's company, particularly as he was a writer who had what she longed to have, a published short story. At the time, he appeared brilliant, and yet, 'One thing was evident to me,' she wrote, 'I was incapable of love. Part of me was as cold as marble. It was as if I had been injected and couldn't feel. I liked Keith . . . but as far as affection went, I could give him none.'

The love of a man was perhaps bound to involve problems for Catherine, given how deeply she had suffered her father's rejection and then Dailey's. How upset she was, hard on the heels of Dailey's rejection, and in need of someone that could meet the romance of her aspirations, was shown in an episode at Tendring that may have had something to do with her swift departure.

One evening, when out walking, Catherine had come upon a woman in a cottage garden; her son was playing nearby. She spoke to the boy, who commented on her North Country accent. One thing led to another and the boy's mother invited the stranger into their home, where she met the woman's husband. Later, Catherine observed that the couple were clearly at odds with one another, 'at opposite poles'. Her analysis was that the wife was rather parochial, while the husband had an interesting mind with no one on whom to exercise it. As a result, she concluded, he treated the wife badly.

Catherine was invited to return to the cottage, and buoyed by the man's response to her intelligence (always the way into Catherine's affections, starved as she had been of serious questioning company at home and at Harton) she began to raise her act to him. He responded, and his wife became increasingly excluded. The climax to this difficult situation came when, one afternoon, all four went to the Odeon cinema in Clacton.

Catherine sat next to the man and, as usual, they became preoccupied with each other, while the boy watched the film and his mother quietly fumed. Mid-way through the programme, the little boy asked to go to the lavatory and his mother asked her husband to take him. He refused. She, smouldering with fury, had no alternative but to take him herself.

When mother and son emerged from the Ladies, they pointedly sat some way away. In the car going home there was a terrible row and when finally Catherine was dropped off at the bottom of the drive leading up to the workhouse, she did what she had always done when shamed (as when she stole a comic from the local newsagent as a child, or watched as Kate stole a length of flannelette from a shop): she vomited on the ground.

On account of this disturbing episode, she had arrived in Hastings determined to put all thoughts of love or marriage behind her. Work was her prime motivation. But she was young (twenty-four in 1930) and attractive, an independent spirit, unusual in a woman at the time, and these qualities together with the no-nonsense self-discipline which now characterised her extrovert personality – though it never completely eradicated the softness at the centre – made for a formidable combination.

She may have believed that she was 'incapable of love . . . cold as marble', but in *Our Kate* she also observes that 'I was a reluctant virgin. I was warm-hearted and wanting love, but determined, however hungry I was for it, not to go the way of my mother.' The impression one has is of a woman deeply in need of love, but mistrusting that she will ever find it in a man, if Kate's and her own experience are anything to go by.

From this period of disquiet and longing came the development of a character who was to become one of her most popular heroines. Anna Brigmore – Miss Brigmore, as she was known to anyone but her closest friends – is of course the governess of Thomas Mallen's nieces, Barbara and Constance, who are ten and seven years old at the start of *The Mallen Streak*, the first novel in Catherine's biggest-selling trilogy. Miss Brigmore comes from a middle-class family fallen on hard times. Her father had used money from his clients in the bank where he worked to keep his family's standard of living high. Miss Brigmore had, therefore, entered service of necessity. She was well educated, strict but fair, a stickler, the 'embodiment of high moral principles, but happily flawed', as Catherine's first literary agent, John Smith, once referred to her.

Miss Brigmore's unhappiness was that her early upbringing had made it impossible for her to find 'bodily expression' with any man who might normally be regarded as suitable for a governess. She yearns for love, and finally Thomas Mallen puts her out of her misery – her 'years of virginity, her personal torment'. We learn of this through Barbara, who hears Miss Brigmore moaning in her room and finds her in bed with Thomas, his hand fondling her naked breast. Miss Brigmore's relationship with Thomas is touchingly real. They remain very close; indeed, Anna takes control of Thomas's destiny when he loses the family estate.

In the early 1930s, however, Catherine's mistrust of men was to be proven time and again. First, it was Keith's turn to disappoint. Fairlight Cove lies on the coast between Hastings and Rye. It is a place of great beauty, where Catherine would love to walk. Later she rode a stallion along the cliff-top there out of stables close to Rye. Yet her novel, *The Man Who Cried*, marks out Fairlight Glen (sic) as 'a cursed place' – a place of infidelity and deceit. The demented Lena Mason follows her husband,

Abel, to a rendezvous there with his lover, Alice Lovina – the very place where, in 1932, the unfortunate Keith dared tell Catherine that he had been deceiving her, that he was married, that he had that very day been to see his wife to ask her for a divorce, so that he could ask Catherine to marry him.

'If he had attempted to push me over the cliff I could not have been more startled,' said Catherine, to whom Keith's outburst was a re-run of Jim Dailey's deceit. It was irrelevant that the poor man was actually freeing himself to marry Catherine. It was irrelevant in the boiler house of her emotions that she felt nothing much for him anyway. He had deceived her, and anyone less than true brought upon themselves all the ire born of Catherine's childhood trauma. He must have wondered what hit him.

At the moment that unsuspecting Keith disgorged his good news, Catherine *became* Lena Mason – she remembered the hate she felt for Keith when she created her demented fictional character, a feeling which, in the novel, leads directly to the brutal murder of Alice Lovina, and in reality almost to Keith's demise, too. She rushed at him to 'push him in the face. If I had done he would certainly have gone over the cliff, perhaps we both would have gone.'

Within weeks another man danced with Catherine at a workhouse 'do', and invited her to be his guest at a dinner party thrown by Mrs Silverlock. She accepted the invitation, but when she mentioned it to Matron, she expressed surprise that he wasn't taking *his wife*. Catherine was dumbfounded. But this was not the end of it. Another chap, again met at a workhouse party, and a bit of a linguist – he had French, German, and was a student of Italian – came to meet her each day from work. And he, too, turned out to be married. Three times her boyfriends were promised to another, four counting Jim Dailey – just as her father had been when he'd promised himself to Kate.

All this is omitted from the published version of Catherine's autobiography, *Our Kate*, and one has to wonder what we should make of these 'affairs' and two others with older men, of which she also makes mention. 'Now I knew there was something wrong with me, something in me that only attracted married men and old men. It would appear that I was only attractive to married men,' she told me. In *Colour Blind* the same fate befalls Rose-Angela when she grows into a young woman, and she, too, wonders what it is about her that attracts them. Was it her voice, 'so like her father's'? Was it her face? Was it the quietness in Rosie which did it for these men, particularly married men? Catherine said that in her case, sex was not an element in any of them, but also that she 'had a name, and the unfairness of it caused me to cry at nights'. She had a name as a loose woman.

One especially embarrassing occasion actually involved the intervention of the soon-to-be-married man's parents. When they discovered what was going on they came to Catherine and begged her to let their son, a grown man (a Sun Life insurance agent indeed!) go. In the end, she could only throw her hands up in the air, although, 'it was no light matter to me at the time – I kept myself buttoned against the cold of mankind'. Again, the impression is of confusion, of disturbance, of a repression in open conflict with what would make this woman happy, of emotions (perhaps to do with her father) too strong to entertain, but in some strange way dictating situations at the conscious level.

It was a situation ripe for exploitation, 'when into my life came this Irish woman, with her big heart and her many endearing faults. I clung to her like a drowning man to a raft.' Nan Smyth came to Hastings from Belfast, where she had left behind a husband and a handicapped daughter called Maisie, after the family had fallen on hard times. She had joined the staff of the workhouse in the same year as Catherine, but had been seconded to the hospital as a scrubber-down, an orderly. She first makes an appearance in the Governors' Minutes at a meeting of the Sub-Relief Committee, when a Contribution Order of six shillings weekly is made to her in the Municipal Hospital.

A year later, a flu epidemic swept the institution and Nan was sent to the laundry in place of a worker who had fallen sick. Shortly afterwards, the Assistant Matron handed in her notice and Catherine was asked to take over her duties. Now, with the duties of three officers on her hands, Catherine asked her staff to do overtime. None came forward, except Nan Smyth.

The irony was that Catherine had been trying to find a way of getting rid of Nan Smyth. She was one of the most disruptive workers Catherine had. Nan's trick was to employ her native Irish humour, so that whenever she created a disturbance and Catherine sought to upbraid her, there'd be half the laundry behind her, enjoying a good laugh. Maybe it was Catherine's very Irishness that somehow gave Nan the confidence that she would, in the end, get the better of her. It was a Friday afternoon, machine-cleaning duties were in progress, the Laundress had been called away, and when she returned, she found no work being done, only this Irish woman doing a sword dance over a pair of brooms.

Catherine was furious and decided to sack her formally on the following Monday, but was diverted from doing so. It was later that same day that Matron gave Catherine licence to take on someone permanent to help her in her various duties, and the Irish woman had applied. Catherine summoned Nan to her room and told her that she was lazy and had done more to impede work in the laundry than anyone, but Nan returned her look, holding Catherine's eyes with her own deep brown ones, and asked her for one last chance: 'You try me, Missis, and I'll show you,' she said in her jaunty, masculine-sounding voice. And show her she most certainly did. Nobody worked harder during that time of stress than Nan Smyth did.

In the 'all muck in together', emergency workhouse regime brought about by the epidemic, Nan, who was in desperate financial straits, saw in Catherine a woman not unlike herself, a woman who, beneath the hard, efficient exterior, had another story to tell, and who might be in a position to help her.

The change in their relationship came through Nan's discovery that hard work and loyalty were the path to reward in her mistress's eyes, and the reward began with the revelation of a shared sense of humour. Where once Nan's ribald jokes and crazy antics had brought Catherine to the verge of sacking her, now a laugh or two, suitably muted, fell on her boss's feelings like salve to some hidden wound.

Nan bent to Catherine's will instead of fighting her and found that the grip of her control was anything but a stranglehold. In the process, Catherine, who was quite a few years younger than Nan, began to find odd comfort in their relationship. Incredibly, they were becoming friends. Anyone who could lighten the burden of Catherine's loneliness, and demand back from her nothing that she was not capable of giving, would have been a candidate for friend.

Eventually the two women became inseparable. 'This friendship appeared to me as a result of prayer, of breathless prayer,' wrote Catherine. Events moved fast. Catherine was still living in the workhouse Lodge, but had retained her rented room in Clifton Road. One day, on a mission to pick up Catherine's racket so that they could play a game of tennis, Nan claimed to have discovered that Catherine's landlady was double-renting her room. Catherine immediately decided to move out of Clifton Road, and the subject came up of taking a flat with Nan.

The flat found was in West Hill, part of the Old Town – one large room, one bed, and a kitchen with covered bath and lavatory. She and Nan moved into it in December 1931 and Catherine set about decorating it immediately: 'The paintwork was dead black and the walls were covered with a dark blue paper. Now, this combination sounds dreadful, but when the room was furnished it was a picture that I have never been able to repeat – heavy dark pink curtains, grey carpet with Chinese spray in corners and black border, modern furniture, but it was the colour scheme that struck the eye.' Catherine felt she had surpassed herself, and when her credit ran out at the local shops, Nan put her few pennyworth in, turning up one day with dozens of huge aspidistras and, reaching from the bath to the door, the most colossal gas stove, three clothes baskets filled with kitchen utensils and a box of corkscrews. Catherine was not amused – 'Smyth kept out of my way for some time.'

Their friendship gave Catherine a new sense of confidence, such that in August, feeling much more settled, she returned home for the first time. She found the New Buildings unchanged, but not everyone had responded well to her. No doubt she would have wanted to give them the impression that she had made a success of her life, more so than had she stayed there. Reny for one, who was now a hairdresser, had not taken kindly to her. However, Kate was not drinking at this point, so they had an enjoyable time together and Kate had shown an interest in visiting Hastings.

After a week's holiday, Catherine returned to Hastings and her friend. To others, particularly at the workhouse, the friendship might have seemed odd, in that Nan Smyth was everything (a working-class skivvy) that Catherine was trying not to be associated with at this time. But the fact was that these two women did come from the same side of the social divide, and in her down-to-earth nature Nan provided the kind of balance to Catherine's pretensions that she had hitherto always relied upon Kate to supply. Nevertheless, at first, aware that the Master and Matron would have questioned a Manager playing tennis with a scrubber-down, let alone sharing a flat with her, Catherine decided it was to be their secret, hers and Nan's. The decision to make the relationship a secret made the arrangement even more promising from Nan's point of view, by making Catherine vulnerable to exposure.

Years later, in an unpublished piece of autobiography, Catherine saw Nan as a protector, a mother figure, even though of the two, Catherine says that she was the stronger. 'I had not known a father or a mother as such, for Kate did not fill the capacity of mother in my mind, and although Nan Smyth was the outward antithesis of anything relating to a mother, it, as I see it now [twenty-five years later] was primarily the function she performed for me . . . [She was] 'naturally lazy, naturally indolent, naturally a liar – a charming one, as are all the Irish – and naturally, an outstanding virtue [she had] a big heart. It was this that I recognised as akin in some way to Kate and before a month was out we were friends – she a scrubber and me head of the laundry.'

A mother's love is unconditional. Catherine did not have to earn Nan's love. She could be herself. She could be as cold as marble. From her point of view, being loved by anyone was a whole new experience, and being loved unconditionally was probably the only way she could be loved at that time. For her part, Nan couldn't afford to place any conditions on the relationship, nor did she wish to. Catherine was her superior. Here was an opportunity to get out of the financial and social mess she was in. Nan was about to move into a flat with her boss, why wouldn't she be prepared to take anything Catherine threw at her, and give back all that she had – namely her love – unconditionally in return?

Both needed each other for their different reasons, but Catherine's need for love ran terribly deep, and however much she felt in control, she was the more vulnerable partner.

Perhaps that's why she soon decided to reduce the factor of risk and be done with the deception. When the epidemic emergency was over, Nan returned to work to the hospital as an attendant and Catherine told Matron that she was 'taking her' as a friend.

This odd turn of phrase, and the need to tell Matron anything, might seem to suggest a degree of guilt, but the impression Catherine gives is that the only lines transgressed were those of class – the manager and the working girl should not normally be seen together. There was no moral transgression. Most working-class women slept two or more to a bed from the time of childhood. Catherine said that it was nothing special sleeping in the same bed, as she had always slept with her mother.

However, that is to overlook the buzz about lesbianism that was in the air at this time. (Marguerite) Radclyffe Hall's novel *The Well of Loneliness* (1928), which openly concerned lesbianism, had recently occasioned a trial for obscenity. The book was banned, attacked and stoutly defended in a sensational trial, and an appeal was refused, despite support from Virginia Woolfe, E M Forster and Arnold Bennett, among others. So, it was not true that two women sharing a bed would not have raised questions in many people's minds, and rather lame for Catherine to use it as her 'excuse'. Indeed, Matron was aghast when Catherine told her they were living together.

It is also to overlook the fact that Nan had a masculine way about her. 'She was rather manly in her outlook and dress,' said Winnie Richardson, who met Nan in later years on a trip to see Catherine in Hastings, and hadn't liked her. 'She had hair parted in the middle and cut straight down,' said cousin Teri, 'and mannish tops.' Cousin Sarah's niece, Rosemary Barker, told me, 'She was very, very masculine. Her face was leathery and she always had a cigarette dangling from her mouth.'

Catherine declared openly that Nan loved her, and agreed that she was a masculine woman, but refuted the suggestion that she was a lesbian. But since John Smith released a taped interview with Catherine about her relationship with Nan, there has been speculation that Nan and Catherine enjoyed a full, sexual relationship. I have even been telephoned by a newspaper for a quote about how Catherine might have responded to the suggestion that she be made part of a Gay Museum, apparently approved by the City of London Mayor, Ken Livingstone. And last year, Catherine herself was back, centre stage, in *Kitty & Kate*, a play by Claire Luckham that did the rounds of the provinces. Billed as, 'A rags to riches story inspired by the dramatic life of much-loved author, Catherine Cookson', it focuses largely on the relationship between Catherine and Nan.

I once tentatively asked Catherine whether she had had a lesbian relationship – not something one often asks a ninety-year-old woman. At the time, I didn't know how close she and Nan had been, but did appreciate how powerful was the intuitional side of her nature, and how attractive it will have made her to her own sex. She made me ashamed at my caution.

'I have had more trouble with women than with men,' she replied, 'and goodness knows I've had enough trouble with them.' She told me of a secretary long ago, and of a French lady who had a 'pash' on her and who invited Catherine to France, all expenses paid. It was one of only a few occasions that Catherine ever set foot abroad, and she couldn't get home quickly enough. Then there were her matrons at the laundry. 'Women seemed to cling to me.' All her matrons had a habit of doing this – she thinks they wanted to mother her, wanted simultaneously to maintain their authority over her and draw on her, rather like some mothers draw on their sons.

A point that those who argue for a full sexual relationship between Catherine and Nan ignore is that the relationship began in the first year in which they arrived at the workhouse, and it was during this self-same period that Catherine 'enjoyed' all those highly heterosexual relationships with men. But perhaps the last word on the issue should go to cousin Sarah, who said: 'If Nan was like they say [a lesbian], she'd have been kind to Kitty and Kitty had not had a lot of kindness, not a lot of love either.'

Only a few months after they began actually to live together, an appeal came from Kate to be allowed to come down to Hastings to visit her daughter, first step in an arrangement that would see Catherine living not only with Nan but her mother, too.

Catherine couldn't say no. Kate assured her that since John's death she had beaten her drinking habit. But still Catherine was on tenterhooks before her arrival. She knew that Kate would want to meet her colleagues and friends at the workhouse, and Catherine feared that all the good work she (with Chesterfield's help) had done to cover up her 'disgrace' of a background would be undone in a trice.

In the event, the opposite was true. Kate was free of drink and on her best behaviour. She went down a storm at the workhouse. Only the matron, whom Catherine had told about Kate and her own determination to shake free of her, took Catherine aside afterwards and told her what she wanted to hear – that it was obvious that Catherine and her mother were poles apart. It was an interesting comment on Catherine's relationship with her boss and suggests that the matron knew how to ensure she got the best out of her workhorse.

The staff lower down the hierarchy warmed to Kate's

unaffected humour and down-to-earth chat, and when Kate, Catherine and Nan repaired to the flat, it must have seemed quite natural to Nan to ask Kate, who was often living alone at number 10 (her husband David McDermott being away at sea), why she didn't come and live in Hastings permanently. I can hear the deafening silence that will have followed, Kate turning to Catherine, Catherine's cheer that all had gone so swimmingly well suddenly frozen with dread that Kate's 'recovery' might be tested on a permanent basis.

That was how it happened. That was how Catherine's short-lived independence disappeared almost overnight. Indeed that, indirectly, was what set her on the road to breakdown, whatever the underlying causes. For Kate did come to live. Embarrassment forced Catherine into formalising Nan's invitation, and later that same year, 1932, Catherine found herself on the way to the railway station to collect her mother. She arrived five minutes late to find Kate sitting on her cases in the forecourt, blind drunk.

'Because I was five minutes late she went for me immediately. I was absolutely horrified to see that she was well gone along the old road. I cried to God, Why? Why have I done this? Straightaway I knew that my new life was shattered.'

In preparation for Kate's coming Catherine had moved out of her one-room apartment and taken a much larger flat in an old building on the seafront with sufficient rooms for Kate to take in paying guests. The northern landlady, used to squeezing three or four lodgers into the one bedroom of number 10 along with Jack, was about to be released upon unsuspecting visitors to middle-class Hastings. In fact, nothing much came of Catherine's idea at first, because Kate spent most of her time down the road at a pub called The Hole in the Wall, almost permanently drunk.

Alcoholism is never completely beaten. Like Catherine's nervous breakdown, dark shadows of which haunt her to this day, Kate's alcoholism could only ever be consigned to the background of her personality by a great effort of will, and when now the craving reappeared after a short break, it seemed to gain a vicious vigour from guilt or whatever else she was feeling deep down, which no alcohol could ever cure.

Kate was fifty. Unlike Catherine, she wasn't in Hastings to build a new future. The move, which pulled her up by the roots from the only life she had known, would never have been easy. In Hastings she was a fish out of water. Also, from the moment she arrived drunk, and probably before, her daughter regretted her coming, and Kate would have known this. It was a recipe for difficulties even without the drink; but with drink, it was a recipe for guilt, bitterness, and, as it turned out, violence at a pitch that inspired the mutilation scene in the novel, *Hamilton*, to which I alluded earlier – mutilation of the daughter, Maisie Carter, by the mother. It happened as follows.

It was Christmastime, the year 1932. Catherine had started a row with Kate about her heavy drinking, but when she realised that everything was coming to a head, she tried to back-track; she didn't want to spoil Christmas. But Kate had already gone too far to retreat. She lined up four bottles of spirits on the sideboard. One was her husband David's rum; another was her own whisky; the other two contained gin and vodka. Kate then took a half-pint mug, poured more or less equal portions from each bottle into it and, mixing it all up, downed the whole explosive cocktail in one. Beside the fire were her husband's boots – hobnailed working boots, which David wore to work at sea – with short nails with large heads set proud of each sole to keep him steady on the metal grid floor of the hold. As the battle between the women raged, Kate took first one of these boots and then the other and hurled them at her daughter with all the anger of a lifetime. Catherine was staggered. The first missed her, but she felt the slipstream of the second on her face. A few millimetres closer and she would have been maimed like Maisie.

Catherine soon realised that she had to get Kate away, away from pubs like The Hole in the Wall. She began her search for a house of her own on the outskirts of the town. One day, as she sifted through the properties for sale, she spotted a notice for a house called The Hurst in Hoads Wood Road, which the estate agent described as a 'fifteen-roomed gentleman's residence'. He must have been a good agent or a lucky one, for the house in question was something of a problem to sell and he had alighted on a description which was bound to make Catherine sit up. The gentleman in question had been Colonel Alexander Burton-Brown FRAS, FCS. He lived there from 1911 with his wife, Ethel Augusta, their daughter, Jean, and stepson, Rupert Noel-Clarke.

Anyone experienced in house-buying would have avoided The Hurst like the plague. It was riddled with woodworm and rot. Its multiple roofs, one giving over on to the other, with gulleys between, promised huge maintenance bills. The prospect of heating the rambling place would have put most people off.

But to Catherine these were just practical problems. More to the point, didn't it have a butler's pantry and a wine cellar and a spacious drawing room with floor-to-ceiling windows which let on to a large garden? It really was the house of Catherine's dreams. And she knew exactly what she would do with it.

That the purchase of property was even on the cards seems extraordinary, but Catherine had always been good with money, and this was payback time. As a child of eight she had bought, for the price of a few pence, her first insurance policy from the shipping offices at Tyne Dock, insuring her life for £50. Now, in 1932, she had a policy with Sun Life of Canada against which she could raise a mortgage of £1,000. She mortgaged this and secured the house even before she had sold the lease on her flat.

The purchase became the subject of gossip. According to Catherine, a doctor let it be known that he suspected she had bought it with money earned between the sheets. Catherine enjoyed telling him barefaced that indeed there had been a time when she had made regular trips to London and Paris to seek out her select clientele. He had retreated rather swiftly with his tail between his legs.

She decided that she would take in guests to help pay for the work it needed, or maybe turn it into a nursing home of sorts. Of course it would take hard work to put right, but she wasn't afraid of hard work and where else could she find a property so splendid at a price she could afford? Above all, it was a house she could love, a square of ground that Catherine could call her own; and it remains a great source of pride to this day. 'I bought it in 1933 when I was twenty-seven years of age, without the help of any man, but through the savings of years and my endowment policy. I mortgaged the policy and bought this gentleman's residence.'

The relationship between Catherine and The Hurst lasted twenty-one years. When finally, in 1954, she and her husband Tom Cookson, who first moved in as a paying guest in 1937, gave up the struggle with it – for it was a struggle from the first day the rains came and washed through those roofs – 'it had eaten up my energy and every penny poor Tom and I were earning.'

The Hurst, or something like it – a grand manor house situated not in Sussex but in the North, not far from Gateshead – is Beatrice Steel's folly in *The Obsession*. Pine Hurst, as it is called, arouses an all-consuming passion in Beatrice and nothing will deflect her indulgence of it. The house becomes 'her child', and her desire for it is driven by a conviction that she alone in the Steele family has inherited from her father traits which give her a feeling for land, and specifically for the house. When Beatrice's mother and then her father die, and it is revealed that her father has gambled away all the family's money, the real risk of losing Pine Hurst turns Beatrice's obsession into a psychosis. It is an interesting autobiographical parallel, but not one which helps to explain Catherine's own nervous breakdown, as we shall see.

Catherine, Kate and Nan moved into The Hurst in 1933, along with Nan's handicapped daughter, Maisie. Catherine had been perplexed about Nan's child from the start. Although Nan assured her that her sister was caring for her, Catherine insisted that Maisie be sent for. The tumultuous interpersonal goings-on between these three women at The Hurst would fill more than one novel. Basically, Catherine became Kate and Nan's meal ticket, and Nan milked her for all she could get.

Catherine was now working a sixteen-hour day. When she came home from the workhouse she began work on The Hurst. And when she had made the house habitable, she began taking in guests, which started a whole set of other problems. Guests came, but rarely returned. 'My mother (now really on the bottle every day) and her monstrous practical joking ensured this. Added to this, when expecting the guests to pay, I was often told that my mother had already subbed half of it. How low can one fall! After two terrible rows I had been placated by my step-father [David McDermott, who was home on leave], a quiet man, to overlook her lapses. Then later, when her domination and drink drove me almost to suicide, I knew in one way or another there must be an end to it.'

Kate's practical joking had to be seen to be believed – 'she would do all kinds of things, like smearing jam on the doorknobs.' She was out of control. This was also the period during which Kate mixed her explosive cocktail from four bottles of spirits, and, as I have described, Catherine narrowly missed being hit by David McDermott's hobnailed boots. On another occasion a French couple – the woman, the one who later invited Catherine to France and made a pass at her – arrived and were treated to one of Kate's pies. 'Kate was a very good pastry cook, not much when it came to sophisticated cuisine, but pies were her forte.' She could be really artistic, creating delicate little foliage effects on the crust. Now, the French like their food, and, although pies are hardly a staple of French cuisine, Catherine would have been confident of their reaction to what was being laid before them, as they sat around the dining room table at The Hurst. It fell to the head of the table to take a knife to the pastry. Gently she eased the blade into the crust before separating the section. All eyes upon her, she plunged a spoon into the depths of the dish. But as the spoon re-emerged it carried with it not a soup of succulent beef, but a pan scourer and a mousetrap. Catherine died inside.

The evening had gone so well. Her guests were an educated couple and had been talking to Catherine about various French writers, whose work she hadn't read but, as ever, was very keen to learn about. Perhaps it was this strand of conversation, and the rapport between Catherine and the French woman in particular, which had set Kate off on her bizarre recipe. Catherine was still bent on improving herself, and Kate and Voltaire did not make for a happy mix, particularly since at this stage, as Catherine admits, her desire for learning carried with it a degree of affectation. The pricking of the bubble of her daughter's apparent pretentiousness may have brought Kate its own reward, but Catherine was furious.

Mother and daughter had different allegiances. Kate was her Northern culture, instinctual, primitive. It was this kind of thinking about Kate which years later would have one of cousin Sarah's boys telling Catherine that she wasn't fit to wipe his Aunt Kate's shoes. Catherine, on the other hand, was dressing herself up in her 'new-natural' culture, fortified by Chesterfield and her own determination to break new ground. The problem wasn't simply a case of Kate being gross (which, owing to the drink, she was), but that her daughter's development and abhorrence of her drinking was alienating her. Kate was a dominant creature, she didn't take kindly to this; and eventually, inevitably, she went too far.

Kate had always needed to dominate. Even in the wake of Rose's death there had been a crescendo of argument and violence with old John to settle who was the dominant partner. But now Catherine was not about to defer in her own house to this drunken parody. One dinnertime, this time on the losing end but refusing to lie down, Kate rose from her chair and let out a scream that would have made Edvard Munch double-take. Catherine's civilised guests were astonished. Kate then took to the stairs and from the landing let out yet more blood-curdling wails. It was a terrifying sign of how deep within herself Kate had joined battle with her daughter.

Afterwards, just as inevitably, Catherine's guests had been understanding. They had a relation, they said, capable of much the same; Catherine shouldn't mind on their account. Whether or not what they said had been true, it was hopelessly inadequate. Civilised, sweet, but there was really nothing more to be said. It was the end.

In 1935, the relationship reached total breakdown. Catherine became suicidal and Kate agreed to her suggestion that she move back to the flat, the lease to which Catherine had not yet managed to sell. Kate saw this not as defeat but as a chance to show her daughter that she could make it on her own. Her one stipulation was that Catherine refit the apartment so that it would take six guests.

For some months their paths didn't cross, and back at The Hurst things settled into a more pleasing routine. When she was not on duty in the workhouse or managing Nan and her guests, Catherine was able to spend more time writing – mainly short stories and sketches of workhouse life – and pursuing her other hobbies of fencing and horse riding.

Then Catherine heard that somehow Kate had swapped the lease on her flat for one on a large terraced house. 'One day I received a note from her asking me to go and see her. At that time I allowed myself only one hour a week in order to take a fencing lesson. On my way there I called on her and I immediately recognised that she was well away. She asked if I would meet her new guest, who was a grammar-school master. I said, "No!" I was in a hurry and I must go. She preceded me along the passage and threw open the door of the sitting room. "This is my daughter, Mr Cookson!" I saw a young man rise from the table where he had been writing. He said, "How do you do?" Why I should answer him as I did I will never know. For I said, "Do you fence?" It was a moment before he said . . . "No." And on this I turned on my heel and walked out.'

Tom Cookson was twenty-four when they met, Catherine thirty; it was October 1936, the month that Ellen Wilkinson galvanised 200 unemployed Jarrow workers to march to London, and presented a petition to Parliament calling for action on their behalf.

Tom was an Oxford graduate, his subject mathematics. He

had been teaching at Hastings Grammar School since September that year. Catherine believes that the reason Kate sent for her was that she wanted to show her off to this educated man. But whatever her reason, Kate certainly never dreamt that she was match-making on an amorous level. Tom was a studious young man, Catherine was older than him with, as far as the world could see, a forceful, extrovert personality. It was an unlikely love match, and had Kate even contemplated it, she would have dismissed the possibility that such a quiet, shy man as Tom would dare to take her daughter away from her. But that is just what Tom did.

Two nights after their abruptly curtailed first meeting, he showed up uninvited at The Hurst and asked Catherine to accompany him to the cinema. Catherine was as surprised as Kate would have been. There was she, a busy woman some years his senior with a personality capable of dealing with anyone from down-and-outs to mental patients on a daily basis, with a guest house (which now included the occasional epileptic patient) to maintain and run, being asked to the pictures by 'this boyish fellow'. But when Tom issued his invitation in his polite, unassuming fashion, Catherine was even more amazed at her response. She said simply, 'Yes, I would. Thank you.'

They went to the pictures and afterwards walked the two miles home, whereupon Catherine invited Tom in and they sat either side of the fire in the study and talked, and talked. By the time the hall clock struck twelve they had been sitting talking for almost two hours. 'What happened then I can't explain. Whether it was he who leant towards me or I towards him I'll never know. But we kissed. I knew in that moment it was right.'

When Kate learned what had happened she was dumb-founded. She and Nan laughed their heads off at Catherine 'and this twenty-four-year-old boy'. Their ridicule of Tom initially concentrated on his physical stature, and how this upset Catherine may be seen in the novel, *Maggie Rowan*, whose eponymous heroine pours scorn on small men. In Maggie's dreams her men are 'tall and strong and virile', having a short husband is something at which people laugh. Tom stood five foot four and a half inches, though in fact his size belied a notable physical prowess.

He had joined Hastings Grammar School as replacement for maths master Michael Jerrom, who had lodged at Kate's before him, but his extra-curricular responsibilities included sport,

Scouts and the Drama Society, and school sport meant football, cricket and athletics. 'Behind T. H. Cookson's cheery countenance lurked a hundred schemes for gingering up the team and outwitting the enemy,' records the school history, and he intitiated the school boxing club, which at one time boasted as many as eighty members.

'He was quite a sportsman,' remembers Edna Humphreys of her brother as a boy, 'though he was small. I still remember his two friends coming to collect him for school and they towered above him and they'd always walk either side of him. It was so funny. But he played football and tennis and water polo at Oxford. Then I've got a photograph of him playing in the Varsity match, football. And I have got his Blue, which he got in football. And of course he played cricket as well.'

'He was a very good footballer,' agreed ex-pupil Tony Weeks-Pearson. 'When I first saw him play it was quite clear from the first few moves he made that he was ace, he was a small, fast, dribbling man on the field.'

So, who was this Tom Cookson? He was the son of Mabel Florence Lear and Thomas Cookson, a verger at a church in Chingford, Essex, who had died in 1915. 'Tom was born in 1912, so was two or three when his father died,' said Edna. 'There was Jack, the eldest boy, Tom and sister Mabel.' The father died just two weeks before Mabel was born. By this time the family had moved to Grays, on the north bank of the Thames close to Tilbury Docks. Thomas Cookson's widow married again in 1920, her husband a plumber's mate called Percy Gusterson. They had four children, three girls – Edna, then Joan and Jean – and a boy who died in infancy. Later, Joan emigrated to Canada and Jean to Australia.

Tom had adored his second father, and learned from him skills of plumbing put to good use when he and Catherine were tackling The Hurst. He had been schooled at Palmer's in Gray's, the local grammar school. 'He always had a wicked sense of humour,' said Edna, which is not something I had noticed in him in later years. 'I must have been eight or nine when he went up to Oxford. There were only two of us [Edna and Joan] when he went and then Jean was born in 1934. I remember them saying nothing about Jean's birth until Tom came home and found her there. Mother had to go to work to keep him at Oxford and so when he came home he virtually looked after us girls. I can remember him shutting me in the cupboard. I must have got a bit cheeky to him, and I remember one day doing it again and shutting myself in the cupboard before he could. There was no smacking, no abuse at all, but I knew the punishment. He was very firm, and I remember he came up to a funeral – was it Dad or Mum? – and Elizabeth, my daughter, was getting ready for her O levels and she was a bit flummoxed with maths and he took her off and when she came back she said, "Oh it's so easy. I know what to do now", and she just sailed through then.'

There are some quirky coincidences of names in Tom and Catherine's life, which seem to bind the two together even before they met. Palmer's, of course, was also the name of the shipyard at Jarrow, which Catherine knew so well. She had grown up within a stone's throw of Cookson's Glassworks on the Tyne, and as Kate drew to Catherine's attention in the 1950s, there had also been a Cookson lead works. 'Yes, do you remember those Rail Crossings top of Western Road on the way to Hebburn? It was up there.' Now, Tom's college at Oxford turned out to be St Catherine's.

This confused me when I first learned of it because St Catherine's was only founded in the 1960s. In fact, in Tom's day, it did not have full college status within the university. It was a Non-collegiate Society, which offered opportunities to win Oxford University degrees to underprivileged students without the means to pay full college fees. As a Society it had no buildings of its own and none of the trademark Oxbridge college traditions, whereas today it has breathtaking Grade I listed architecture, designed by Arne Jacobson, the famous Danish architect, a moat and the largest student theatre in the university. Tom, I discovered, gained a First Class degree in Mods and two years later, in 1935, just as Kate was being dismissed from The Hurst for her drunken antics, graduated with a good Second Class Honours degree in Mathematics.

Winning a place at Oxford University was a big thing in a working-class family like the Gustersons. 'It wasn't just a big thing at home,' said Edna, 'he was one of the few in the Grays area. He and Frank Gubb went up together. I remember the preparations. He had this trunk and enough clothes in it so that he would not have to do any laundry for the entire term. When he came home, Carter Paterson would bring the trunk and there was all the dirty washing. My mother seemed to be washing for weeks and weeks and weeks.

'After Oxford he taught at the grammar school in Newmarket

for about a year,' continued Edna. 'Then he went to Devonport, Plymouth, and was at the grammar school there. They were only temporary jobs. His first permanent position was at Hastings.'

So, like Catherine, Tom had come from a poor background, and in the crucial years (three to eight) he had grown up without a father. The elements in Tom, noted by everyone, were a gentle firmness and a selfless, supportive nature. Perhaps these characteristics were fostered in his role as surrogate father to his siblings; certainly they were proven in his position as schoolmaster.

When I pursued Tom's highly individual interpretation of his role as teacher in and out of the classroom with some other of his pupils, they offered the following reports:

'He was my teacher in the A stream. He was very small, a very tiny guy, but he had a presence about him that was quite compelling. There was something very gentle . . . and yet he had the ability to command the attention and respect of a group of thirty adolescents,' said Steve Blower.

'Mr Cookson was my maths master. I remember him as a teacher who had a knack of explaining in a very understandable manner . . . He was very quiet in manner, but was well able to control us if we tried to get a bit unruly,' said John Finch.

'I remember him stressing that we should not worry about being confined in the C stream because we might well end up in the best seat,' said James Davidson. ' "Boys in the A stream," he said, "would go on to serious occupations, earn little money and probably ride bicycles to work. Boys in the B stream would be teachers or civil servants and drive secondhand cars. But you in the C stream are going to be the businessmen and drive brand-new cars." He was absolutely right. I went into the army, then set up in the pub trade, sold up and retired by the age of fifty-two!'

When I told Tony Weeks-Pearson that I was writing a book about Catherine, he put it this way: 'Books should really be about the Tom Cooksons of this world. Because, you know, Tom is at the heart of this in relation to Kitty, not just as a husband but as a complete factotum, whether it was cooking or as amanuensis or whatever. Everything that Tom did, he did for her . . . It wasn't just giving up his time for me and dozens of other boys, listening or advising or spending time with them, it was just the same with anyone he met, and it was the same with

Kitty Cookson. I always thought theirs was a more professional relationship of husband and wife – his aiding her – even more so than it was with us. You see, you used to forget that he was a teacher, he took a personal interest . . . very supportive.'

'Tom was a gentleman,' said Edna, as if nothing more need be said. 'He was gentle and he was my brother. You could rely on him. Kitty was the powerful personality, but he gave her the strength to do it. He was there for her. He was strong. Most probably he needed someone with her type of personality to give him the urge to do it. She wasn't Tom's first girlfriend. There was a girlfriend locally while he was at Oxford. So, he nearly escaped!'

Tom represented something to Catherine that neither Kate nor Nan could understand, nor wanted to when, to their horror, these two dependants sensed that this wasn't just a passing flirtation. All Catherine's development, which Kate took as pretension, was being brought to ground in Tom, who gave Catherine sturdy roots on which she could graft her future.

Certainly there was also a physical attraction. He was captivated in particular by Catherine's voice – 'something strange to my ear . . . vibrant with life. I had heard nothing like it before.' There was also 'a lilt or inflection, an inheritance from the North,' which completely slayed him. Catherine also admits that she found Tom 'attractive-looking', but more than this, in Tom, Catherine glimpsed her own fulfilment. 'This man was someone I knew I'd been waiting for all my life. He had a mind which was not only brilliant in his work but which met my searches.' In Tom, Catherine had, at last, found someone with whom she could lift her life to a level at which she had dreamed she might live when first she had left the North.

Tom recalls being amazed at the vigour of Catherine's commitment to her 'fight against superstition, bigotry and intolerance' – her fight not against her people's exploitation by their capitalist bosses, which was the common cry in the 1930s, but against the ignorance, prejudices and hypocrisies which she had suffered firsthand, and which she perceived kept her people in strait-jackets self-sewn. At the time, she was reading two authors who seemed to back her in this fight. When Tom first arrived at Kate's lodgings in the late summer of 1936, Catherine had been away in Paris, visiting the French woman to whom Kate had served her mousetrap pie. The woman had introduced Catherine to the writings of Voltaire, a leading figure in the

Enlightenment, the eighteenth-century movement towards freedom from superstition and intolerance. Shortly before Catherine met Tom, she had been reading *Candide*, which had particular relevance to her doubts about Catholicism. They had also discussed Plato and Socrates – Catherine had been reading – and he saw that this wasn't intellectual pretension. His amazement was threaded with admiration that this 'person who had left school at fourteen' was so obviously 'consumed with a desire for learning'. What had struck Catherine was Socrates' integrity – his refusal to budge from his position when he stood accused – even though he was to drink the poisoned cup: 'Like Christ, Socrates never wrote a line; like Christ, when they brought him before them, he stuck to his convictions.' She was inspired too by Plato's idea of 'this spring of knowledge – out there are concepts which have a real existence, distinct from the material world, and on which we draw – a spring of knowledge into which we can all dip . . .', as she put it to me. With her deepening doubts about Catholicism she warmed to these philosophical ideas: 'I felt I could follow Socrates,' she said to me, 'I felt I could follow him without fear.' At the age of twenty she had coined a phrase, ' "I learn each day by gaining a greater knowledge of my ignorance". I thought I was very clever. Now I discovered that Socrates had said similar words to his judges in the fifth century BC.' Excited by the idea that she might tap into this spring of knowledge, she saw that with Tom she had the makings of a dialogue. The quest she was undertaking need never more be a lone quest. Tom gave Catherine all the things she needed – nurturing, even parenting, for Tom was someone to whom she would be able to show her vulnerable side. Perhaps parenting was what Catherine had been seeking in her relationships all along.

In return, Catherine gave Tom a new confidence. 'I knew not only did I need him, but he needed me even more.' Tom was 'quiet', shy and reticent. But this kind, quiet man had not been overawed by Catherine's abruptness when they first met, he had pursued her. He jokes now that he can't imagine where he found the courage to do so, but he knows that he found it in Catherine.

Integrity was the point at which Tom, the academic, and Catherine, with her firsthand knowledge of life, met intellectually; the shared value to which their lives had led them, albeit along two very different paths. It encouraged their perception of each other as two sides of the same coin. I don't believe

Catherine expected ever to meet anyone who would contrast and complement her at one and the same time, or even that she could have created a character who could perform such a role, before she met Tom. Catherine and Tom were at opposite poles, and yet precisely because each was the antithesis of the other, they knew almost at once that they were made for each other, for 'in the channels where the intangible but real life runs, we were one, and we recognised this.'

Theirs was a dovetail attraction. She discovered in Tom the beauty of love as a two-way process, giving as well as taking. Above all, Catherine needed to give. Not since hanging on to her grandma's skirts as a child had she known real love. There is nothing simple about working out this strongest kind of love, and Catherine recalled many arguments, mostly about who was in command – 'In the end we decided it was better to be second mates . . . He is the flesh below the hide.' There is a lovely irony in Catherine's first salvo, 'Do you fence?', for though Tom claimed not to, they proceeded to fence together for years, and their long union, and especially Catherine's work, benefited from their fencing. When Catherine said, as she often did, that Tom was the only one who had been of any help to her in her work, she meant it, not because her agent and editors and publishers didn't help, but because Tom's help has been at a fundamental level, at the level at which the very shape of her writing was formed. In the end, all her novels are about creating harmony out of disharmony, unity out of disunity, finding serenity through love.

When Kate saw all this going on it became clear to her that neither she nor Nan could any longer count on Catherine as the fulcrum of their lives, and the two women teamed up to make sure the match wouldn't happen. Their laughter turned to ridicule and malice; they even resorted to opening mail in search of anything that might be used to come between him and Catherine. The temptation is to see more than a bit of Dorrie Clarke, the twisted, resentful busybody in *Kate Hannigan*, in the pre-war Nan Smyth. She it is who steals six letters from Kate Hannigan and gives them to Stella Prince in order to prevent Kate marrying Rodney, the love of her life. Nan and letters and bitter resentment certainly go hand in hand. On her deathbed she would direct Tom to a bunch of them in a drawer, letters which, as we shall see, had been saved with one purpose in mind, to break up Tom and Catherine's relationship from beyond the grave, even a quarter century or more after they were married. 'I could write a book about what happened during the next two years,' said Catherine, 'and eventually they did part us for a time . . . In all Kate's stages of drinking I think this was the lowest.'

Readers of Catherine's novel *Hamilton* may remember the awful slyness of the Stickle family who inveigle themselves into Maisie Carter's house after her mother commits suicide. Their purpose, to drain Maisie of her inheritance, is obviously different from Kate's and Nan's, but the parasitic pressure they exert on their quarry bears the hallmarks of the period in Catherine's life when she was 'feeding' Kate and Nan in an emotional and material way and they were draining her. They (like the Stickles) fancied they controlled her, rather like some members of an orchestra fancy they exercise control over their conductor, but the need is greater on their side. Neither Kate nor Nan could survive without Catherine; deep down they knew that, and they responded with as much venom as did Maisie's persecutor, Howard Stickle.

What resolved matters for Catherine and Tom was that Kate found that she couldn't make it on her own. One day a letter arrived at The Hurst in which Kate hoisted a white flag. She would return to the North if Catherine would free her from her lease commitment on her house. Catherine agreed, though the deal wiped her out at the bank. Kate had lost; in fact, very soon she was to lose everything. In February the following year (1938), her husband David McDermott's body would be found in the Tyne. He had been blown from the quayside on his way back to his ship, weighted down into his watery grave by bottles recovered from his pockets.

Tom, meanwhile, had taken off for Austria, where he was to spend the school summer holidays. In theory, he was due to return to lodge with Kate from the beginning of the new school year in September 1937. Now that she was giving up her guest house, Kate suggested that since it was all over between him and her daughter, perhaps Catherine would let him lodge at The Hurst. On the day, a Saturday, that Tom walked through the front door of The Hurst, 'we knew immediately we were one again'.

Nan, however, was still running the place with the help of a housekeeper called Mrs Webster, and incredibly, when Tom returned, the same old animosity started all over again. This time Catherine acted; but it wasn't an easy decision. What would become of Nan? What would become of their business at The Hurst when Nan wasn't around to manage it? Catherine couldn't be at the Institution and run The Hurst at the same time. Nevertheless, she moved decisively and dispassionately. She mortgaged The Hurst and, so that Nan could set herself up in business, bought her a house (which would be signed over to her shortly after the war). Then Catherine sold some land which had belonged to this property, taking half the amount to recoup some of the cost of the house and giving the rest to Nan. At the point of Nan's departure there were seven guests in The Hurst. Nan took three of them, leaving Catherine with 'two mental patients, a penniless army captain, Tom, and no money in the bank'.

Tom's sister, Edna, has vivid memories of visiting the house at around this time: 'We spent a week in Hastings just before the Second War was declared, there was Joan [sister] and myself and a neighbour went down. I remember the gorgeous grounds, the big kitchen. Oh I can picture it! You went in the front door, study on left, then there was the drawing room, grand piano across the window, the dining room. It was a big hall and there was a huge fireplace and the stairs. When we went there, there was Pansy and about three people Catherine was looking after. Pansy seemed twopence short of a shilling. There was also the house-keeper, she was deaf – Mrs Webster. She lived in the servants quarters at the top of the house. I remember the place at the top of the house, under the turreted roof, which was demolished after the war because it was damaged. Mrs Webster did the cooking as well. I never met Nan Smyth. I don't think she was on the scene at the time.'

One of the 'guests', a man in his late thirties who was soon to die, was remembered especially because of the impact he had on Catherine's confidence as a writer. He was reckoned to be something of an intellectual, a word much bandied about in those days, and he and Catherine would have long discussions about books and ideas, so it was perfectly natural for Catherine to ask him one day whether he would read one of her stories. She had not stopped writing since leaving the North, and there were stacks of short stories and sketches of life in the workhouse, written (so Tom told me many years later) in the style of the Hamilton series, which she kept in a cupboard on the landing. The fellow read one of these and whatever he actually said, Catherine was so upset that she burned all her work on a fire.

That year, in August 1939, Catherine gave in her notice at the workhouse, returned to run The Hurst full time and despatched Mrs Webster to help Nan. It was a bold move on the eve of war, which was declared with Germany the following month, whereupon The Hurst was requisitioned as a home for the blind, with Catherine in charge.

All this time, Catherine had suffered bleeding from the nose. No doctor had diagnosed a cause and none had found a cure. The battle with Kate and Nan had taken its toll emotionally on a body weakened by this trying, tiring illness. Now, under treatment by a doctor for her 'nerves', she had to cope with twelve blind male evacuees from the East End of London and it was hard, unrewarding work.

Then one day Catherine received a letter, which brought news of the evacuation of the grammar school to St Albans in Hertfordshire, an event which threatened to split her and Tom up again. On opening the letter she made an immediate decision. Tom was already over the threshold on his way to school when she ran out of the front door after him and called out to him that they should marry on the following Saturday. Tom came back to her, took her hand and then turned and ran for joy down the road to school.

For two or three years before this, Catherine had been seeing the parish priest in an attempt to resolve her increasing doubts about Catholicism. The priest would come to The Hurst, play the piano, stay to tea and then wonder at Catherine's reservations about the Church when clearly it made for such a jolly time. Now, when she asked him to marry them, he told her that he wouldn't unless Tom became a Roman Catholic too. Tom was a Christian, a member of the Church of England; his father had been a verger in Essex. But that wasn't enough. He was a Protestant, she was a Catholic. The priest wanted Tom to turn. Tom, for whom integrity was all, would not. Together he and Catherine put it to the priest that they would be married in a register office. In the face of this possibility, the priest compromised and Tom signed a document saying that he would bring up their children in the Catholic faith.

But then, of course, there was Nan. Catherine and Tom agreed that she should not be informed until after the wedding. Catherine may yet have been scared of what Nan could do to destroy her happiness with Tom. She had seen what she was capable of – the back-stabbing, the blackmailing, the dirty dealing – and Nan had told her that if she married Tom she would kill Catherine or herself. Certainly, Nan was kept in a state of ignorance of what was about to happen until the morning of the day itself.

Catherine always said that Nan did not have a hold on her, that all the badness was born out of Nan's love for her and she would never completely disown her. But it is likely that Catherine feared that she never *could* completely shake herself free from Nan. And now, on the morning of the wedding, while Tom was at school – he had Saturday-morning classes at the grammar school; they were due to be married in the afternoon – Catherine left The Hurst and made her way to the house that she had bought for Nan, to tell her what she was about to do.

What exactly went on behind closed doors between Nan and Catherine on the morning of her wedding, 1 June 1940, we cannot say for sure, but the scene was set in a particularly violent frame by the fact that Nan's forceful traits had been recognised by the British Army and she had been made a sergeant major in charge of the quartermaster's store. Nan would, in time, be stationed in South Shields and see something of Kate, but now, in Hastings, as Catherine arrived, there was a munitions truck standing outside her house, and when, some time later, Catherine emerged through the front door with Nan seething with rage and looking after her, she was convinced that at any moment she would hear the crack of a rifle and feel the kick of a bullet in her back. According to Catherine's first literary agent, John Smith, to whom she related this incident, once out of sight she fell against some railings sobbing with relief.

There was no such relief for poor Tom, however, who had, meanwhile, arrived at The Hurst after school to be told that Catherine had gone to see Nan. He feared the worst. At the eleventh hour, after years of patiently winning Catherine over and extricating her from the woman's evil grasp, Nan had won.

When Catherine appeared, and told Tom that she was free, they fell into each other's arms but barely had the energy to make it to the church for the ceremony.

They married nine months into the Second World War and two weeks or so before Catherine's thirty-fourth birthday. 'I had married a Protestant. Perhaps we were married in a Catholic church, but under protest, which was all done very suddenly because Tom's school was under orders of evacuation, and I couldn't be left behind. The priest threw the ceremony at us. There were only eight people present and it was only on the promise that I would get him to turn.'

The priest's attitude of disapproval towards the marriage and the atmosphere at the ceremony distressed Catherine, confirming her doubts about allegiance to a Church which could alienate a Christian in such a way. But the deed was done and the papers signed. Now, surely, she need have no doubts as to her identity, Tom had made her a Cookson and for that alone she was proud.

There could not have been a worse start to Tom and Catherine's marriage, however. On their honeymoon journey to London, they ran into battle-scarred British and French troops at Tonbridge station, their terrible condition bringing home the ghastly reality of war.

France had fallen. However heroic may seem the evacuation of Dunkirk today, it was a terrible and messy business for those actually involved. There had been nothing to prepare the couple for what to expect, no television pictures or feature-length reports. Catherine was in floods of tears when she arrived in London, where she and Tom took a room in the Charing Cross Hotel.

The city was in the grip of war-time recession and the atmosphere was depressing. If France had fallen, how long would it be before England was invaded? Catherine and Tom planned to go to the theatre, stay the night in London and then go on to Grays in Essex to visit Tom's family. They chose a production of *Ghosts* by Henrik Ibsen, but were among only a handful of people in the audience. The play closed the following day.

The visit to Tom's home seems to have gone rather better, but when the couple returned to Hastings soon afterwards, their downbeat experiences had taken hold of their health: Tom had flu and Catherine was suffering terrible nosebleeds. The following weeks were spent packing up The Hurst in preparation for their evacuation with the Grammar School to St Albans.

They arrived in St Albans in July, where they took a flat in Victoria Street, across the road from the library. Edna Humphreys remembers visiting them around this time. She slept on the divan in the lounge. She remembers in particular walking with Tom around town in the vicinity of the cathedral and meeting the Grammar School boys, who would doff their caps when they caught sight of her brother. She was only seventeen or eighteen, but was aware, too, of a certain unrest in Catherine.

In an extraordinary quirk of fate, with the bitter taste of the wedding ceremony still fresh, she and Tom had immediately received another dose of religious mania. 'I took Tom on our first Sunday morning there to Mass. There was a young priest at the altar, and when he stood up to give the sermon, he said the theme of it was "hell's flames". He went on to state that hell was no figment of the imagination. His actual words were: "Hell is a burning fire, where we will be sat on gridirons for ever more. And get that into your head . . . This is no fable or imagination!" How I kept my seat and kept Tom there I don't know. He was a man recently down from Oxford, and I had brought him to listen to this ignorant pig of a priest, spouting the very topic I had been fighting against for years. We never went back.'

Her problems were exacerbated in the month of their arrival after a visit to the doctor. She was told that she was pregnant. Catherine couldn't believe it. She and Tom had made love only once – on their wedding night – how could she be pregnant? She didn't want to be pregnant, not living in their little St Albans flat with the war going on all around. She convinced herself that she couldn't be and she went to another doctor, who confirmed what she wanted to hear, she wasn't pregnant at all, she simply had constipation. He prescribed her a strong laxative.

In November a letter arrived from the North. A friend reported that Kate was ill and that Catherine should come immediately. London was being battered nightly in the Blitz. The trip north, in the war-time blackout, proved an exhausting experience, and reopened old wounds. She recalls, 'My mother was very surprised to see us. It was a false alarm from a false friend. She had nothing but a sniffly cold.

'As I would soon learn, I was indeed five months' pregnant, added to which I was having regular nosebleeds.' The flow of blood was so bad that it drenched the pillow on their bed.

When it became obvious that there was nothing wrong with her bowels, that indeed she was pregnant, Catherine was sick to her heart that the laxatives might have affected her baby. She went into labour three months before term, on 7 December 1940, electing not to go into hospital but to have a midwife at home. The baby, a boy, was delivered by Tom while the midwife was taking a rest after a long and dreadful labour. He was born dead.

Catherine and Tom were absolutely overcome with grief. It was a tragedy for which neither was prepared, 'particularly so because our child, not having lived, could not be buried in sacred ground. It was buried in a common grave.' They had named him David long before he was born. Catherine couldn't get the sight of him out of her mind. He had looked so small and yet perfectly formed, everything in place as it should be, and the very image of Tom. In a diary she began to keep in February 1942, she wrote that she refused to believe the Catholic dogma that babies who die before they are baptised end up 'in Limbo'. She would have laughed at the Church's about-turn on this in October 2005, had she been alive to see it. Today, Roman Catholics must no longer believe in 'Limbo'. She once said to me that she couldn't abide turncoats, particularly religious ones. Tom had taken Catherine to see David's grave, and a man had told them that the child was laid 'together with three men and an old woman, who I gathered had come from the Union [the Workhouse]'. Catherine had wept, remembering how sweet David had looked on the one and only occasion she had set her eyes on him. Then she consoled herself that the old woman would have looked after him.

Far from content within herself, she worried that she might have damaged the baby by not accepting she was pregnant, and damaged his chances of survival by not opting to give birth in a hospital. Most of all she worried that David's death was a sign that her decision to marry a Protestant had set the wrath of God against her.

That Christmas, Tom and Catherine went to stay with Tom's mother Mabel. Edna was living in the house with her husband Bill. 'We had the front room. Kitty had lost David. I remember I was expecting Elizabeth and I was messing about working at something, when Kitty said, "*Stop* doing that, you'll lose your baby!" You see, they didn't realise it was the blood was doing it.' No doctor had told Catherine that she was among that 15 per cent of women whose blood status is Rhesus negative. Obstetrics were nothing like as advanced as today antenatal services were primitive by comparison.

This was the first of a series of emotional traumas which

must have made Catherine feel that her whole life was cursed. Over the next four years, between the end of 1940 and the summer of 1945, she lost three more babies. What she, as a mother, felt at such a loss was one thing. What she felt on Tom's behalf was even worse. Her marriage, far from resolving any problems, seemed only to be dragging Tom down into her old vortex of pain. These four terrible losses underpinned the persecution of herself which brought her to breakdown in the same year that she lost her fourth child. Catherine was strong. Strife was her 'yeast', the culture in which her achievements had been grown. But this was not the same. In this it was not just her alone.

She began having nightmares in which a judgemental, black-robed priest appeared. These terrifying dreams dredged up from her past the voice of the 'missioner', her Father Confessor who consigned her to hell for admitting that she didn't like the taste of God on her tongue. She began to imagine that her and Tom's tragedy was the result of her questioning her faith. She was floundering in the same mire of superstition as her people.

As always when at a low ebb, Catherine decided to work her way out of it. With the happy chance of the City Library within walking distance, she decided to extend her programme of self-education. She drew up a list of books which ranged over English literature from Chaucer to the 1920s, and the verve with which she went about it astonished her husband. 'As in every-thing she tackles,' Tom remembers, 'she persevered working through that colossal list.'

The list included Plutarch, Thomas Carlyle, Clarendon, Macaulay, Johnson, Boswell, the great figures of early Saxon literature, such as Caedmon, Bede, Aldhelm, Boethius; Chaucer, Langland, Wyclif, writers through to Shakespeare, Milton, thence Dryden, Steele, Addison, Swift, Goldsmith, Defoe, Fielding, Smollett, Pope, and her beloved Romantics – Coleridge, Wordsworth, Byron, Shelley, Keats – and then even those who were shaping modern thought, from Darwin to Marx and Freud.

Catherine began to see knowledge as a deposit on which she would draw for strength, looking for answers to deep questions, the existence of God and the purpose of life, brought to the fore now that 'the dread of war was afloat'. In this she was following her tutor Chesterfield. 'Let me most earnestly recommend you to hoard up, while you can, a great stock of knowledge,' he writes to his son, 'for though, during the dissipation of your youth, you may not have occasion to spend much of it, yet, you may depend upon it, that a time will come when you will want it to maintain you'. Ideas, concepts, quotations become valuable property stored in the lumber room of the head, a stock list, much as the seventeenth-century novelist Daniel Defoe has Robinson Crusoe make inventories of his possessions for the purpose of survival. In 1941 Catherine was still cast away on her desert island, and with Chesterfield as her Man Friday she set about increasing her intellectual stock in the hope that it would help her find a way off it.

Chesterfield's advice was useful in one respect at least. The *Letters* encouraged her to form her own judgements on what she was reading. 'Use and assert your own reason,' he urges Philip. 'Reflect, examine and analyse everything in order to form a sound and mature judgement. Great learning, if not accompanied with sound judgement, frequently carried us into error, pride and pedantry.' Catherine rumbled those writers who lost her in a fog of verbiage.

On this determination to educate herself she would build the key existential theme of her historical novels, but interestingly the novels returned her to a conclusion quite foreign to Chesterfield. In *Tilly Trotter*, education of the working classes is recommended as a cure for superstition. The idea is that, by showing people how to think for themselves, education enables them to escape the control of others and to be themselves. Descartes' self-evident intuition, 'I think, therefore I am,' lies at the heart of it. The French philosopher and mathematician was one of the seventeenth-century precursors of the Enlightenment whom Catherine had been studying.

In *The Black Velvet Gown*, another novel set in the nineteenth century, Catherine explores a number of related themes: the fear among those in power in society that education of the working classes would diminish their control over them, the rich promise which working-class people were convinced education held out to them, and the success and failure of education in delivering that promise.

Miner Seth Millican takes it upon himself to learn to read, despite his boss's disapproval. Further, he teaches his wife, Maria (known as Riah), two sons (Davey and Johnny) and two daughters (Biddy and Maggie) to read and write, so that they will never need to earn a living down the pit. But when Seth dies during a cholera epidemic, and his family find work and lodging at Moor House, the home of an impoverished gentleman (Percival Miller), Riah interests Tol Briston, a worker on the big estate nearby called The Heights, in learning to read, and Tol's sister, Nan, accuses her of unsettling Tol. What will education do for Tol other than make him aware of the hopelessness of his lot in life?

When Percival Miller overhears the row between Nan and Riah, he announces a proposal to further the education of Riah's children with two hours' tuition a morning. Daughter Biddy turns out to have a large appetite for learning, but it doesn't improve her station in life. At the end of it all she is only able to secure a place in the laundry at The Heights, the lowest position in the servant hierarchy. For Riah herself, education stands between her and her growing attraction to Miller. Education is all he ever thinks about, other than Riah's son, Davey, who takes to Miller's curriculum about as eagerly as a horse to brine and, realising that he is becoming the special object of Miller's attentions, responds by taking a scythe to him.

Education is no all-purpose panacea, and may be a dangerous tool. The educator concocts his own prescription to cure ignorance, and, as Miller admits to Riah, his motives are not wholly altruistic. He is educating her children not only 'for their own good' but to give himself 'some kind of an aim'.

Up at The Heights, where grande dame Mrs Diana Gullmington rules the roost, Biddy's learning is causing a sensation of disapproval. When, in a game of forfeits in the servants' hall, she recites a poem by Shelley, family members who come to watch are alternately dumbfounded and hostile. Afterwards, a friend of the family called Laurence (the son of Diana's sister-in-law, Grace Gullmington) counsels Diana's teenage grandchildren, Paul and Lucy, not to mention Biddy's performance to their parents, fearing their disapproval of literacy among the lower orders. As it is, Biddy is threatened with dismissal and her books with burning, and Paul and Lucy's hostility turns into an open vendetta. One Sunday, when Biddy is working in the laundry, Paul and Lucy burst in and taunt her for studying French and Latin. Biddy flares up and points out their provincial accents, whereupon Lucy slashes Biddy across the face with her riding crop and ends up in a tub of washing before Biddy is trussed up by her wrists on a drying rack with linen torn from the sheets, raised so that only her toes touch the ground. Biddy is found later, unconscious but still alive.

Behind all these shenanigans runs a serious dialogue between Laurence and Grandmama Diana Gullmington. We learn of 'great stirrings' outside the closed world of The Heights – strikes, riots which soldiers have been brought in to quell, merchant ships subjected to naval guardianship, even the murder of a mine deputy, a historical reference to the murder of Nicholas Fairles in 1832, a particularly gruesome business where the principal got clean away but which caused enormous class tension at the time. Education is seen as spelling the end of the old social order by Grandmama, who, as I have already mentioned, sees the placing of human beings in a social order as God's work and as implying that reason has no place in the life of a servant. Laurence, on the other hand, takes the progressive view: he is for people using their own minds.

England remained so far behind Europe in the matter of educating its people that even in the late nineteenth century it was criticised for deliberately withholding education from the working classes in order to keep them in their place and their expectations low. Technical training was permitted only because 'this kind of learning would not encourage workmen to be dissatisfied with the station in life into which they had been called by a wise providence,' as S. J. Curtis wrote in his *History of Education in Britain*.

Implicit in *The Black Velvet Gown*, however, is the message that education does not guarantee success in the world, at least not in nineteenth-century England. Nor would Catherine's problems a century later be solved by her programme of education in the flat in St Albans. If there is a final conclusion to the debate in the novels it is in favour of intuition and knowledge ground out of experience – 'wisdom without learning' – which is what Dr Rodney Prince divines in uneducated Kate Hannigan and is the source of her allure. Once again, it is an autobiographical conclusion. It would be Catherine's own experience as a writer that the channels of creativity can be blocked by too much rational analysis. She would watch, for example, as her flesh-and-blood northern characters 'wilted under Tommy Cookson's correct but stilted English' when he gave her a course in syntax and grammar. In the early twentieth-century Tyneside novels Catherine alerts us to the categorical difference between intellect and imagination, between reason (capable of dissecting things into infinity) and intuition (capable of reaching a truth with a marvellous economy).

While in St Albans, Catherine also began work on a book of rhymes for children and paid a visit to the local art school in search of an illustrator. The art teacher told her that none of their students was up to such a commission and suggested that she might like to learn to draw. She tried, only to discover that she couldn't draw children, a telling enough comment on recent wounds. She returned to the school and informed the teacher that she had enjoyed the class but had decided that instead of children she would draw stone. He must have wondered what on earth he had taken on. But Catherine found herself in perfect sympathy with this primitive material. As anyone who has seen her drawings of St Albans Abbey and Hereford Cathedral will appreciate, she does indeed have an extraordinary ability to make stone look like stone. Three-dimensional, rich in texture, it is alive to the senses, tempting us to see these artworks as a rehearsal in techniques which, in a different medium, would bring her fame, once she had learned how to redraw herself with equal honesty.

Eight months after the loss of their first child, in August 1941, Tom enlisted in the RAF and together they moved to Leicester for his training.

Catherine had not been to church in more than a year and her mind was besieged by strangely oppressive fears as her faith fell away from her like flaking skin. The Church's doctrine on mixed marriage, its adherence to stories of hell-fire and its strategy of maintaining allegiance through fear and guilt infuriated her. But she could not let religion go. Transubstantiation now seemed not just misguided but even repulsive to her. It is a first precept of the Catholic Church that in the Mass the bread and wine literally turn into the flesh and blood of Jesus Christ. Try to accept this, truly accept it, and you can begin to see where her problem lay. People who pay lip service to their religion and worry, for example, if the church is cold, or who go there without truly believing the dogma or because attendance is a mark of social respectability, will find it a challenge to understand the fears which beset Catherine at this time. But in the stormy sea of Catherine's self-doubts, which her childhood had bequeathed her, her faith had been the one certainty. Its erosion cleared the way for self-doubt to gain the upper hand and in just four years her fears would become so unbearable that something had to give.

In Leicester, where she rented digs while Tom was away at training camp, she decided to do something about it. 'One Sunday morning I made myself go to Mass and I came out of that place so angry I could have exploded . . . The climax came when I was leaving. There were double doors and when I closed one I saw this large notice there and it was headed "On Mixed Marriage". It went on to say that mixed marriage was not recognised by God and the only hope the Catholic part of it had was if they turned their partner into a Catholic, if they brought their partner into the Church. This was what I must work at every day, because the Catholic party was living in sin, and knew only too well the outcome of that! I was so furious . . .'

But still she couldn't let it go. She couldn't just turn her back on it. This was where reality lay: if it didn't, then there was nothing. 'The fight went on within me. I lit candles to Our Lady, who I understood to be the mother of God . . . and I bought a number of Masses. Oh yes, you had to pay for having a Mass said . . .'

Later that same year, 1941, Tom was moved to Cranwell in Lincolnshire and Catherine discovered she was pregnant again. She wasn't to know that the chances of a pregnancy running to term were slim. She had undergone no tests. She did not know that her blood group was Rhesus-negative or that a Rhesus-negative mother carrying a Rhesus-positive baby, the child having inherited its blood group from the father, could experience problems.

Knowing none of this, Catherine saw the pregnancy as a blessed second chance, until she suffered a miscarriage. Then, in 1942, Tom was posted to RAF Madley in Herefordshire and she took digs in Hereford, at number 1 Ryelands Street, where, once more, she turned her hand to drawing and keeping a diary. When leave was due to Tom, she would save her rations and wait on tenterhooks for his arrival. One weekend, in February 1942, was particularly memorable. Somehow she had managed to get hold of 'soup, rump steak (my whole week's rations), bacon and sausages, fried bread and then a trifle' for his supper, but he didn't eat as much as she wanted him to. He had been too excited just to see her. Afterwards they sat back and Tom talked of his plans for The Hurst after the war, what they would do to the garden, while Catherine basked in their just being together, and thought, 'What does any of it matter.'

In the morning, Tom has gone and Catherine wonders whether they have made a baby. She receives the news of the fall of Singapore and sinks into a deep depression for the mothers of the sons who are lost. Then she begins to talk to her hoped-for child, her would-be Valentine baby, naming him then and there, Valentino, though she would rather have had the name David. The following day she receives a letter from Tom, expressing his love for her, and imagining her voice 'playing the most wonderful music in my ears'. It isn't yet two years since they were married, and Catherine considers that Tom has already swept clean all the hurt of her early life from her mind.

There was no Valentino. They lost their third child in 1943, and Catherine was alone once more. She was advised not to become pregnant again. This posed a separate problem. It was a sin against God to practise contraception, to prevent life – another ticket to damnation. She knew she would have to take her problem to a priest. The priest didn't tell her to exercise celibacy; he told her to leave the sinning to her man. What kind of hypocrisy was that? How could the priest suggest such a thing? He had struck at the very heart of her doubts. He was dodging the issue because the doctrines of his church were at odds with life, real life.

Catherine's problem with religion was that she had been brought up in a rigidly, even ruthlessly, disciplined Church, some of whose doctrines she had doubted from the start, which had filled her with guilt. But religion had answered a need in her, a fundamental spiritual need, which would never leave her. Now that the disciplines and doctrines were suspect, what did that mean for the validity of the spiritual answers which that same Church had given her? These priests were reducing the whole thing to a child's game. Leave the decision to your man. Let him go to hell. Why didn't they all grow up and get to the heart of the matter?

Deep down, what she was after was truth. Catherine had once before been cheated in a matter of love, love for two people whom she had known and believed in as her mother and father. But parental love was as nothing to this love, the very essence of feeling, which she had discovered in her relationship with the Holy Family, and in particular with Christ's mother, the Virgin Mary, through whom she had always dealt. Mingling with her feelings of outrage was a kind of aggression, little stabs of aggression. She was not a child any more, but what they were doing to her was tempting her to lose faith altogether, to lose faith in those whom she had loved and had loved her. Like the first time, it was the negation of all that had been true.

Chapter Seven

Catharsis

The years since 1932, when Kate had arrived in Hastings to live, had been a nightmare of drink, recrimination, argument, fights and hard physical work. Work getting Kate organised, work (from 1933) getting The Hurst into some sort of shape, work making it turn a profit as guest-house-cum-home, and through the whole period long hours of toil each day at the Hastings Institution, which, until Catherine's resignation in July 1939, formed the backbone on which all other work was ribbed.

Tom has said that, for his wife, work was the essence of being, it galvanised her energies. But those energies had been wasted by her illness: 'I had been losing blood practically every day since I was eighteen.' They had been wasted by the extraordinary campaign waged by Kate and Nan over Tom, and by the terrible loss of three babies in the three years that she and Tom had been married. They had been wasted, too, by the battles raging within her, not only about religion, but also about herself – 'my illegitimacy was hitting me harder than at any other time'. She was being torn apart by her two sides, which she identified with Kate and her unknown father. Sublimating the first, her nightmare side (Kate), she could apprehend her other side, her 'new nature' which promised an alternative destiny, a fulfilment longed for and prepared for by reading and following the strategy of refinement devised by Lord Chesterfield. And yet, despite all her feverish doing – drawing, painting, educating herself – that side of her seemed to be leading nowhere. Only Kate remained real: an awful, negative reality. Fulfilment on almost any level was denied her. Tom alone provided succour, 'the strange delight of knowing that she was wanted', as she would write in *Kate Hannigan*.

Her life was going round and round like a fairground carousel, Tom holding her tight round the waist lest she fall off. Every so often people popped up in front of her, offering false avenues of escape. 'I recall there was a very civilised priest in Hereford and he talked to me so quietly and nicely, and strangely we became friends. But it was no good.' A printer who liked her drawings of St Albans Abbey and Hereford Cathedral suggested she turn her hand to postcards. Another printer agreed that her drawings showed talent; why didn't she illustrate Arthur Mee's *Kings' England*? Catherine took up both offers, but the postcards made her only a halfpenny each, and the illustrations for Arthur Mee's *Kings' England*, sized one inch by one and a half inches, kept her eye to a magnifying glass all day long and rewarded her with a cheque for five pounds and conjunctivitis. A kindly, talented painter called André van der Meersch offered her lessons in perspective (which she might have used in her life as well as in her art), but he was an old man and died. No one, it seemed, could stop the endless, sickening motion of the less-than-merry-go-round, which was leading in ever-decreasing circles, closer and closer to the grinding engine-house of her mind.

Physically, odd things had begun to happen. She became thin and wasted; the veins in one leg became inflamed (she had contracted phlebitis); her anxieties lost any reference to specific preoccupations – religion, illegitimacy – and stared back at her in the mirror of her mind with merciless intent, confining her to bed, even paralysing her legs. Then one day she fell; and for a full two weeks she stayed in bed, staring at the ceiling. Catherine's fears had got her where they wanted her, alone in her lonely room, Tom away at the RAF camp, her unsympathetic landlady pacing the floor below. And they set about their business with surgical precision.

She saw her life as a hopeless stream of attempts to anaesthetise herself against the hurt she felt inside, which she associated with the stigma of illegitimacy, and which, up to now, had always driven her on. All the effort of her bid for freedom, her leaving Tyneside, her reading, her writing, her art, all the hours pushing herself at the workhouse, the effort of getting The Hurst up and running, where had any of it got her? Fragile respectability, a veneer, a momentary sense of achievement which left unfilled the vacuum inside, the aloneness to which she had been consigned by lovelessness and the rejection first by her father and then by her mother at birth.

The hate and resentment left by the 'fracture' of her birth was more deeply rooted now than they had ever been, for every approach to unity within had failed. Her writing and her art had got her nowhere. Her love for Tom had been cauterised by the loss of three babies. It was not enough for her to suffer the lovelessness of her own birth, she had to have a body impervious to the love of its own offspring. Even the Church had failed her. That self-proclaiming fountain of love had labelled her a sinner – she, the Catholic party in the relationship, was living in sin, 'And I knew only too well the outcome of that! I was so furious . . .'

Bit by bit, lying there in her room, she began to peel away the veneer of respectability and seek out the lovelessness inside, identifying and picking over a list of repulsions, headed by Kate coming down on her from a great height, her warm, whisky-soaked breath fouling her nose and throat, that slack mouth of hers grinning at her as it uttered a befuddled 'give us a kiss'. Or Kate's boyfriend, a young lodger called Mulhattan, who came from Birkenhead and sat little Catherine on his knee. She was quite used to knees. She would love to sit on her grandparents' knees. One of the reasons why people wanted to lift her on their knees was because she was so small, and pretty of course, too. That day, when she was sitting on Mulhattan's knee, parting his hair and plaiting it, she suddenly noticed there was something about this fella's knee that wasn't quite right . . . she yelled at him and then he got her in his arms and carried her to a leather chair, where he set about kissing her in a terrible fashion. Stiff and petrified with fear, something bursting inside her, she begged and cried to him to stop, that she knew what he was going to do, and that she would tell her da.

There followed a terrible fight when her granda returned and the man was never seen again, but her drunken mother and the lodger Mulhattan were far from being the only corruptions of love little Catherine knew. There was, too, the time when she was repeatedly made to kiss a tobacconist, who kept what was known as a house-window shop, in Lancaster Street. He and his wife mopped up the out-of-hours-custom of the main shop in Philipson Street. Catherine would be sent to get tabs for brother Jack or baccy for old John, maybe late in the evening. The shopkeeper was small and white-haired, a man well into his sixties. After the first time he kissed her, Catherine stood in the backlane pressing herself tightly against the wall with her legs tightly crossed and bit into her lip, for the fear in her was making her want to go to the lavatory. She determined never to go to the shop late in the evening again. But needs must, so she got into the habit of holding the door open ready to run, and the man got into the habit of withholding her change until he had what he wanted. Her nightmares were frequent during this period. The business was terminated when the family left the New Buildings in a rush. Why, little Catherine never knew nor cared, the relief was so great.

Catherine began to be overwhelmed with feelings of hopelessness, lovelessness, self-loathing and hate. As she put it to me, she began to want to 'wreak retribution on somebody or something, especially for losing the babies'.

Things that had happened in her past had left such an accumulation of marks upon the landscape of her life that the thin social veneer with which she had tried so hard to smooth it over now inched away from its surface, revealing the marks and sores. Resentments became putrid, foetid, like little germ factories building into one massive boil, self-pity, hate, aggression as dreadful, nameless terrors swimming together to spawn its angry head.

She lay helpless, bound to her bed like the timbers in the Jarrow Slacks, prone in the mud, one of a row of skeletons unearthed in the graveyard of her mind. Then she sank, wallowing, choking in the black mire, and knew for the first time that there was no escape. Trapped beneath the surface of the mire she looked about her at a madman's world of twisted, grotesque creatures, sprawled at all angles, weirdly suggesting motion but horribly still. She gazed into the face of a man whom she had known as a child, a man who sold coal but who had no legs, and she saw her own horror in that man's face – it was misty, the face had gone, but the feeling remained. Her feeling turned to rage, rage against Nature, rage against God, rage against Kate.

These are images culled from the novels, from *Kate Hannigan*, *The Blind Miller*, *The Fifteen Streets* and *Feathers in the Fire*.

Catherine said to me once, 'Strange, isn't it, that I have never written about my breakdown.' But it is all there. Confined in her room in Hereford, she too dreamed fantastic dreams in which she was wallowing among strange, faceless, reptilian monsters, which transformed themselves into hands.

Many of her novels explore mental stress, but none comes as close to offering us a glimpse of the author's spiralling descent into hell than *The Garment* (1962). Driven to the point of breakdown by her husband Donald, Grace Rouse begins her final descent when she shows herself vulnerable to every nuance in her husband's slyly destructive treatment of her. What was once sickening in his behaviour towards her now appears sinister. But everyone else is won over by Donald's jolly exterior, giving no credence to Grace's apparently paranoid version of events. The agony of the insane is that their version is true and yet no one but they can see it. Madness is not a blameless world, it is a world in which the madman is not allowed to place blame. A doctor friend warns Grace that if she continues to bottle up her anxieties they will come to a head in her brain like a boil. It is the same image Catherine uses to describe her own breakdown.

One morning in August, a silly scene with Grace's son Stephen results in some insolent behaviour, condoned by Donald, which in Grace's troubled mind seems to complete a picture, a jigsaw of truly paranoid impressions that her children have entered Donald's conspiracy and are united against her. Then, that afternoon, Donald suggests re-employing the gardener, Andrew MacIntyre, into whose arms he had previously driven Grace. Alienated, alone, she sees this as Donald trumpeting his control over her lover and slamming the door on her one avenue of escape. It is Donald's final manipulation, and all hell breaks loose.

Driven to the precipice of insanity by her husband, Grace turns to her friend, Dr David Cooper, but it is too late, she is too far down the path; not even he can help. When Catherine turned to Tom he could do nothing to stem the tide either.

One day, after he had returned to camp, Catherine was gripped by a terror she could neither place nor understand. Her heart raced, her limbs trembled, she felt sick and was sure she was going to die. She had been found lying on the bed, stiff, wild-eyed and silent. Later, she would discover that the terror had a name – *nervous hysteria* – but no one told her that at the time.

In breakdown, there is no pretence. All the face, all the gentility which guards against truth in a civilised world melts away in the heat of pure rage. It is, in a way, a cleansing. The boil bursts and all the putrid, foetid resentment of a lifetime pours out. Ever since Catherine could remember, whether it was her disgust as a child at Kate shoplifting a part-bale of flannelette or a fear so strong in adulthood that it made her sick lest she go out and take the life of a child, Catherine must cleanse herself of it. She literally vomited her fear away. Alienation, nausea, repulsion, purification compose a major theme of the novels. Nervous breakdown is the ultimate evacuation, not of the stomach or bowels, but of the mind, in her case an involuntary purging of all the filth of her childhood experience. Potentially, it is a cathartic experience; but, as with a boil that bursts, healing is neither instant nor guaranteed. Putrefaction may set in.

In *The Obsession*, nervous breakdown turns Beatrice Steele into an animal, prowling around the house, whispering, scratching at locked doors with her nails like a crazed dog. In *The Garment*, Grace Rouse yells out, screaming mouthfuls of saliva and abuse, goading, terrifying. Kate is one object of her abuse – she is screamed by name. At first I made no connection with the minor character in the novel, Kate Shawcross, clergyman Donald's admirer. Read it as I did and the autobiographical content of Grace's awful purgation is alarmingly clear. In any case, it includes other elements, which have a transparent autobiographical reference – for example, her resentment about fetching the coke, or her slipping into a Geordie accent as she spews out her oaths. All pretence is over as she bares her claws and the real fury begins.

She is restrained on her bed by her husband, who shouts at their son Stephen to fetch 'Uncle David' at once. It's a moment when one identifies wholly with the child, the shock of seeing his parents out of control. So often it is a man called David, the name of Catherine's dead child (who might have turned her own world round), who offers succour to her mentally unstable fictional heroines. In *Maggie Rowan*, David discovers Maggie's sister Ann in convulsion before she is taken to the asylum. In *The Blind Miller*, where the narrative returns Sarah Bradley to Catherine's 'locus of self-destruction' – the Jarrow Slake – it is David who allays her fears, hugs and reassures her that it is only a dream. But now there is no dream, only nightmare reality. It is a terrifying scene, brought to a close by Dr Cooper with his

The staff at Hastings Workhouse, to which Catherine went as Head Laundress in 1930. She is seated on the far right. The Master and Matron of the workhouse, Mr and Mrs George Silverlock, are three and four seats away from her.

Looking out over Hastings Old Town towards the pier, where Catherine went to watch the then famous healer, Harry Edwards, perform a demonstration. Later, she became convinced that her close association with Edwards facilitated events and solved problems in her life.

In 1930, the year in which Catherine arrived at the Hastings Workhouse, stewardship was handed over by the Guardians of the Poor to the local Corporation. As the picture shows, the inmates' uniform remained the same, and indeed it continued to operate as a workhouse until 1948, when the National Health Service was introduced and turned it into St Helen's Hospital.

Catherine, shown far left, organised picnics for the female inmates within the precincts of the Hastings Workhouse. It was quite a novelty for a member of staff to go to the trouble of relieving inmates of having to stay in their wards most of the day, and is mentioned in Matron's Report of 9 April 1931.

Tom Cookson is on the left of Mabel and Jack, the three children of Thomas Cookson, verger to a church in Chingford, Essex, and Mabel Florence Lear. Thomas died in 1915, two weeks before his daughter was born.

Tom Cookson in RAF uniform during the war. He had gone for a commission, but Catherine hadn't wanted him to fly and 'put the kibosh on it,' Tom told his half-sister, Edna Humphreys.

Catherine and Tom on a honeymoon visit to Tom's family in June 1940. The couple had beaten a path across a blacked-out country to London and met evacuees from Dunkirk along the way.

Tom and Catherine married on 1 June 1940. 'I had married a Protestant. Perhaps we were married in Catholic church, but under protest . . . The priest threw the ceremony at us. There were only eight people present and it was only on the promise that I would get Tom to turn.'

Catherine's friend, Nan Smyth, is seated on the far right, next to Kate and then Catherine, in this tennis group on the lawn of The Hurst. Clearly it was an odd friendship as perceived from within the workhouse – Nan literally a scrubber, Catherine head of the laundry – and Matron was aghast when Catherine told her they were moving in together.

Nan Smyth in later years. 'She was very, very masculine. Her face was leathery and she always had a cigarette dangling from her mouth.' Catherine declared openly that Nan loved her, but refuted the suggestion that she was a lesbian, adding that it was nothing special sleeping in the same bed, as she had always slept with her mother

The Hurst in the 1930s, when Catherine bought it. It was a disaster of a property, woodworm, rot, and in hopeless disrepair, but it represented something important to Catherine. Amazingly, this girl from a penniless family on the Tyne was only twenty-seven when she bought it.

Catherine with two of her 'paying guests' at The Hurst. To make ends meet, she turned the house into a cross between a guest house and home for invalids. 'They had blind people staying and mentally handicapped people,' remembers cousin Sarah, as well as other guests.

Catherine fencing with a guest on the terrace of The Hurst. She took an hour-long fencing lesson each week, part of a rigorous regime she kept, which also included riding.

Tom Cookson on scout camp with fellow masters from Hastings Grammar School. 'It was a school troop run by a very good parcel of men,' remembers Tony Weeks-Pearson, a pupil at the time, 'the chief of which was the deputy head, L. H. G. Baker. "Cookie", like the rest, were assistants to "Com" Baker. Kitty was a good painter and would come to camps. I remember making her an easel out of the forest wood, branches and stuff.'

Catherine in the period leading up to her breakdown and admission to St Mary's Psychiatric Hospital, Burghill. 'I put on this front,' she said, 'this act that everything was quite normal. But underneath I was writhing in fear.'

syringe, the husband nursing his torn and bleeding face at the end of the bed, the patient cursing him into oblivion.

'When the boil burst and my head made into a whirlpool of terror,' Catherine said to me, describing the scene, 'I knew something had to be done.' It sounded all very rational. Catherine always maintained that it was she who had suggested confinement in St Mary's Psychiatric Hospital, Burghill, that she had been quite willing to go, but this was not the case.

In the original draft of *Our Kate*, she uses the 'boil' metaphor again, and the boil bursts at the very moment that it is suggested she should see a psychiatrist. Then, when subsequently the psychiatrist arrives and suggests that she should go for treatment, fear runs riot.

Her treatment at Burghill included ECT – electro-convulsive therapy – the electric current once so powerfully administered that it lifted her off the table. In 1945 such places were not what they are today, and Catherine's experience resonates with images of cold stone stairs, of waiting her turn for treatment on heavy wooden forms, of the glare of arc lights, of the effort afterwards of lifting her legs (made unnaturally heavy by the current) back along the corridors to her bed, of the smell of urine in the wards, recalling the desolation and misery of the infirm wards at Harton and the bitter memory of the urinals opposite the dock gates from which that woman had emerged, laughing, arm-in-arm with three men. In *The Blind Miller* Catherine gives Sarah Bradley the same experience in prison, where the smell of urine permeates the air.

Each night Tom would ride fourteen miles on his bicycle to visit her, this after riding fifteen miles back and forth to the camp and their digs. After five weeks Catherine was allowed out for a day. 'I recall that the nice priest from Hereford saw me and cried out, "What on earth are you doing here?"'

Chapter Eight

The Creative Force

Catherine walked out of the mental hospital with one thought in her mind: to get back to The Hurst. She arrived home on her own, determined to get the house back into shape and to work, work, work, so as to divert her energies from fearful introspection and aggression. It was June 1945. She lived alone there for nine months, fighting her battle out, Tom unable to join her permanently until his demob in the spring of 1946.

Upon opening the front door for the first time in five years, she was struck by the most appalling smell and must have wondered whether it was some kind of nightmarish imagining from the depths of breakdown. For the smell that pervaded the place was the smell of urine. There was a mixture of relief and revulsion when she discovered that there was a full chamberpot in each bedroom. 'The home had been occupied only during the last few months by an officer's wife, who had used it as a guest house for other officers.'

The whole place required a complete overhaul. It was a depressing and lonely time. Catherine was, of course, on tranquilisers and sleeping pills, her need for which she found repugnant, but which she could not deny. During the day she would try to get house and garden back into shape, proceeding according to Kate's dictum that the only way out of a depression was hard work. But hers was no ordinary depression and the house needed no ordinary repairs. There was damage to the roof from incendiary bombs and one of the turrets was dangerous and would have to be removed. As for the garden, it had lain untended for five long years.

A woman living opposite told her that she would never fully recover from her breakdown because she could not open her soul to joy. However true a reflection of Catherine as company at this time, it was the worst thing she could have said. Then in early autumn she discovered she was pregnant and all the uncertainties that had attended the first two pregnancies after David's stillbirth returned. How she longed for Tom to share the burden of her ordeal.

Instead, Tom's mother arrived and was appalled to find her living in the basement of the house opposite. She eased her back to The Hurst, whereupon Catherine suffered another miscarriage.

Desperately sad, but aware that one slip would have her back in Burghill, or some hell that was similar, she pinned a chart on the kitchen wall to record each day how she was doing. The lowest point of the graph marked the day when she prepared for suicide.

At the end of her tether, she made ready in the bathroom of The Hurst to take all her sleeping pills at one go. She made all the preparations and at the last minute, thinking of Tom and what it would do to him to find her there, she flushed them down the lavatory. Momentarily she felt better. She found herself on her own, with no medicines to cling on to, and it felt good. She took it as a sign of the way she must take: no dependence, no props, her future was up to herself.

This was a crucial point, a turning point, the first big positive move, a declaration that henceforth it was Catherine alone against her breakdown. There was no room for bravado, nor was there any. It would be an act of will. Even if she only had a few hours' sleep each night, she knew she would never go back on her decision to do without pills.

Each new day she would don two dressing gowns and a huge pair of Eskimo-like boots and wrap a big woollen scarf around her head, and set to work 'in that freezing barracks'. Even heating one of the cavernous rooms took the physical effort of chopping up wood from the garden trees. The Hurst had no central heating of any kind and had only one large fireplace in the drawing room and a number of small ones in other rooms. 'It was after the war,' she explained, 'and we were still on coal ration of a ton a year. So I spent at least an hour a day sawing old trees down and sawing them up to keep some kind of warmth in one room. This was besides cleaning the place, cooking, washing by hand (no machines of any kind, not even a wringer) and writing in every spare minute . . . writing, the locked shelter in which once you get the door open you can live,' A safe place to be herself – like Annie Hannigan's 'little square house' sanctuary in the backyard, or like the 'hiding place' for which Reginald Farrier yearns in *The Wingless Bird*. Returning from the trenches in the First World War, emotionally shot to pieces, Farrier appeals to his brother's widow Agnes Conway to provide it, with a quotation from Psalm 32: 'Thou art my hiding place; thou shalt preserve me from trouble; thou shalt compass me about with songs of deliverance.' Catherine, though, was not reading psalms any more.

Still she was sick with anxiety every minute of every day. Her chart showed that Catherine had known only one day free from fear in the first year she was back at The Hurst.

She began by writing plays. 'But after having written the third play I questioned myself as to what I really knew about the characters.' They were cardboard, two-dimensional, mostly plucked from the upper middle class and living the kind of existence which Chesterfield might have known at first hand, but which was largely foreign to Catherine's experience.

But occasionally she did experience moments of electric creativity. Catherine described one such moment in a collection of recordings issued on tape towards the end of 1996, which includes a song called 'Falling Leaves'. She was sitting at a baby grand piano in the drawing room during a break from her gruelling, self-imposed, fourteen-hour working day. Tall windows looked out on to the lawn, bordered by trees and an old rhododendron hedge. As she was staring mournfully out at the garden, a gust of wind stirred the trees and set free a fall of leaves, which floated past the window, caught in a ray of clean, clear autumn sunlight. Instantly Catherine was infused with a feeling of sheer joy, 'as swift in passing as the leaves themselves'. Fleeting moments such as this offered an exquisite peace that was new and seemed to awaken something inside her. She composed the song 'Falling Leaves' there and then at the piano. The moment of joy was distinct from anything she had ever felt, and it was instantly creative.

Sensitised by nervous breakdown, Catherine had become so acutely aware that it was almost inevitable, given her obsessive propensity for action, for doing, that if she could draw on this power, which she perceived interlacing people as well as things, it would transform her writing. A few moments of creativity – around this she began to write poetry – were interspersed with awesome moments that brought an ecstatic but at the same time frightening insight into things, breaking things up into energies, intensities, drives, as if there were 'a power passing through and interlacing all things,' as Catherine put it. This fearful awareness never left her. Years later she described it to me, using imagery from a dream she had at this creative time of flying up a telegraph pole, looking along the conductor wires and flying to the next before sliding back down.

Here was raw spiritual experience, the like of which she had never known in the context of religion. 'There can be no God in the way religions describe, but there is a power out there. There is something,' she said. 'I myself have touched that something. Call it spirit or soul or what have you; it might be only a means of electricity . . . I have for some time looked upon it as a great cable of electric wires that run round the world and through us, and you can tap your own wire, you can plug into it . . .'

In the mid-1950s, Catherine and Tom would own a bit of woodland. When taking a break from her writing, she would sometimes walk in among the trees. She knew that if she stopped and leant for a moment against the big bole of a particular oak she would feel her tensions slipping away into it. Putting this together with her description of the spirit in things, I was reminded of D. H. Lawrence's description of the same power, which appears in *Fantasia and the Unconscious*: 'I come so well to understand tree-worship,' he wrote. 'All the old Aryans worshipped the tree. My ancestors. The tree of life. The tree of knowledge . . . This marvellous vast individual without a face, without lips or eyes or heart . . . Here am I between his toes like a pea-bug, and him noiselessly overreaching me, and I feel this great blood-jet surging. And he has no eyes. But he turns two ways: he thrusts himself tremendously down to the middle earth, where dead men sink in darkness, in the damp, dense under-soil; and he turns himself about in high air . . . A huge, plunging, tremendous soul . . .'

In *Sons and Lovers*, Lawrence refers to the same magnificent power when Paul Morel, who represents Lawrence himself, is lying on the ground next to Clara Dawes, a married woman with whom he is having an affair. The grass stems close to their eyes are 'curving and strong with life in the dark'. It is in the grass, it is in the peewit calling, it is in the warmth of Clara's breathing and in her eyes – 'life wild at the source staring into his life, stranger to him, yet meeting him'. Recognising this makes Paul afraid, as it did Catherine, but there is also a kind of satisfaction. It gave them 'rest within themselves ... to know their own nothingness, to know the tremendous living flood which carried them always'.

In the spring of 1946, when Tom returned to The Hurst, he was not alarmed at her spiritual energy. He encouraged his wife's writing, and that Catherine should join the local Writers' Circle, which met at the Rougemont Hotel (since demolished) in Harold Place on Hastings sea front. Getting out among fellow writers was a crucial step. Members had to read their work out loud to the rest of the Circle. Catherine's nerves were so bad that when her turn came she had to stay seated, giving the excuse that she suffered from rheumatism. After each reading there would be a discussion, in which other members offered criticism and pointers for future work. She found that the stories she took were often well received. She gained confidence from this and enjoyed analysing and commenting on others' work, the experience underpinning and informing her solitary efforts. But there was a mountain to climb.

Before Tom's return Catherine had counted the hours and the minutes until she could hold him in her arms again. But now that he was back she was once more expected to be a school-master's wife, a role which carried with it certain obligations. For example, she was expected to attend school functions, some of which interrupted the strict schedule to which she kept, and at times she resented this. Also, these events took her out of the house into potentially discriminatory company and she felt far from confident. She had always felt she had to dress up in her best bib and tucker, and thrust and parry wittily among the masters and their wives to maintain her (and especially Tom's) standing. This was one of the areas where Chesterfield had served her well in the past, but now, since her breakdown, there was always the danger that her nervous disorder would without warning crack the facade.

In *The Obsession* Catherine uses Beatrice Steele to explain the awful unpredictability of her state of mind. Walking down a street, Beatrice suddenly experiences 'that tired feeling' which invariably preceded an attack. With it comes a feeling of dread: 'Oh, my God! Not here!'

One day Catherine was walking down Queen's Road in Hastings on her way to a masters' and boys' cricket match at the grammar school. Stopping at the Fifty Shilling Tailor's, where she had to cross the road to reach the cricket field, her eyes fell on a brick lying in the gutter. It was one of a number left there by men working nearby. She eyed the brick, a rough, particularly pink brick. Then she turned to the Fifty Shilling Tailor's and eyed its shopfront window, a large, particularly smooth expanse of plate glass. The desire to hurl the brick through the window was so strong, and Catherine hovered on the edge of indecision for so long, that one of the workmen noticed something was up.

'D'you want to take it home with you, missis?' he asked her.

She told him that no, she didn't want to take it home, but she could think of another use for it. Fortunately, the workman had defused the situation. Catherine walked quietly across the road and took her place among the schoolmasters, charming them with ironic remarks about cricket and the performance of her husband on the field, all the time wondering inside at the kind of creature she had become.

Going out into the town terrified Catherine for another reason, too. The emotional pain of four miscarriages had left her with an aversion to babies and a terrible, uncontrollable urge which threatened to take her at any time. 'I am a kind person, I wouldn't hurt a fly,' Catherine said to me, 'so how could this kind, caring, loving individual have the terrible desire to pick up a baby from a pram outside a shop and run off with it, worse still, to take hold of that baby and dash it to the ground?'

It was ten or fifteen years before Catherine could hold a child in her arms, and during this time she underwent three operations on her womb. Even people close to her failed to understand what her losses meant to her. I recall Catherine telling me of a visit one Christmas by Tom's parents. There had been a baby in the visiting party and they had tried to get Catherine to hold it. She had declined, making light of it, and so they had pressed her again, and again, and when she continued to refuse they had become upset. It was some time – long after the holiday was over – before she was forgiven for her apparent coldness.

Catherine's unravelling of this tortured period of her life was so honest, so absolutely public and open, that one feels those dealing with cases of involuntary baby-snatching would do well to take note. A principal reason for spelling out the terrors of her nervous breakdown was the obligation she felt later in life to her faithful readers. If even one of those millions felt, as a result, that they were not alone in their particular hell, her harrowing revelations were worthwhile, she felt. She would say that she had no satisfaction in writing the novels other than meeting the dictates of her urge to write, but it was for Catherine the height of success 'if in the process of writing I say something worthwhile, something that might make someone laugh or cry or think – most of all I hope it makes someone think – and often I have letters that tell me that they do . . .'.

Catherine's breakdown, fraught with her loss of faith in God and precipitated by the death of her babies, was the culmination of an identity crisis which had led, with Aunt Mary's assistance, to her upstart years, to Lord Chesterfield, to hiding behind a veneer with which she felt able to face the world and hoped to rise in it.

Her recovery was to be inextricably bound up with her writing, which now would reflect fundamental changes in her way of thinking about herself. As I have already noted, in the early novels Catherine puts humanity on the slab and wields her scalpel to cut away hypocrisy, envy, bigotry, pretension and superstition. But before she could do this she had to set about herself with similar precision.

Discarding her plays with their wooden, upper-class characters was the first cut. It was a cut into pretension, into her dear Lord Chesterfield, into the veneer that covered her true self and which Catherine's reading of him had fashioned. Staring at herself in the mirror one day, berating herself for her weakness – a favourite therapy – a little girl with long tresses tied up in plaits came into view and for the first time she saw herself as she had been as a child before the truth of her illegitimacy and the dissemblance of her mother and grandparents had been made known to her. She saw pathos and innocence and truth in this image, and the writer in her was inspired to write a story. It was about a girl from the North who had no father and whose playmates destroyed her little world by telling her that the man she thought was her father was not. She called it 'She Had No Da'. This, she could see, worked better. She had brought her writing back to herself, and it worked.

With this cut Catherine learned the most painful lesson of her nervous breakdown – that if she was ever going to write anything worthwhile, she would have to 'strip off the pseudo-lady' and be herself. Her road to recovery was to be something of an existential odyssey: this cut meant that she was coming to terms with who she was, the fact that she was Kate's daughter, Kate's illegitimate daughter, the fact that she was a product of the environment which contained her drunken granda, the Pawn, the beer, the cinder tips. The decision was a turning point. She dropped her mask, opened the locked doors of her mind and out poured the lives of real folk she had rubbed shoulders with for her first twenty-three years . . .

A young member of the Hastings Writers' Circle remembers being particularly impressed by her approach. Joan Moules (née Longfellow), nineteen at the time, who went on to write novels and biographies, as well as running a Writers Circle of her own, remembers, above all, Catherine's demand for realism in others' writing: 'She was the one in the group you remembered – dramatic! Catherine was a brilliant critic. She talked about your story, about the characters, about the setting. Would they have done that? That sort of thing. Realism! She didn't touch on the grammar or the construction of sentences. It was totally the story, what came out in the story.'

At the same time, Catherine never lost sight of her alienation from the society of her birth. For whatever reason – her father, her artistic nature – she was, like Meursault, the hero of Albert Camus' classic existentialist novel *The Outsider*, 'wandering on the outskirts of life, solitary . . .'. This was an important creative stance for her. Catherine always said that the physical and cultural distance gave her the objectivity her creativity needed.

It was a creative position achieved by another with a good deal less searching, because he realised from the start what set him apart from his people. D. H. Lawrence left his home in Eastwood, a mining village eight miles from Nottingham, in 1910, two decades before Catherine left her working-class roots on Tyneside. A few years later he gave the following words to Ursula Brangwen in his novel *The Rainbow*: 'I have no allocated place in the world of things, I do not belong to Beldover [Eastwood] nor to Nottingham nor to England nor to this world, but they none of them exist. I am trammelled and entangled in them, but they are all unreal. I must break out of it, like a nut from its shell which is an unreality.' Like Lawrence, Catherine in 'escaping' from Tyneside was fleeing not so much from a place as from the unreality of her existence in it. She was out of place in it. Now she only truly belonged there in her imagination. Her escape had been from unreality into 'the channels where the intangible but real life runs'.

Her understanding of this was assisted by a complete overhaul in her spiritual life. Far from contradicting or excluding her new spiritual awareness, this insistence on realism denied her any false props, which, of course, included her religion, railed against in the asylum at Burghill. At her wits' end, before her descent into hell, hadn't she discarded all intermediaries and gone to the man at the top? 'I put it to God the Father: if he wanted me to remain a Catholic he should give me a sign. He did. I had a breakdown.'

Now she was determined to put the pieces back together again. 'During this period,' said Catherine, 'I read anything which might help my state of mind, from philosophy to *How to Keep Nerves in their Place*.' In recovery she began to make sense of a spiritual dimension without recourse to Catholicism, thanks to a book by Leslie Weatherhead, *The Christian Agnostic*. The Christian agnostic was 'a person . . . immensely attracted by Christ who seeks to . . . meet the challenges, hardships and sorrows of life in the light of that spirit, but who . . . feels that he cannot honestly and conscientiously "sign on the dotted line" that he believes certain theological ideas about which . . . the Church dogmatises.' This fitted Catherine like a glove. With Weatherhead, Catherine could move on from Father O'Malley's vengeful God of the Old Testament.

Not long after Tom returned, Catherine's cousin Sarah Lavelle came to stay from Birtley, a Durham pit village. Sarah was a shy girl in her early twenties, brought up on unquestioning Catholic principles, the youngest of eight in a large, loving family. She couldn't believe the intensity with which Catherine lived life, and had no idea that her cousin had just come out of a mental asylum. Sarah's religion came under the microscope, and Catherine's robust treatment of her shook Sarah badly.

'It was a different world altogether. I first met Kitty in 1946 when I had a recurrence of osteomyelitis [a bone marrow disease] and Aunt Kate wrote to her and asked if I could go down to recuperate. It was not long after the breakdown, but I didn't know that at the time. I think I was down there for a month. I had been brought up a very strong Catholic, so she took me to church on Sunday, to Mass. Oh, it was horrendous really! When we came out we met a few people and started to chat, and she said, "Well it does nothing for me," and I said, "Well, it's the way I've been brought up." I was just educated at an ordinary Catholic school, a very good school, but here I was talking about my religion with Tom, with his MA from Oxford, and Kitty, who was self-educated and very strong in her opinions. So they started on about the Catholic Church and all the pomp and everything, which was their point of view and I was trying to put my faith across to them, and I was so upset because I had never had any friction like that before. I had always sat in the corner, being the youngest. Even when Jack first married me he said to me, "Don't you ever answer back?" (He's sorry he said that now.) They were running my faith down and I was trying to defend it as best I could and I found it very difficult. Of course Tom was gentle, but Kitty was robust, and I thought I have got to get out of this house. This was the very first weekend I was there! And then I walked in the evening to Benediction and when I got back the wound in my leg opened up, so she said, "That's what you get for going to church!"'

Sarah wasn't to know the turmoil going on inside Catherine's mind. One day in 1948, Catherine threw her head back and challenged her religion head-on, sending 'to blazes and bloody damnation . . . God, dogma, the Catholic Church, the Devil, hell, people, opinions, laws, illegitimacy . . . and fear. Bugger them all!' As she says, 'It was a brave show,' but really splitting away from the last 'thing she had to cling on to' wasn't easily effected.

Weatherhead recommended his readers take the very direction that Catherine then took: 'Few writers on Christianity have taken psychic factors into account,' he writes, 'presumably because formerly the whole subject was bedevilled by cranks, cheats, fanatics and the self-deluded.' But Weatherhead went on to predict that doing so would bring astonishing rewards: 'Surely if there is one field of enquiry . . . relevant to Christian understanding, it is that of psychical research.'

So it was that Catherine attended a seance at the House of Healing in Hastings, a well-known Spiritualist Centre in the town. She was impressed when 'contact' was made with two people she had known – she writes in detail about this in *Let Me Make Myself Plain* (1988). Later, she returned to the centre and received treatment for a painful sinus below the eye, which her doctor had indicated would need an operation. There was a laying on of hands, again the session worked, seemingly miraculously.

Subsequently, she went along to watch the then famous Harry Edwards heal. 'He was doing a demonstration in the theatre on the Hastings Pier,' she recorded. 'I was one of hundreds watching him straighten limbs. People using walking sticks would be helped up onto stage, then walk down unaided. Whether by manipulation or by some other means, this tubby and ordinary-looking man was actually enabling people to walk again.'

Harry Edwards' power of healing was first exercised in the Middle East, where he was serving in the British Army and cured the son of a Muslim priest. In 1946, he set up his headquarters – still in existence today – on a 14-acre estate called Burrows Lea in the Surrey stockbroker belt at Shere. Counting royalty among his many clients, he attracted thousands to mass healing sessions, including one in Manchester attended by 6,000. The press denounced him, but people kept coming, and, like Catherine, seemed convinced that he had a special touch. He continued healing for forty years and died in 1976.

Catherine began corresponding with Edwards, the association apparently facilitating events and solving problems in her life. Most dramatically, she ascribed to Edwards a cure in 1953 that obviated the need for her to undergo a hysterectomy. Catherine met him only once, but always said that Edwards gave her the confidence 'to rely on that inner voice that is always waiting to be heard . . . I began to believe, as Christ said, that the Kingdom of God is within one, and if I had faith in this it would be sufficient for my needs.' She made the Harry Edwards Spiritual Healing Sanctuary Trust a substantial bequest on her death.

Tom cut a path of compromise where he could, always encouraging Catherine to put her intellect to work. There were others ready intellectually to meet Catherine too. Muriel Hilton lived with her husband, the minister of the Unitarian Church, in the same road as The Hurst. An extraordinary woman, Muriel, who wrote a monthly column in the Unitarian journal, *The Enquirer* (a paper that had a big influence at the time in literary circles), befriended Catherine. She was able to talk about the great writers of the day from personal experience. She even knew John Masefield, the Poet Laureate. She was a striking personality, but absolutely the antithesis of Catherine.

'The thing was,' recalled Tony Weeks-Pearson, who arrived as a pupil at the grammar school shortly after the war and knew both Muriel and Catherine, 'that the two women were opposites. Hilton exercised a calming influence, a reassurance, at least for a few minutes (which was itself something of a miracle in Kitty's case). The Cooksons lived up the top of Hoads Wood Road and Muriel and Denbeigh lived, until their deaths, down the bottom, so they would meet at bus stops and things. Having said how calm Muriel was, she also had a tremendous sense of fun, and so close was the relationship that they would burst into laughter spontaneously, like girls, when they saw each other in the distance, which was extraordinary in two women so apparently responsible and mature.'

In the summer of 1946, Tom took Catherine on holiday to the Norfolk Broads for the first time. They went with another master from the Grammar School, Bill Bennett, and his wife. It was an attempt to get her away from the gruelling schedule she set herself of ten to twelve hours a day. She claimed to hate the water, and it is true that until they came to own their own swimming pool in 1954–5 she could not swim. But this was to be the first of many boating holidays and the novel she wrote years later, called *Rosie and the River*, in which Fred and Sally Carpenter are recognisably Tom and Catherine, suggests that all tensions flew away when she was on the water. Indeed, in the mid-1950s they bought a boat of their own and christened her the *Mary Ann Shaughnessy*.

Over a decade they holidayed on her, Catherine always refusing to admit that she was enjoying herself. I have it from family friend Dr Manuel Anderson that the boat was bought at auction in Blyth, a coastal town to the north-east of Newcastle. It was a twenty-six-foot cabin cruiser, coloured white up to the superstructure, which was brown with a cream roof, and to Catherine's delight, 'the wheel was very much like that of a car steering wheel'. She fell in love with the craft, and was distraught to discover that 'by the time she got to the auction,' as Mannie recalls, 'a bid had already been accepted'. That night, however, Catherine had a dream that if she took her rosary and put it in a box on board, it would be hers the next day. She did, the bid fell through and she got the boat. Besides anything else, the story shows that for all her bravado at walking out on the Church she was still sufficiently involved to carry a rosary with her when travelling.

Dr Anderson, his wife Rita, and two daughters, Sylvia and

Marian – 'those two pairs of lovely legs,' as Catherine referred to them – holidayed with Catherine and Tom on the *Mary Ann Shaughnessy*, on the Cam at Stretham, close to Soham, deep fen country – 'everyone interrelated and deeply suspect,' according to a boatman I met down there.

These holidays also produced Catherine's novel *The Fen Tiger*, in which her preoccupation is the deep-down character of a people who once lived by spearing fish among the reeds and fiercely defended their watery land from those who would drain it, and their spirit out of them.

The hotel where Catherine, Tom, Bill and his wife stayed is now called The Lazy Otter, but was then The Royal Oak Hotel. Dr Anderson and his family stayed at a pub nearby called The Green Man, with a permanently drunken goose called Nicholas. It is now a private house.

During one holiday, probably in 1957, Dr Anderson was asked by Catherine to draw up a list of ladies lavatories in the Shields area by way of research for her novel *Fanny McBride* (the heroine, you may recall, becomes a lavatory attendant). 'Forty years of friendship and what have I got to show for it?' he laughs today, 'a book dedicated to me about a ladies lavatory attendant!'

In fact, as Catherine told me, the novel, published in 1959, was inspired by him. 'In those days I used to stay at his home in South Shields when I came up to give talks,' she said, 'and he would get up in the middle of the night if any of the old girls were dying, and he would go to them and comfort them. I thought that was simply marvellous. He told me that one of the saddest things was on visiting day to go into the ward in the hospital and see patients sitting there just staring into space with no visitors even though some of them had big families. This image stayed with me and touched a strong spring in myself, because I have always been lonely. Kitty was born lonely, and that day he told me about those women in the ward I immediately understood what they were feeling, and I had to bring this out. In *Fanny McBride* this *is* brought out. The whole family stay away, except for this one man, we call him Philip, who she didn't like because he was an upstart.'

Another way in which Tom set about trying to help Catherine back on her feet was by bringing the energies of his relationships with his pupils back into The Hurst. 'Tom took students in,' recalls cousin Sarah, 'not paying students, just lads he wanted to help who were at the school. They had a lad called Gub and another lad, there was always someone. They looked after their education in the evening. They didn't stay over, but Tom would do so many hours in the evening with them. So, there was always a lot going on.'

The joy this gave Catherine was inestimable. 'I've lost four babies but I've brought up more babies than in an orphanage,' she said to me a few years before she died. 'There were always boys at the house. One came every day for his lunch and he stayed two years! Another came when he was sixteen and he didn't leave until he was twenty.'

In 1946 Tom became the third ASM of the school's Scout Troop, which clearly was no ordinary scouting organisation. 'That troop was as vital an influence on us as the school itself,' remembers Tony. 'It was a school troop run by a very good parcel of men, the chief of which was the deputy head, L. H. G. Baker. "Cookie" [Tom's nickname], like the rest, were assistants to "Com" Baker. Baker actually had two nicknames, one a school one and one a scout one, which is indicative of the place. "Strube" was his school nickname, after the cartoonist. He was a maths teacher as well. "Com" was short for Commodore. They had these naval titles, not sure why. There was a Coxswain and a Bos'n. I don't remember Cookie having one, but he probably did. That troop won all the competitions. And they did this elaborate scout pantomime annually. Kitty was a good painter and would come to camps. I remember making her an easel out of the forest wood, branches and stuff.'

Tom's pupils became their family, and the one family element in Catherine's memories of East Jarrow – New Year's Eve, when ships' horns, dock hooters and church bells all rang out simultaneously, was revived in their drawing room. Tony remembers one occasion in particular: 'We must have been sixthformers at the time and were invited up to the house. We all had a special relationship through scouts, either troop or patrol leaders. The big thing that I remember, apart from the fact that I took a girl with me, was that Kitty made sure that I was the one to perform "the first footing", I brought in the piece of coal. I remember Cookie; we saw the man in a new light that night. At a certain stage in the evening he took hold of my girlfriend who was a keen dancer, probably did it to make her feel at home because she wasn't anything to do with the school. She was a ballroom dancer and they did the Apache, it was French, a kind of wife-beating drama performed in a sleazy, low Parisienne, Tango style, chucking the woman across the floor . . . The Hurst was a very handsome house at the top of Hoads Wood Road. They took the carpets up and Cookie had his shoes off and I remember him slipping and going for a burton right across this floor and into the wall . . . in a very graceful, slow way, no side about him of course.'

Such events were the mainspring of what Tom was trying to create for Catherine at The Hurst. As her readers know, Christmas and New Year are always moments of quiet expectation in the novels, when the tussle of life is suspended and hearts are opened. Catherine's first novel is built around successive Christmas Eves; it is a clever device that has us share this warm feeling of expectation.

It is unlikely that Catherine's extraordinary literary output could have been maintained had her time been taken up with a large family clinging to her skirts. But her novels cannot be said to have filled the vacuum. Their dogs, however, did help. First came Bill, who is celebrated in a couple of the novels. In *The Menagerie*, Willie Macintyre has a dog called Bill, a bull terrier. Newcastle United and bull terriers are Willie's life, and his love for Bill is down to his perception that the dog shares the character of his favourite football team. Willie had had another bull terrier when he was a boy, but it had developed mange – bull terriers, we learn, are born with it in their blood. Catherine actually caught mange from her Bill, a Staffordshire, brindled bull terrier, and had a particularly nasty time getting rid of the disease: Tom had to paint her, head to foot, in a kind of sheep dip solution. In *Fanny McBride*, Corny, Fanny's grandson, has a dog, an unfortunate mixture with a bull terrier's massive chest and a whippet's slimline hindquarters. He is a light brushstroke in Catherine's picture of personal identity and inherited traits which preoccupies her in so many of the novels. Then there was *Bill and the Mary Ann Shaughnessy*, in which, Catherine revealed, all the episodes are true – they really happened 'to some extent, except meeting the baddies'. But for the real Bill's identity we must turn to *Hamilton* (1983), a richly comic novel and the first of a trilogy (*Goodbye Hamilton* and *Harold* followed in 1984 and 1985 respectively).

Elsewhere Catherine describes Bill as 'our child, a tearaway, a bad lad – but a loving lad', and his appearance in Hamilton gives us a graphic and accurate description of the way Bill on his lead would pull Catherine off her feet and whisk her through

Hastings in his slipstream. Again, she records in the novel the memorable occasion when Bill slipped his collar and she raced after him up roads and down alleyways in the sedate town, to the amazement of onlookers, eventually to discover him at the butcher's where he is 'rewarded' with a bone.

Bill was a rascal and Catherine loved him. When he died in Tom's arms at nine years old, both she and Tom were devastated. After Bill came golden labrador Simon, and after he died, again in Tom's arms, they had a poodle called Sandy, who appears in *Goodbye Hamilton*. Years ago, not long after we first met, I was a bit surprised to come across a photograph of Sandy sitting with Catherine and Tom in their garden. Catherine hadn't exactly come across to me as a poodle sort of person. But Sandy was a child to them, as Bill had been. Poodles, she will tell you, are not dogs at all; they are children who never grow up. While Sandy was with them, Catherine became a patron of the Newcastle Dog Shelter and fell for another poodle, a hopelessly unkempt and rejected bitch called Sue. They took her in and spruced her up, and the dogs so took to one another that the Cookson home was never more replete with doggie love.

If the joy which these dogs gave them is a measure of Tom and Catherine's capacity for love of children then it is a sad measure too of the tragedy which denied them their own and goes some way towards helping us to understand the pain of their loss, which precipitated Catherine's breakdown.

At the end of the 1946, on Catherine's return from the Broads, she felt ready to embark upon writing a novel and started what, four years later, would be published as *Kate Hannigan*. She knew that she couldn't write as well as the poets to whom Miss Barrington had introduced her and she feared that she would never make a living from writing because of what she calls her syntactical naivety. Deep down she feared that although she could appreciate the beauty of words she didn't have the education to organise them in the syntactical framework which she thought would broadcast their sense.

As far as the mechanics of language were concerned she saw Tom as everything she wasn't. His scholarship in Latin and mathematics gave him a scientific, analytical approach. He could describe the job done by commas, colons, semi-colons, verbs, adjectives and adverbs, and he knew the grammatical rules which were a mystery to her. So it was that she would 'tell Tom the story in order to set it in my mind. I would then put it down in longhand, then reassess and correct it, after which he would go over it.' It was a reasonable idea, but it produced 'grammatically correct sentences, which made my characters gutless . . . And I fought him. Oh yes, I fought him to do the thing in my own way because I knew my way was right.'

One can't help but feel sorry for Tom in these battles he was made to fight, but eventually he saw how important it was for him to lose them. It was all part of the loosening of the bonds, a further freeing of the creative channels. It was crucial to the flow, sometimes torrent, of Catherine's imagination that her characters didn't have to leap barriers of stilted English. If she had deserted what linguistically was bred in the bone she would have been as lost as a writer as if she had deserted her people.

More than a century earlier, the Northamptonshire poet and day-labourer John Clare had expressed a similar linguistic unease, and in his best work had discarded even punctuation, which he called 'that awkward squad of pointings'. It had an extraordinary effect, giving his melancholic descriptions of rural childhood loss a poetic quality, and is one of the secrets of their power and truth. For Catherine, freedom from linguistic analysis helped facilitate a spontaneity, an intuitive contact with the creative power in her, of which she was permanently aware.

Years later, the process of discarding any obstacles between the stories in her mind and the written page was made complete. In May 1961, after writing the first fifteen or sixteen of her novels in longhand, she developed 'writer's cramp and a frozen shoulder, and thought my writing days were over'. Tom suggested a way out, which would give her further release from the mechanics of writing. 'It was then I resorted to a tape recorder, which I have used ever since.' Catherine cannot recall which was the first novel to be written in this way, only that *Katie Mulholland* (1967) was definitely spoken, not written down. The era of the 'Grundig Dictator' had begun, the dictating machine, actually a Stenorette, on which all future novels were composed, and which can be seen amongst other effects on permanent exhibition at the South Shields Museum. What it meant was that Catherine had stepped back into the tradition of oral storytelling which had been part of Catherine as a child, when Rose would tell her stories and sing her songs and rhymes that she had heard at her mother's knee long before the Tyneside towns of Jarrow and Shields were established.

'A new world opened up for me,' Catherine recalled. 'Do you

know, really, I think I am a frustrated actress. Because I act every part. I do every bit of the dialogue. This is mostly done when I am sleepless. It might take me up to two o'clock in the morning. And Tom will say, "You're not still at it. For goodness' sake, get yourself to sleep, woman!" And then the following morning I wake up and wonder why I am tired, forgetting that I have lived a number of other people's lives in the night. But I start now and whatever I have thought of last night, I put it down on to tape. It might not be exactly in the same words that I used in the night because my mind at night delivers brilliant answers to questions, but,' she laughs, 'they are very mundane in the morning when I attempt to put them down.'

Struck by the picture of her talking to her characters gathered around her bed in the dead of night, I asked if that wasn't rather unnerving sometimes. 'Only when they start making love to one another,' she said. 'What happens is this. I take two, four or six characters and place them in a certain environment, and it is the environment that affects their characters. That started, I then find the end. I always find the end of the story before I begin it. Not to do so would be like going into a station and asking for a ticket and I'm asked, "Where to?" And if I didn't know, then why was I asking for a ticket? What I do next is to go to the pictures. By this I mean I conjure up every scene and every character in it as if I was looking at a film and I act these characters.'

Writing her stories about the girl from the North who had no da helped Catherine see that she had been 'over-sorry' for herself, made her realise that the bitterness she felt about her early life had constricted her creativity. Now, with a clearer sense of her own identity, her people had come into ever sharper focus. 'There was a mass of people crowding my mind that I knew inside out. These were the people I had moved away from, to put it plainly, didn't want any truck with. Yet there they were, dozens of them, hundreds of them, their characteristics shouting at me.'

As words poured out of her onto the page, sometimes seemingly involuntarily, she became ever more convinced of the spiritual dimension: 'I simply cannot say where all the ideas come from, but I have not finished one book before I am working on another in my subconscious . . . I don't know whether someone up there is supplying me with them. I believe in the subconscious mind. If I'm puzzled I go to sleep and say, well, get on with it. And within a couple of days it's worked out.'

People who knew Catherine at this time spoke of 'a radiance about her'. She was becoming an unstoppable force, for now her purpose was clear. She began to see her people for what they really were: 'the fact that work was their life's blood; their patience in the face of poverty; their perseverance that gave them the will to hang on'. She acknowledged 'their kindness and open-handedness' as well as 'their narrowness and bigotry . . . And the women. Stoics would be a better name to give to the females of that time, my early time, because for most of them along those river banks it was grind in one way or another from Monday morning till Sunday night.'

From this new perspective came fresh insight. She began to see that her people's strength, like hers, was born of suffering, that warmth arose out of the cold hunger of their needs, humour out of the dreariness of their existence, that love blossomed from their seedbed of pain, that a deep-down sensitivity was a facet of their vulnerability to brutal experience and drew them together. A balance of pathos and humour, the antithetical form of her collection of stories, which years later became the Mary Ann series of novels, was intuited out of the same perception of the way the world worked.

Her first novel, *Kate Hannigan,* is a triumph of compassion over bitterness on Catherine's road to recovery because Kate Hannigan herself, who is above all a sympathetic character, was inspired by a side of Catherine's mother – an element which she had first intuited as a little girl of six whirling around a lamppost on a rope in William Black Street, but an element buried ever since under a welter of hate. Since returning to The Hurst, Catherine had received letters twice a week from Kate, but she had rarely replied, believing she was finished with Kate, this woman who had conceived her in selfish pleasure, and, as she saw it, was responsible for the state of mind in which she now found herself. Catherine may not have forgiven Kate, but she had begun to understand her. Kate Hannigan represents Catherine's first literary contact with something fundamental in the make-up of her mother's character, a facet of her spirit which she had glimpsed occasionally as a child and inspires Kate Hannigan and many other of her characters too.

The realism on which Catherine was insisting did not extend to an injection of Kate's real character in the novels. Kate Hannigan may seem to us to be Kate Fawcett because her illegitimate daughter, Annie, seems to be Catherine, doing all sorts of things that we know Catherine did when she was a child, and her parents Tim and Sarah seem to be John and Rose, but in fact there is no character in any of the novels that is Kate, either as Catherine saw her mother or as others saw her. The psychological trick that Catherine pulled – quite possibly out of necessity, as she couldn't yet face her mother as she was – was not to write about her as a person, or even any longer to consider her as such in real life, but to transform her into a symbol.

We have all these facts in the novels, particularly in the early ones, facts which equate to facts of Catherine's childhood, and so we imagine that all she is doing is giving us her childhood in readable story form. But these facts – the fetching of the beer, the going to the pawn, all the things in the novels which are true to life – are events in a mythology. Catherine's purpose in gathering them together is not to write autobiography, any more than the purpose of Greek myth is to chart the political and religious history of the Aegean. The word 'myth' is a confusion in the modern world, because many have lost sight of its meaning. 'Mythic' is used too often to mean something which we have come to believe that is not true. Whereas, the very mark of myth is that it is true in a deeper sense than when I tell the truth, it is true in the sense that an arrow runs true.

A myth is a poetic representation, an image that gets to the heart of what, in this case, Catherine's Tyneside is all about. More truly than any history can, myths embody who we are. Losing sight of the myths at the core of our nature, as T. S. Eliot warned the Western world in *The Waste Land* it had done, is to lose touch with our authenticity.

It is in this sense that although Catherine's early novels deal with her personal history, their purpose is not to record events like documentary, but to unearth the image of Northern culture 'that comes from way back and threads the people of this particular area,' as Catherine once put it. And this is most clearly seen in the image the novels give us of Kate, who embodies the archetypal spirit of the North.

Kate appears in many of the novels, as she does in the first novel as Kate Hannigan, not dishing out sweets at the door in exchange for potato peelings, as Winnie remembers her, nor as the harridan Catherine remembers, forcing her daughter to suffer the indignity of taking John's trousers to the pawn, but as a symbol of something deep in the subconscious of Tyneside people, as 'a symbol of earth, of home, of blood, of race . . . of the deepest ground from which life emerges and to which it returns'.

In the first novel, Rodney Prince sees this clearly in Kate Hannigan. It is why he loves her. He realises that what he sees in her has to do with the reason why he has decided to come and work among the Tyneside poor. When finally he and Kate come together it is a celebration of that same something.

There is very often a figure in the novels who performs this function, a woman in touch with the spirit of Tyneside – every instinctual female figure (often, but not always, called Kate) from Kate Hannigan through Lally Briggs in *Pure as the Lily* (a sheer expression of 'wisdom without learning', the very hallmark of working-class culture) up to Kate Makepeace in *Dinner of Herbs* (a personification of the harsh lead-mining Northumberland countryside, out of which Catherine's people came).

On the face of it, it is extraordinary that Catherine should choose the woman she claimed she hated more than any other, and whom she blamed for the agonies of her mental breakdown, to put at the fulcrum of her books in this way. But Kate was the obvious candidate. She was Catherine's mother, she was the root of Catherine's problems and her needs.

What's more, Kate had always signified something special in this way. Catherine would remember the moments when her mother seemed to have a line into the spirit of East Jarrow, like the time when, quite sober, Kate had spontaneously seized Catherine's hand and run along the bank of the Tyne, chasing the clouds as they scudded over the moon, before collapsing into her daughter's arms, laughing fit to burst, or when Kate and other women of the New Buildings would dress up as men and go beating the bounds, as had been done on the Tyne since time immemorial.

Kate's instinctual nature meant that she was her environment in a way that Catherine, with all her desire to uproot, could never be. This instinctual, natural self was not lost to Kate, as it was to so many in the process of civilisation, and it is what gave her 'wisdom without learning'.

In Kate the lines of communication were open to poetic truth in a way they never were to the daughter, and perhaps there lay Catherine's real, subconscious regret of the mix-up that stole her mother from her at birth. With the enforced separation she was cut off from her true fount of inspiration.

Now, following her breakdown, Catherine's need was to write and to get back to the fount. As for Jimmy in *Pure as the Lily* – her need went beyond the desires of the torturous days of childhood, beyond the rejections that had been heaped on her and she had heaped on others, beyond the self-recrimination, beyond this past life into something only dimly comprehended, but well-deep, and her birthright. Jimmy found the answer in instinctual, unaffected Lally. Henceforth, there wouldn't be a day or a night when Jimmy and Lally were apart, and now the same would be true, in an imaginative sense, of Catherine and Kate.

Catherine was coming to terms with the fact that Kate belonged to the East Jarrow community in a way that she never had. When she thought of Kate, now that she was back home and Catherine was renewing her acquaintance imaginatively with people she had not seen for twenty years, it seemed that her mother embodied the spirit of her community, and Catherine knew that she needed to draw on that. She needed to come home, to the home that Kate knew, to the mother she had always refused to know.

If she hadn't done so, she would never have come to write the novels that she did. Years later, she would acknowledge to Tyne Tees Television the debt that she owed her mother in this, giving her mother credit for that side of her that enabled her to write and to be 'a little bit of a poet'. This seemed like an amazing advance, certainly it was for the fiction, but to consider that she might owe her mother a debt, when she had always imagined that her talents sprang from her 'gentleman' father, was an extraordinary turnaround.

Perhaps Catherine's awareness that she lacked this intuitional, loving aspect of Kate, which time and again resolves fractured lives in the novels, did lie among the roots of the hate she felt for her. Certainly, envy is often a key emotion. But what did it matter now, for Catherine had the imagination to deliver it to her readers. In that sense she enabled a partnership between mother and daughter in her fiction that had not been possible in real life. They came together in a way they never had before.

The long, torturous path to completion of her autobiography, *Our Kate*, which went through many manuscript versions over many years before seeing publication, is the path to understanding the myth that she was creating. Dr Manuel Anderson, who was then Consultant Physician at the Ingham Infirmary in South

Shields, was witness to this process of imaginative recreation, or mythologising, of Kate's world: 'It must have been in 1952 that I invited Catherine to give the presidential address to the Writers' Circle in Shields and so began the habit of Tom and Kitty staying with us whenever they were in the area. She wanted to try her speech out on us first. She had only a few notes, a list of dates on a tiny piece of paper and she delivered it fluently, an emotive piece about her early life, ending with the words, "Thank you Kate for giving me life." All three of us were in tears, and the following day the audience at the Town Hall were also in tears. She then returned to our home and repeated it verbatim (!) into a tape recorder.'

Dr Anderson and his wife Rita and Catherine – all three of them were in tears. So important did her mythology of the North become to Catherine that she struck off anybody who didn't respond to it. When Tom's parents were made to listen to the tape as visitors to The Hurst, 'They listened to it all through, sitting next to one another on the couch – that is what Catherine told me,' Dr Anderson said to me, 'but they couldn't see it – eyes down, blank expressions.' They were not moved at all. Pretty soon, they were no longer on The Hurst invitation list.

How essential Catherine's developing mythology was in the creative process was shown when she discovered that she couldn't write powerfully outside it. She had been walking along the London Road in St Leonards when a woman approached her, a county type dressed in 'tweeds, brogues, a Henry Heath hat and a collar and tie'. She was pointing her finger at Catherine as she marched towards her. Catherine was startled, but convinced herself that the woman must be pointing at someone behind her. The woman came to a halt – 'her finger still pointing' – and relieved Catherine of any doubt as to whom she was after, with an 'Ah! Mrs Cookson! The regional writer!' In her high-falutin voice, she informed her that she had read her books and demanded to know why she insisted on writing about that awful Tyneside, when here, on her doorstep, was a far more attractive proposition.

Typically, Catherine took it as a challenge and actually set about tackling Hastings, searching for its soul among the few fishermen left from older days, people she felt might lead her to the spirit of the place. Fishing had been the traditional industry of the town, but it had long expired. In the mid-seventeenth century 239 out of 280 heads of Hastings households were involved in it. But from the 1830s, with the end of the smuggling boom, and with increasing competition from mainly French fishing boats, the place began its slide into tourism. Catherine found she couldn't write about it with any strength at all.

Within the context of her mythology of the North-East, Catherine's female characters emerged as 'strong, they always come through,' but there is much more to them than that. There is sensuality and womanliness and a generic potential which puts them in charge of her fictional world. Something of this potential has to do with fertility – mammiferous womankind, like Kathie McQueen, with her 'huge breasts', or the buxom Fanny McBride. In *Colour Blind* the young cripple Tony marvels at the 'great cones of flesh hanging out from open blouses as the women sat on their front doorsteps suckling their babies'. In Catherine's fictional world, fruitful, fertile, intuitive women coexist with physically tough, sometimes impotent men whose work is largely uninspirational. The few male artists who do appear are either exploiting dark images of Tyneside for their own gain or drawing on women in some way, usually emotionally. The women, on the other hand, are weavers of the emotional web of life, in touch with its source and not dependent on men in the same way. In the majority of the novels we have a clear sense of men's dependency on women, of the fact that, despite the male, macho myth of the North, the women are in control. Ego is a male problem, a form of hypocrisy which dulls intuition, twists and obscures truth, and is an expression of impotence. Clergyman Donald Rouse's behaviour in *The Garment* is a study in this.

At the root of his wife Grace's emotional problems, which drive her to a nervous breakdown, is Donald's ego. It dominates her life. First, it prevents him admitting to Grace that he is sexually impotent (his name – Rouse – is wonderfully ironic), his weird interpretation of sex carrying bogus religious connotations which keep intercourse at bay. Then it allows him to convince himself that he has achieved acts of union sufficient to explain the appearance of his wife's first two children (by farm worker Andrew MacIntyre, into whose arms Donald's ego has driven her). Finally, on the third occasion that Grace is made pregnant by MacIntyre, when there appears to be no possible excuse for Donald's deceiving himself into believing he is the child's father, Grace revels momentarily in the infusion of honesty and truth into the scene. But even then Donald manages to cast a pall of deceit over their lives, this time from the pulpit. Truth in the novel is confined within the terrors of Grace's breakdown, shut away from the world as she herself is when the asylum gates close upon her.

Catherine has written of the potential in a relationship between a strong woman and a man who is prepared to set himself free of his ego. But she is not a feminist. 'I do not agree with the way the movement tries to denigrate men, to take their manliness away,' she once told me; she likes working with men, though she won't have male bosses. Nor does she glorify women. In *Bill Bailey* (1986) we read that 'men can be vile and cruel but they don't create as much harm as women who are sweet and poisonous', and Bailey's down-to-earth personality and chipper sense of humour overcome cold, ruthless Eva Brown (it takes a careful reading of the novel to connect her name with appropriate Hitleresque images as it is never spelt out in full, both names together, and the surname is only mentioned once). Again, in *A Dinner of Herbs*, Kate Makepeace tells us that all females are blood-thirsty: 'It is as old as the hills . . . where the female of the animals are concerned, they are more fierce than the male. It's the protective instinct in them, I think.'

We see this protective instinct in *The Invisible Cord* (1975). Molly McCabe is a splendidly ebullient character in the mould of Fanny McBride. Her dim son, Georgie, makes seventeen-year-old Annie Cooper pregnant. Their offspring, Terence (known as Rance), kills his own father brutally and becomes involved in pushing drugs. But motherly instinct – the 'invisible cord' which joins Annie to Rance – prevents her from turning him in. Again, in *Fenwick Houses* there is a sense of the aberrant potential of the instinctual, mythic Tyneside mother figure in Phyllis Dowling's suckling of her son, Don, another psychopath, long after he is able to feed himself.

The powerful feminine principle encompassing love and hate, compassion and cruelty, fruitfulness and destruction, on which Catherine draws for women characters as diverse as Fanny McBride, Mary Walton (in *Pure as the Lily*) and Mary's mother, Alice, who, as I said earlier, brings about the disfigurement of her daughter's lover, the burning alive of her daughter-in-law and the early death through drinking of her son, can be found crystallised in the poet Robert Graves's grammar of poetic myth, *The White Goddess*.

His Goddess is the ultimate creative and procreative force, embodying all things and their opposites in the name of truth – kindness and cruelty, beauty and terror, life and death – both sides of Mother Nature, and a rather different concept from the male Christian God, who is all-good and, as a statement of Nature, required the Devil for completeness.

Graves presents the Goddess as the feminine principle which inspires the true Muse poet. As an object of worship, he traces her back to a Sumerian matriarchal civilisation around 8,000 BC, when the idea of a procreative male divinity was patently absurd. She occurs in ancient myth under many guises, but her fundamental association is with the goddess Ariadne, the daughter (or younger self) of the ancient Cretan moon goddess, Pasiphae – which brings us back to Kate Fawcett and those strange moments of imaginative release, moon-riding with her daughter along the Slack bank, and the 'primitive weirdness' which Catherine associated with her mother as a child, when suddenly Kate and her friends would dress up in men's clothes and dance crazily through the streets.

Three novels in which Catherine uses the moon as a symbol of imaginative or creative or supernatural power, two of them explicitly connecting it with artistic inspiration, are *The Whip*, *The Moth* and *A Dinner of Herbs*. In *The Whip* Emma Molinero's artistry with whips and knives has its roots in the supernatural. She has a penchant for making night sorties to practise her art, and one night, while throwing her knives against an oak tree in the cold, silver light of a full moon, her special communion with her muse is disturbed by Peggy McFarlane and her illicit lover, a farmer called Hudson. Peggy rises out of the shadows screaming, and it is weird, 'unearthly . . . like someone coming out of the grave'. Peggy describes Emma as a devil with horns and black from head to toe, and claims that her devil's dagger just missed her heart. The scene ends in chaos with the clouds closing over the moon.

Throughout this novel Emma is persecuted, as Catherine was, by the 'something' that set her apart from her playmates and which marks her out as an artist. In her disturbing world of sexual repression and sadistic violence, Emma dictates messages to the subconscious drives of the other characters, arousing envy and resulting in her own exploitation. On the farm she is worked like a horse and her oppressors seem to want to break her spirit as if it were the free spirit of a wild horse, to make her one of them. They try to dominate her, abuse her, even whip her as they would a horse, this creature with a sixth, intuitive sense.

The horse is another symbol of creative inspiration. Hamilton is the name Maisie Carter gives to the horse which appears in her imagination in the novel of the same name, and which later inspires her to write novels. It first appears to Maisie after her mother's violent attack on her, mentioned earlier. It is a black horse with a richly flowing name and a shiny coat like a seal's; it carries a white spot on its nose and has white feet. Catherine had come into contact with horses nearly half a century before the novel was published. Around the time she was taking fencing lessons she had also taken to visiting a stables four or five miles out of Hastings, near Rye. Initially she had run into a bit of trouble with her riding kit. She had answered an advertisement offering for sale a pair of secondhand riding boots. They turned out to be a size too small, but she managed to squeeze her feet into them. When she sent her measurements to a tailor's to make up her riding breeches, they came back many sizes too large. Eventually she sorted it all out and she and her horse came together. She began to enjoy their walks along the cliffs, only one section of the course causing any difficulty. On the way home, horse and rider had to negotiate a gap in a hedge so narrow that Catherine had to take her feet out of the stirrups. Once through the gap, there was a steep descent to the stables, and Catherine would feel the horse tremble in anticipation of the canter home. On one occasion she dared to ride bareback. Horse and rider were as one until Catherine attempted to dismount, threw the wrong leg over the horse's back, overbalanced and fell backwards into a trough of silage.

If you accept that the horse is a symbol of creative potential – which it certainly is for Maisie and elsewhere in literature, myth and psychoanalysis, where it symbolises the 'voice of nature' with which artists, healers and gurus make contact and which rational man has tried to dominate and exploit throughout history – then there are some wonderful allusions to Catherine's struggles to find intuitive contact with her muse in this story of her relationship with her horse. The horse also brings us back to the moon, because the original horse goddess, Rhiannon, who 'becomes horse' in one of the legendary stories of the *Mabinogion*, and is the forerunner in myth of the Roman horse goddess Epona, is but another 'self' of the inspirational moon goddess.

The Moth (1986) is, to my mind, Catherine's best novel in her later period of writing. Readers, or viewers of its television adaptation, will recall that twenty-four-year-old Robert Bradley, on his first Sunday in the rural hamlet of Lamesley, trespasses on to the Thorman estate near Foreshaw House. It is already dark when he comes upon the estate and sees how wild and rundown it has become. But then a shaft of moonlight catches his eye and lures him in beyond the dilapidated boundary fencing. Once inside, he comes to a lake, and the sublimity of the scene – the still water, the clear night sky and the moon riding high, shining deep into the water – holds him spellbound. He is about to leave when he is suddenly surprised by what looks like a large moth apparently floating towards him through the air from a belt of trees. Mingled with Robert's feeling of wonder is fear, and even as the form is illuminated he remains uncertain whether it is human. Not until the creature comes close does he notice that it is propelled forward by feet and that its supposed wings are the folds of a cape held outwards by human arms.

The hooded figure, a girl, is unutterably impressive. Besides her femininity (dark sweeping eyelashes, oval eyes, pale skin and full but thin-lipped mouth) he senses a strange ethereal quality which defies analysis and possesses him completely. The vision speaks. For a moment he is awed, but she puts him at his ease and he learns that she has a sister called Agnes and that her parents own Foreshaw House. The contrast between Robert's earlier supernatural apprehension and the mundanity of this exchange of information brings to his mind the possibility that the girl (she tells him her name is Millie) is touched in the head. Later we learn that Millie's great-aunt was in and out of asylums. In *The Whip* there is this same connection between artistic inspiration and madness – moon-struck Emma is worried that if she is caught throwing her knives she will be tied up in chains and thrown into the madhouse. And we have already seen how Catherine's breakdown influenced her imaginative perceptions. However, Millie is not mad. She has come out of the little house of her imagination for a while, and because Robert has never found the way into his, it troubles him.

Millie talks to Robert of her love for the moon, and as she does so it disappears from view, leaving only its reflection in the lake, apparently unsourced. She gives the moon mythic status: it has the power of alchemy. He finds what she says strange but at the same time alluringly beautiful. Then she makes physical contact with him: she takes his hand. He finds himself shaking, but she chats to him so normally that he doesn't draw back. She even reassures him that she isn't mad. She is there because the moon is there; when the moon comes out she comes out too. Millie has him in the palm of her hand. It is a masterly performance.

It is Millie, of course, who will draw Robert to his destiny, luring him to work at Foreshaw and inspiring him as he learns to transcend the barriers of the class system of maids and mistresses, manservants and masters, which characterised Edwardian England. Catherine's mainstream themes, explored in the early novels, are all here. But what is new is contained in the dreamlike sequence which introduces Robert to Foreshaw Park and his life's destiny, and is Catherine's recognition, symbolically in the image of the moon, of the power which guides her.

The fourth novel to suggest a supernatural element in what drives Catherine to write, and one which at the same time presents the writer as transformer of the cruel side of her 'goddess inspiration', is *A Dinner of Herbs*, again one of her later novels. The title comes from Proverbs xv, 17: 'Better is a dinner of herbs where love is, than a stalled ox and hatred therewith.' *A Dinner of Herbs* is a *tour de force*. In more than 250,000 words, characters and generations come and go, but pace and interest never flag. Throughout, the hatred which clawed Catherine down into the depths of breakdown simmers beneath the surface. It is part of the landscape of her characters' lives, occasionally erupting in terrible violence. At the centre of the novel is Kate Makepeace, one of a long line of herbalists. Thick-set, of medium height, with dark wisps of hair and wrinkled skin, Kate is in her late sixties when the novel opens, but strong of character and wise of mind, a kind of personification of the land in which she dwells – hard, unyielding Northumberland lead-mining country, but 'knowing' of all things which have marked it since creation.

Roddy Greenbank is brought to Kate by his father Peter, whose wife has died. Kate agrees to keep an eye on him and 'tell him the paths that lead straight in his mind, and where health is to be got from the ground'. Kate becomes a touchstone in the lives of Roddy, his friend Mary Ellen, and a boy called Hal, whose father Roystan stands accused of robbery and who is, with Peter, first to suffer at the hands of the Bannamans, for whom hatred will be seen to be an inherited trait.

We first meet Kate as she emerges from the shadows, a witch-like creature, strange, magical. Peter tells us that Kate 'was always a good one with the moon,' and he and Roddy watch as the moon comes out from behind the 'black skirts' of the clouds and washes itself in the water. Peter, who once lived and worked here, has watched the moon 'riding alongside us many a night, skipping over the waves'. Later, smelters say that it is as well to keep on the right side of Kate or you'll likely get boils on your neck. Jed Pierce, who chases five-year-old Mary Ellen, develops a huge carbuncle on his backside after a warning from Kate that if he continues to harass her he'll not be able to sit down. 'She had powers . . . it was well to keep in with witches.' This is the classic image of the witch which, in legend, is embodied in Cerridwen, the creature who, according to a recipe contained in the twelfth-century romance *The Vergil of Toledo*, boils up a cauldron of inspiration and knowledge and leaves it to simmer for a year and a day, adding to it magical herbs gathered at the correct planetary hours. She makes a boy – Gwion – stir the brew and one day three drops fly out and land on Gwion's finger. At once he understands the nature and meaning of all things past, present and future. Realising what has happened, the witch Cerridwen pursues Gwion, translating herself from screaming hag first into a greyhound, then an otter, a hawk and finally a black hen.

As *A Dinner of Herbs* gets under way, however, we see fewer intimations of the witch in Kate and the Earth Mother comes to the fore. She becomes all-love, in touch with bountiful, healing Nature, and Mary Ellen, Roddy and Hal all derive their strength from her, its purpose to transform the destructive hatred of the Bannamans. Associations with both sides of Catherine's awesome inspiration, and her resolving role as a writer, are clear.

One special moment with Kate Fawcett, which I have left until now to describe because of its relevance to the character, as well as the source, of Catherine's inspiration, concerns Kate's favourite song, 'Thora'. This song, you will recall, was her 'party piece', enacted at family gatherings at number 10. Aunt Mary and Uncle Alec would be there, 'Mary at her disdainful best'. Also there would be Kate's Aunt Maggie Hindes and her son Jimmy. Catherine would die with shame and disgust as her drunken mother strained to hit the top notes, 'her head well back, that slack lower lip of hers wobbling'.

But one day she and Kate were sitting silently in the kitchen, working on a clippy mat on a weaving frame which stood between them, and in a very soft, quiet voice, the firelight playing on her face, Kate began a rendering of 'Thora' which had an utterly different effect upon her daughter. 'The song, like Kate, was beautiful that day,' and it brought tears to Catherine's eyes. 'I wonder now,' Catherine says, 'whether her "Thora" was speaking out about her kind of pain.' On this occasion Kate was not drunk, nor was she playing to an audience; she was sharing with her daughter a vision of her promised land. The song is worth printing in full in order to appreciate what that meant:

I stand in a land of roses,
But I dream of a land of snow,
Where you and I were happy
In years of long ago.
Nightingales in the branches,
Stars in the magic skies,
But I only hear you singing,
I only see your eyes.
I only hear you singing,
I only see your eyes.
Come, come! Come! to me Thora,
Come once again and be
Child of my dreams,
Light of my life,
Angel of love to me –

I stand again in the Northland
But in silence and in shame.
Your grave is my only landmark
And men have forgotten my name.
'Tis a tale that is pure and older
Than any the sages tell.
I loved you in life too little,
I love you in death too well.
Speak, speak, speak to me Thora,
Speak from your heaven to me.
Child of my dreams,
Love of my life,
Hope of my world to be!

'Thora' is one of the songs Catherine sings on the tape which, as I have already mentioned, was issued towards the end of 1996. It is sung from the heart, with power and with an inconsolable longing, as if she would be at one with her mother in her mythic snow-covered land of the North, with its stars and magic skies.

I had read the lyrics before, but I did not know the tune and it was only when Catherine insisted I order a copy of the recording and I heard it sung in that pressing, urgent way of hers that its significance dawned. Immediately I was reminded of a book I had read years before, *Surprised by Joy* by C. S. Lewis. What came to mind was Lewis's description of a particular 'moment of joy' in his childhood. Coincidentally, he, like Catherine, was a fan of Longfellow, and it was while Lewis was idly turning the pages of Longfellow's 'Saga of King Olaf' that he came across his translation of a poem by the nineteenth-century Swedish poet Esaias Tegner, which seemed to the boy to encapsulate the strange spirit of Northernness which the heroic saga was all about.

'Instantly I was uplifted into huge regions of Northern sky,' Lewis wrote. 'I desired with almost sickening intensity something never to be described.' Years later, when he saw one of Arthur Rackham's illustrations in *Siegfried and the Twilight of the Gods*, Lewis recalled 'the stab, the pang' of pleasure-pain that the moment gave him. 'Pure "Northernness" engulfed me,' he wrote, 'a vision of huge, clear spaces hanging above the Atlantic in the endless twilight of Northern summer, remoteness, severity.'

His joy is awe-inspiring, and the poetic image which inspired his strange pleasure-pain (so similar, I felt, to that implicit in Catherine's rendering of Kate's song, which had cried out her mother's pain and longing) is the very same which all-knowing Gwion gives us of a distant land where countless souls await resurrection in the Fifth Age of the World when Christ will release them. It is an image of the magical, snow-covered grounds of the remote Castle of Arianrhod in the Corona Borealis, a constellation in the northern skies, and the stronghold, no less, of Robert Graves's Moon Goddess of poetic inspiration.

This heroic and yet tragic image of Northernness, yearning for resurrection, seems to encapsulate that element in Northern culture 'that comes from far back and threads the people of this particular area,' which Catherine unearths in her novels. She feels it in the voices and emotions of her characters as they speak to her, but it is rooted in Kate, who embodies both the cruel and beautiful aspects of the powerful feminine principle which inspires Catherine's work. It was essential that Catherine was able to come to terms with being part of her mother, because in the process she found her muse. She had no need to look for the groundswell of character in myth and weave it into her novels. Once she had acknowledged her true identity and her creative channels were freed, she had a direct line to it through kinship with Kate, the woman who, as Catherine confirms in the dedication to her first novel, 'found her expression through me'.

A trip Catherine made to the North in 1952 is worth relating because it gave her unexpected contact with this heroic, tragic spirit of a people awaiting transformation. She was visiting her coal-mining cousins in Birtley and had upset them with remarks about the price of coal in the South. Her granda, quick to dismiss anyone else's achievement, had always scorned miners. He 'used to say that all pitmen hewed more coal at the corner end, or at their games of quoits, and pitch and toss, than they ever did down the mine,' and tongue-in-cheek she had taken his part. 'The result of our verbal battle was that they challenged me to go down the mine.' Terrified at the prospect, she was led to the coalface by cousin Peter, who was a deputy at the Betty pit in Birtley.

In *Maggie Rowan* she gives her experience to Ann Rowan, who is challenged by sister Maggie to go down the pit and face up to her fear for husband David Taggart's safety, and also because Maggie hates her sister, who 'hasn't the guts of a chicken'. Like old John, Maggie thinks of all pitmen with scorn, 'as bigoted, ignorant clods, hewing more coal at the corner ends, in the bars or on the allotments than they did down the pit'. Restless and bitter, plain girl Maggie Rowan is a reject. No one believes that she could have normal desires. She is starved of love. But her unattractiveness clouds the real issue, which has to do with confusion over her identity. She knows she is different, but until she learns that she is not Nellie Rowan's daughter she can't begin to understand why. So she hits back at her people, rejecting their bovine existence, their stupid and coarse boisterousness and humour, while all the time putting her earnings carefully away, waiting for the day she can be shot of the lot of them and get herself a place on Brampton Hill, where the lights shine like stars in the sky. The relevant issue here is not just Maggie's identity but that of the mining community. The pit is the underworld of myth, 'the darkness and silence of the eternity of the damned'.

Catherine is down there for three hours with the miners, and when she emerges she embraces the daylight and feels ready to pin a medal on every man jack of them. For her, as for Ann, the experience has been nervewracking, but it has brought revelation too. Like Maggie, whose experience informs her that 'the pit is like me in some ways, or I'm like it, deep and dark, always clutching at something to lighten the darkness,' Catherine is inspired by her experience to write a novel which apprehends 'the deep, black source from whence all these little contents of lives are drawn'. The phrase is D. H. Lawrence's, but it might as well have been Catherine's.

There are many reasons why the perception of Catherine's work as romance is misplaced – for example, the richness of her narrative, the issues involved in it and the characters who drive it. But it is this inspirational contact with the very essence of environment and character which lifts her work out of any category, romance included, and is the fundamental secret of her mass popularity. She had tapped into the collective unconscious of her people and, thence, into primitive drives of her personal unconscious, too.

The cold violence and cruelty in many of her novels are an essential part of this vision and we should not be surprised or shocked at Catherine's honest but apparently damning claim (which is made in all seriousness) that she is capable of doing absolutely anything that she gives her characters to do. Once, when her mother was staying at The Hurst, she considered having Tom tie her to the bed for fear that she would not be able to restrain herself from walking across the landing in the night and murdering Kate while she slept. Catherine is part of what inspires her, as well as its instrument – a fact which has an unsettling effect even on her husband when she is writing. 'I have to shake my head when I watch her working,' Tom has written, 'the words just come out of her mouth . . . you watch this gift materialise.'

Like the poet John Clare, her inspiration is food and drink to her, but it is not an easy relationship. Clare himself had dreams about his goddess, his 'guardian spirit' as he called her, a 'soul-searching beauty . . . a woman deity [who] gave the sublimist conceptions of beauty to my imagination', identifying her with his lost childhood love, Mary Joyce, his 'simple Enchantress', 'my witching love', 'the Muse of every song I write'. But when his goddess inspiration showed Clare her other side, of cold violence and cruelty, which he describes in his poem, 'The Nightmare' – 'Huge circles lost to eyes, and rotten hulls/Raised with dread groans from the dread "place of skulls" ' – he couldn't assimilate it and began his descent into insanity, never to recover. Catherine made her recovery from a similar descent and the richness of her work is living proof both of that descent and of her return.

It isn't easy being at the beck and call of this inspirational drive, and there have been times when, far from deriving satisfaction from it, she longed for relief from it. 'I can honestly say that I don't get any real satisfaction from any of them. It is very odd. The only thing I get satisfaction from is the urgent desire to write and write and write. I see my brain as an old machine that requires daily oiling and the only way I can keep it going is to oil it with words.' During a particularly desperate period she too had a dream. She had been bleeding badly and had reached rock bottom, and made the decision to give up writing. 'I went to this place,' she told me a decade ago, 'I went to this place and I said to whatever was there that I am tired and that I just want to let go. But as I said it I thought, Why do I ask? Because I knew that I would not get the answer that I want, and this voice said to me, "You are going against your nature. All right, if you give up, you'll give up and you'll go, you'll go very quickly, because it isn't your nature to give up . . ." And this voice went for me, it said, "Tomorrow morning get out of this bed. No matter what you feel like, get out of this bed. Start checking what you have written, get on to that tape."

'And I said, "But I'm too ill to get up."

'And this voice said, "We know how ill you are, but you tell Tom of your decision."

' "But I haven't made a decision," I said.

' "But you have . . ."

'And this went on for an hour.

'The next morning I told Tom exactly what had happened. I told him the exact words because it was still so fresh . . . I could hardly stand on my feet, but I got up and I stayed up for half a day, and when I got back into bed – I always have my tape recorder beside me, but it had been three months since I had finished that part of the story and I had forgotten where I was – and I mumbled into this thing, "Sarah, I'm not sure where I was in this story, but start a new chapter. I know what has to happen. Start a new chapter." And from then it went on . . .'

Back in 1950, when she was faced by her publishers with rejection of her second novel, *Annie Hannigan* – 'This, in my opinion, was even better than *Kate Hannigan*' – she got a sharp taste of the power of inspiration. 'I got a letter from Murray Thompson [her publisher] to say that they would take this book but it wasn't as good, in their opinion, as the first. They would do what they could with it. That inflamed me, those words. I know now why there were doubts about it because I was still expressing my feelings about the Catholic Church. What was more, I was also going into the mind of a young man, thinking about his sex life and thoughts concerning it. Hearing it now, his thoughts were quite poetic, but Mr Thompson must have thought they were a bit way out. That is the only thing that I can think made him question the book.

'Anyway, I remember crying my eyes out and getting on the phone and saying, "I won't have it accepted on those conditions. Send it back!" I think it was one of the bravest things an author has ever done, specially when starting out as ignorant as I was of how difficult it was to get a book published. I can see myself coming out of the little cubbyhole under the stairs where the phone was and going into the drawing room. I was terribly upset, not only that I was not going to let them publish the book, but I knew that I hadn't another story in my mind. There was me, who was never without an idea, never without a story to tell to someone, yet my mind was utterly blank. I thought I was finished. I sat in the cold, icy drawing room. I remember Tom had just gone to school. There was no one to talk to. I tried to think of what I would do next, but my mind was an utter blank. Never before that, and definitely never since, has my mind known such a void. I felt I had nothing more to say, I had nothing more to talk about. I had no more tales to tell. And then I became angry inside. Why, why, now that I had written those two books, was I empty of an idea for a story – or for anything else, for that matter?

'Why I did next what I did, I will never know. But quite suddenly, and this might sound quite sentimental and dramatic, I threw my head back and looked up at the ceiling – don't forget that at this point I had rejected God, oh, definitely – God with the Catholic Church had been thrown out of the window. And I'd said so openly. I had yelled at God that I was finished with belief in the great fable that his followers had established and I would fear no more – brave words when I was full of fear about everything . . . Anyway, as I said, I threw my head back and looked up at the ceiling and cried aloud, "If there's anything there, give me a story!" Now, was there anything more senti-mental or highly dramatic than that? . . . and stupid!

'Believe this or not, I sat back in the chair and there came to me, within the following hour when I was almost frozen stiff with cold, the whole story of *The Fifteen Streets*, right from the opening to the very last words. Every character, every incident and definitely the background. It was all there. I won't say I couldn't believe it. I just accepted it. I knew here was a complete story and I must get it down straight away. I went from there into the dining room, where I usually did my writing on the table, and with my frozen fingers I wrote the title, "The Fifteen Streets". From that moment until months later when I finished that story, I can say with truth I never altered a character, an incident, or anything else in the whole plan. I worked on it practically night and day. I worked on it through bleedings and flu and desperate tiredness, but I got everything down as it had been given to me when I asked for it on that particular morning.

'Strange to say, that book is alive today and has started the career of many actors. This very week it has been performed in a little village hall, one of many village halls that has produced it as a play. I had to smile when one day I received a cheque for one pound two and something which was the profit from a show of *The Fifteen Streets*.

'Well, that mightn't have been a miracle, but it came from somewhere, from some spirit deep within me, that is below the subconscious. Perhaps it was the first time that I recognised that I had a spirit that was an individual thing, not connected with any doctrine. It came from somewhere, but certainly not from the religious picture of the Omnipotent.

'I do believe that this same spirit is in every one of us; it is how we use it that matters. But you have to be able to recognise it first.'

I once put it to Catherine that her skill as a storyteller was in healing the fractured lives of her characters. In reply, Catherine told me the story about her return trip to England after visiting her lesbian friend in France in the 1930s. 'When I was returning from France, I was so thankful to be going home that I lay back in the carriage and closed my eyes. Suddenly I felt a hand on my knee. I thought, Oh no!' She had just escaped the unwanted attentions of her French lady and now she was on her way home, sitting in the railway carriage, minding her own business, and there was a hand on her knee. Catherine opened her eyes to see a woman, a stranger, leaning towards her. The woman said, 'You know, you could be a healer.' That was all Catherine needed. She stood up, grabbed her bag and travelled the whole way home standing in the corridor of the train.

Thinking of the feminine principle, the polarity between the 'good' and the 'bad' woman, the 'healer' and the 'destroyer', I asked whether, on reflection, the woman could have been right. She then told me that on a handful of occasions she had proven it, 'but I was afraid of it'. There were instances at home with Tom. He had had a pain in his hand. 'He couldn't play the piano, he had tried all kinds of things, but nothing worked.' She had taken Tom's hand into hers and then placed her other hand upon it. Her fingers had moved over it, not consciously in any particular way. She had done it because she remembered that years before her cat, Tigger, had been in pain and she had done something similar, and the animal had seemed to recover. She had drawn no conclusions whatever from this, but, when all else failed, had slipped into doing the same with Tom without thinking, and it had worked. She found, too, that she had the ability to put Tom to sleep for hours when he was suffering a migraine. Then one night, when she and Tom were living near Hexham, Catherine's solicitor and his wife had a breakdown in their car. The wife was brought to their house in a terrible state, while the solicitor waited by the road for the AA to arrive. Somehow Catherine got the woman under control and, using the same technique she had used on Tom, put her to sleep on the sofa. Hours later, when the solicitor returned, he couldn't wake his wife up. No one could. For some time all attempts failed. Catherine decided never to try such a thing again.

Chapter Nine

Resolution

The period between Catherine's return to The Hurst in 1945, following her discharge after six weeks from St Mary's psychiatric hospital in Burghill, and the end of 1946, when she embarked upon *Kate Hannigan*, was of inestimable importance. In this period she performed the painful psychological surgery which enabled her to go to work on the environment in which her characters subsist and act out their dramas.

However, although it would be a neat conclusion to say that writing *Kate Hannigan* quelled her mental anguish, it did not. Catherine became herself when writing. But not until the early 1960s, after her first twelve novels had been published and the first two films of her work had been released, did she begin to feel more than intermittent relief mentally outside the safe house in which she worked. Nevertheless, what it took to clear the way for *Kate Hannigan* – which amounted to a complete return to self, a dependence on nothing and no one other than herself, and the spiritual/inspirational release which attended this – was the first step along the path to that recovery.

More important to her recovery initially was a series of broadcasts that she gave on BBC Radio's *Woman's Hour*, the first two of which took place before publication of *Kate Hannigan*, a series of programmes during which she 'came out' about her breakdown and was astonished at the audience feedback she received. Off her own bat she contacted the programme and suggested a first broadcast about learning to draw. Entitled, 'I Learned to Draw at Thirty', it went out in 1949, the same year that Macdonald accepted her manuscript, and it was so successful that it was followed by a second, 'Making Dreams Come True', broadcast on 30 January 1950. *Kate Hannigan* was published that June, by which time she had written (and had had rejected) her second novel (now available as *Kate Hannigan's Girl*), and had begun to write her third, *The Fifteen Streets*. In the same month, May 1951, that *The Fifteen Streets* was accepted for publication, she broadcast a third BBC script, called 'Buying Secondhand Furniture', following it a year later with 'Get Your Nerves Under Control'.

The placing of *Kate Hannigan* with Macdonald, her first publisher, was a speedy and straightforward affair and was occasioned indirectly by her attendance at a lecture at the local library, a talk on how to write a novel. The speaker was Charles Christmas Bush, a successful thriller writer of the time who wrote under the pseudonyms of Major Christopher Bush and Michael Home. The talk was disappointing. All that Catherine could remember was his theme, that anyone capable of drawing up a laundry list is capable of writing a novel. The poor man couldn't have known that he had touched on such a raw nerve. Catherine had been drawing up laundry lists for the past decade and a half, yet the writing of her first novel had taken the nightmare of mental breakdown to perform.

She let him have it. There in front of his whole audience, she gave it to Major Christopher Bush on the nose. He must have wondered what had hit him. He had probably thought he was in for a nice cosy evening, no sweat, no bother. He'd earn his fee, serve the good ladies of Hastings the encouragement they craved and depart. But, to give Bush his due, later that same evening he would see the error of his ways and play a crucial role in Catherine's rise.

After her outburst she beat a hasty retreat down the stairs and through the door out into the cold, rainy, windswept night. Once outside, she felt so bad about what she had said that she returned to the upper room to apologise. Bush not only accepted her apology; he also admitted that the laundry-list theme was an easy solution he had used for years on such occasions, but gave her his assurance that he would not be using it again. Catherine then told him about the three chapters of *Kate Hannigan* she had written, and he suggested that she send them to his agents, Christy and Moore, a prestigious agency which included among its clients, George Orwell, whose *Nineteen Eighty-Four* was published that very year (1949).

This Catherine did the next day. John Smith, a new boy at the agency, read them and wrote to Catherine that she should send him the rest of the novel when it was finished. It was enough to have Catherine devote every single minute of her waking days to the task, which took her a full year to complete.

When John Smith received the manuscript he sent it to Murray Thompson at Macdonald, who, as I have said, read only the first chapter and told his secretary to return it to the agents because he felt it was too strong for any genre he published. His secretary looked at the top page and was caught immediately by the power of Catherine's writing, took it home that night and sat up reading it, unable to put it down until the very last page. The following morning she suggested to her boss that he had made a mistake in rejecting it, and in due course Catherine heard from her agent that *Kate Hannigan* had been accepted for publication. It was a moment of supreme triumph, dampened only by Macdonald's offer, a royalty advance of one hundred pounds of which ten pounds would be retained by Christy and Moore and ten pounds was earmarked for Catherine's typist. Catherine would discover that her agents would also charge her for the postage on submissions sent on her behalf to publishers abroad. In the end her net advance was close to seventy pounds. The book has been in print ever since and has earned Catherine vast royalties, but at the time it did little to supplement the couple's income, which was around forty pounds a month, Tom's salary as a grammar-school master. That, however, was hardly the point. She had won through; she had found her métier.

In *Hamilton*, we get a marvellous picture of the fledgling author Maisie Carter's relationship with her publishers. Like *Kate Hannigan*, Maisie's first novel is richly autobiographical. Unlike Catherine, however, Maisie falls in love with her first editor, Nardy, whom she eventually marries in *Goodbye Hamilton*. Catherine's relationship with her long-term editor, John Foster White, was indeed close, but only professionally so. To everyone who has been instrumental in her career she is intensely and appreciatively loyal, and in John's case she showed her appreciation by dedicating her award-winning novel *The Round Tower* to him and ensuring that he remained editorially involved until his death in 1997.

What is true to life in *Hamilton* is the excitement of Maisie's first trip to London to meet her publishers, and we also get a taste of the family atmosphere in which Catherine has always enjoyed, and insisted upon enjoying, having her books published, even when publishing them became a business equal in size to a light-engineering company and now, when her work earns more thousands of pounds per hour for her publishers than any other single author's. Called to London to meet Murray Thompson, Catherine arrived as excited as Maisie Carter, but on the wrong day: there had been a mix-up of dates by Catherine's agents. She lunched instead with Thompson's secretary, who had been responsible for the book being taken on, and while she enjoyed a pleasant lunch with this woman it had been a great disappointment not to be fêted by her publisher. Catherine never had an inflated sense of herself, but respect was an important ingredient in all relationships she felt were worth pursuing. Before long, if she would have lunch with her publisher, he would be available to her even if she turned up a week early.

Then, in 1953, a letter arrived at The Hurst from Aunt Sarah (Kate's sister) which brought her up short with a bitter taste of reality. Kate was drinking herself to death and had developed stomach cancer. 'The doctor told her that Kate didn't have very long,' Sarah's daughter told me, 'and my mother wrote to Kitty, and Kitty didn't want to know, she didn't want to come up and get her.'

Catherine couldn't face the reality, but Sarah insisted that Catherine do so. At her wits' end, Catherine wrote to Harry Edwards. Tom had told Catherine that she would never forgive herself if she didn't get Kate back down to Hastings, but when the decision was made the problem arose as to how to get her down, for they had no car. Harry Edwards told Catherine not to worry, it would all be taken care of, and 'what followed', she recalls, 'was on oiled wheels'.

Kate had been living in Brinkburn Street in South Shields, one of the streets to which Catherine had gone as a child to an 'outdoor beer shop' with the Grey Hen. When first she had arrived there, in 1937, Kate had found it difficult to find work, her age and figure, bloated by drink, counting against her, though she was still capable of a ten-hour working day. Eventually she had been taken on by a doctor called Carstairs, who, with his wife, remained Kate's friend and employer right up to her final illness.

Now, she was bedridden, puffed up with dropsy; her liver was almost eaten away and she had a bad heart. But 'with the help of ambulances and a night sleeper I brought her back to The Hurst'. It was an extraordinary journey. When they arrived at Newcastle station, a posse of porters jumped to it and winched Kate's great body on to the train, using a luggage lift. At King's Cross an ambulance appeared and raced her across London to Charing Cross station, where the paramedics used more traditional means to get her on to a train to Hastings. Another ambulance made the last leg of the journey, to The Hurst.

Suddenly the real Kate was lying in the bedroom upstairs. 'Oh lass, I'm back home,' she cried when they laid her on the bed.

Except she wasn't, for the real Kate had ceased to exist for Catherine. She found that her perception of her mother had changed since she had translated her into this symbol, she no longer hated her, she even allowed her to drink the occasional whisky! In fact, having re-created Kate in fiction, Catherine found that she wanted to be with her mother and talk and, for the first time, listen to what she had to say.

The experience kept Kate alive for three years. 'Those years were the happiest of her life. But I had to become her gaoler, never left her. I allowed her a bottle of beer a day and now and again, unknown to Tom, I would slip her a miniature whisky. Knowing what I'd gone through, Tom hated even the thought of whisky.'

Four days before she died she said to Catherine, 'I've been a wicked woman to you, lass.'

'Pity made me contradict her.' Catherine told her mother that the only one she had hurt in her life had been herself. Kate died peacefully on 23 September 1956.

One would think that in her latter days, when Catherine and Kate got to know one another, Kate would have told her daughter who her father was. Not so, according to Catherine.

In John Smith's view, Catherine probably did know who her father was by this time, but never wanted to meet him: 'She didn't want to because that would have brought him down to earth. She said she did, but . . . I don't know.' The father was part of the myth she had created, which said that he was the side of her that set her apart as genteel.

It is possible to detect through Catherine's writings a whole spectrum of feelings about the father she never knew. In her novel, *The Gillyvors* – gillyvors, she tells us, are flowers known as nature's bastards – there is anger, fury even, that a father can consign his daughter to an eternity of ridicule and disdain as baseborn. But as early as 1929, she seems to have come almost to a point of forgiveness, writing in notes kept in the Cookson Archive at Boston University, that her father could not have known at the time what suffering his selfish passion would cause her.

Years later, in *The Man Who Cried*, she discovered in the ecstasy and misery of Abel Mason's tears the possibility of a mutual sense of loss: her father, who knew that Kate was with child, may have suffered, too. In so doing she came nearest to expressing her love for him. The novel was written in the 1970s.

'I was told that my father was "a gentleman". My aunt Mary said, "He wore an astrakan collar and carried a silver-mounted walking stick and black kid gloves, and oh! he did talk lovely."' So had begun the myth surrounding Catherine's father, whose absence charged her whole life and career. What is so extraordinary about it is that the wondering who he might have been is so much more interesting than any of the solutions that have been put forward since.

Childhood friend Irene Harding said, 'We were told he was the son of the gentry house where Kate worked, oh quite nearby, that's what we were told. She never did admit it.' John Atkinson, another kid from the area, had a different story: 'What I got told was that Uncle John used to lodge there [at 5 Leam Lane] when my other brothers used to lodge at my house, he used to take her out drinking . . . He'd have been twenty, this was when the McMullens were living beside the Twenty-Seven. John Mather, my mother's brother. Bit of a gaffer in the docks. He could be her father.'

Catherine got fed up with people putting their own relatives forward. Meanwhile, writers made their own theories. As her father met Kate when she was working at the Ravensworth Arms in Lamesley and was a gent, nearby Ravensworth Castle came under scrutiny. There was a suggestion of a visiting aristocrat from Belgium, and someone else linked him to the Belgian artist who appears in *Colour Blind*. Early on, Catherine did put her artistic streak down to a genetic inheritance from her unknown father.

In the novel, the artist, Michael Stanhope, is engaged in a series of paintings of street life on Tyneside. He lives on Cassy's

Wharf off the Mill Dam bank in South Shields and 'never paints owt but men and boats'. The novel's heroine, Rose-Angela, works for Stanhope and meets the Tyneside characters he brings in off the street to his studio.

This notion of Catherine's father being a street-life painter, though later discredited, is apt. It is in line not only with her surprise ability to paint, but also her ability to immerse herself in the spirit of Tyneside in the novels. She makes the point in *Colour Blind* by having Stanhope observe a daily ritual of immersing himself, literally, in the River Tyne.

More recently, after a meticulously detailed search through official documentation, Kathleen Jones mounted a convincing case in *Seeking Catherine Cookson's Da* (Constable, 2004), that Catherine's father was one Alexander Pate, born on 4 December 1879, in Lesmahagow, south east of Glasgow, son of Samuel Pate, a coal miner and horse dealer, and his wife Ann. According to Jones, Alec, as he was known, used his mother's maiden name (Davies) to Kate, because he was already married when they conceived Catherine. It is 'Alexander Davies' that appears on Catherine's birth certificate.

Alec picked up his characteristic slick appearance and smooth-talking patter in the milieu of horse racing. Working variously as bookie and salesman, he made his real money gambling; Jones tells us that in the 1930s and '40s he was known to bet thousands on a horse. The fact that he became a house owner while still a gambler suggests that he had his wits about him and the emotional wherewithal to cope with inevitable misfortune along the way.

As for looks, he was a killer, described by one of his granddaughters as a Rudolph Valentino lookalike. Incredibly, we are told that he did use a silver-topped walking stick, just as Catherine's Aunt Mary had described. The stick was passed on to Alec's son by his first marriage (Catherine's half-brother).

With this image of Catherine's father in mind it is possible to bring to life an emotive scene in 1906 when Alec visited Kate at the tiny one-bedroomed slum flat in Leam Lane, Tyne Dock, not knowing that she was pregnant. Her aggressive stepfather John McMullen, who had whipped Kate's sister Sarah for spending a night out in Newcastle, will have raised the roof over Kate's pregnancy. Now the dastardly perpetrator was standing at the front door! A scene of ugly violence – typical of McMullen – was surely in store.

Alec, experienced in making his play as a salesman according to the demeanour of his clients, had clearly sensed the atmosphere and adapted to it. He will have been helped by Kate being over the moon to see him, the more exalted when Alec demured not at all when he was presented with the fact of her pregnancy. Kate's mother, Rose, seeing Alec for the first time, will have been struck by his dapper appearance, charm, and solicitous attitude towards Kate. It would take quite a performance to get round Rose, with all her experience of hardship, but Alec had a head start with his well-groomed appearance, which suggested he didn't lack money.

Likely, Alec played the inverted snob to McMullen – well-to-do but still identifying with his working-class roots – McMullen was known to be a sucker for that. He could always muster respect for someone who had made good but could still invite him for a drink. Perhaps Alec asked him along when he invited Kate out for the day to Newcastle races, secure in the knowledge that Rose, thinking of her daughter's needs, would have dissuaded him. A day at the races was the perfect end-game. Alec struck exactly the right pose to ensure high spirits in Kate and that her step-father would let him out of the house in one piece.

Had McMullen known that Alec was already married, he would surely have taken the poker to him. He had married one Henrietta Waggot five years earlier. It wasn't long before Henrietta discovered the up-and-down existence she had let herself in for. On three occasions their accommodation was stripped bare by bailiffs. It was then, apparently – in need of an alias to avoid his creditors – that Alec began to use his mother's maiden name, Davies.

There was no realistic chance of his marrying Kate in 1906, but two years later, following various other affairs, Henrietta booted him out. In 1909, Alec returned and begged her for a divorce, but alas not to marry Kate. By then, his amour was Jane Williamson. They married that year in Darlington, but not with Henrietta's blessing. She refused Alec a divorce and he married Jane as a bigamist, under the name of Davies.

In the early twentieth century, divorce was almost impossible to obtain for the working-class poor, and respectable girls wouldn't live in sin, so many were driven to bigamy, or worse. In 1911 Hawley Harvey Crippen, rather than commit bigamy with his lover Ethel le Neve, poisoned his wife, Belle Elmore, who had refused divorce. He concealed her mutilated body and disposed of it piecemeal. Before being sentenced to hang, Crippen said, 'The world knows what happened afterwards, but does not know the agony we both suffered, the frightful torture of two hearts beating one for another but divided by the most cruel barriers.'

Alec died in Scarborough on 25 June 1948, as Catherine was completing her first novel. Scarborough was a good place to hide in the 1930s, being on the east coast, blinded to the west by the steep rising, largely untrod expanse of the North York Moors, and with poor roads north and south. The railway brought crowds in summer, but Alec Davies was unlikely to be disturbed by unwelcome reminders from his past. Also, it will have appealed to his taste for stylishness, for, since the town's spa waters were discovered in the seventeenth century, it had been the haunt of Royalty and landed gentry, and still some of the old stylishness remained, Scarborough's Spa Ballroom and Promenade Lounge having been built as late as 1924. Cause of death was the rare haemorrhagic telangiectasis bleeding disease that assailed Catherine from the age of eighteen. The hereditary nature of the disease is a key element in the theory's viability.

Had Catherine not been rich enough to buy a laser for Newcastle's Royal Victoria Infirmary, which stemmed the flow of blood when she began to bleed internally during the 1980s, it is certain she would have died earlier in the same ghastly fashion as Alec, bleeding internally. But, ironically, she wouldn't have been rich enough to buy the laser had not her father abandoned her and set her on the troubled road that led to her success.

In 1953, the year in which Kate arrived at The Hurst for the last time, Catherine's fourth novel to be set on Tyneside, *Colour Blind*, was published and she was writing two others inspired by the spirit of the place, *Maggie Rowan* and *A Grand Man*, the first of the Mary Ann stories. 1953 was also Coronation year, and *A Grand Man* was the novel that first elicited a royal expression of interest in Catherine. John Smith sold the film rights in the novel to J. Arthur Rank, and when the film was released in 1956, as *Jacqueline*, Buckingham Palace requested a copy of it for private viewing. It turned out that the Queen Mother was a big fan. She was of course a Bowes-Lyon. The John Bowes partnership with Charles Mark Palmer of Jarrow was the fulcrum on which the industrial revolution in the North-East turned. Queen Elizabeth the Queen Mother knew all about the spirit of Tyneside.

Unfortunately, *Jacqueline* and the only other big-screen movie ever made of Catherine's books (*Rooney*, about a Tyneside dustman, filmed in 1958), were seriously marred by the producers' decision to remove both stories from Tyneside to Ireland.

Catherine went to Belfast to work on the script of *Jacqueline* with Patrick Campbell and Liam O'Flaherty. She enjoyed the process of scriptwriting and learned a lot, but found the milieu of film-making wasteful. She even returned the change from £50 given to her in advance as expenses, a move that seems to demonstrate how alien to her the world of movies was.

It was a particular shame because these two novels had the realism and comedy that seemed to be what audiences wanted at the time. In British film, the early fifties belongs to Ealing Studios with their comedies, *The Lavender Hill Mob, The Man in the White Suit* (both 1951) and *The Ladykillers* (1955), and later in the decade audiences would turn to the hard realism of Jack Clayton's *Room at the Top* and Tony Richardson's *Look Back in Anger*. Catherine's novels had the realism and the comedy rolled into one. But the films of her work lacked the spirit of northern working-class people that was their key. It was, perhaps, not surprising that Rooney did not engage British filmgoing audiences in his new guise as a champion Irish hurler. After the film appeared, Catherine refused to deal with Rank ever again.

With the sale of film rights to *A Grand Man*, Tom, Catherine and Kate left The Hurst, 'which had eaten up my energy and every penny poor Tom and I were earning,' and moved to Loreto, a house on a private road only a few minutes' walk away. 'There were about another four big houses and a bungalow on the road. One of the big houses had been owned by a millionaire. He had three daughters. The family broke up because there was a question of religion . . . the daughters turned Catholic. One became Mother Superior of a convent at St Leonard's. The other built a house for herself quite next to the one she had left. The third one, whom I called "my Miss Harrison", not to be outdone, built her house some distance away down the road and called it Loreto.

'It was beautifully built. She had had the bricks hand made and the pointing was an art in itself. She had something wrong with her skin and as I understand had to wear a mask of white ointment on her face. She was looked after by a nurse (frequent nurses, because they didn't stay), a cook, a maid and a gardener. Finally there was this one nurse who was middle-aged, and the dear lady was also attended by a very acute insurance agent who must have told the nurse that if she meant to stay she should make the old girl see that her future was secure. The outcome was that Miss Harrison left her the house and all the furniture, which I understand held a lot of antiques.

'But I don't think the nurse was there more than a year and a half . . . Anyway, the house went up for auction, but it wasn't sold. Then one day, when I was being driven about by a house agent in search of a new house, I saw a For Sale board outside. There we were, driving along this private road, and I pointed out this sales placard outside the house with its long winding drive. "Oh," he said, "don't go in for that place, it's always up for sale," and he wouldn't stop and show it to me. He had another in mind. But something attracted me to the place and when later I got rid of him I waited for Tom to come home from school and said, "I want to show you something . . ." We walked the ten minutes or so from The Hurst in Hoads Wood Road and as we made our way down the drive to this house, we knew immediately that we wanted it.

'The agent for the house told me its history. It had been built in 1938 and this was 1954.' He also told Catherine that the nurse had turned down a number of people who had made offers on the property; she wasn't just determined to get what she was convinced the house was worth, she wanted it to go to 'the right people,' she said.

By arrangement with this agent, Tom and Catherine were shown around the house by the nurse, and Catherine saw its potential immediately. She loved the wrought-iron-framed windows and could see that while some people might be put off by the darkness inside, that could easily be remedied. 'The house seemed dark because everything in it was brown. All the lovely woodwork had been painted brown. But we knew we wanted it straight away. I knew immediately what I would do with it.' As they neared the end of their guided tour, the nurse led them towards two rooms marked 'Private': one was her bedroom and the other turned out to be a sitting room. Recalling what the agent had said about this woman turning prospective buyers down, Catherine immediately went into action. 'I said, "Oh no. No thank you. We can see what the house is like without intruding." That must have got her. Anyway, we made an offer and she got on the phone to the agent.' There was some to-ing and fro-ing about the size of their offer. As far as Catherine could tell from one side of the conversation, the nurse seemed to have taken to them, but the agent didn't advise her to accept their offer at that time.

'As we were about to go a man came in – we had seen him stop his car, a big limousine. Apparently he went round the house and decided he might take it. The nurse was wavering, I understand, when all of a sudden the hall light went out and she asked him would he put a fresh bulb in for her. He was standing on a ladder when the phone rang and it was the agent who at that moment told her that she should let us have the house, as we were the only really earnest ones willing to pay anything near what she wanted. And she said, "All right," and looked up at the man putting the light bulb in and said, "I'm sorry, I've just sold the house." What did he do? He must have been a pig of a fella. He had been about to put the light in, but he didn't do it. He came down and thrust it at her and walked out!

'Anyway, after a lot of legal business we moved our last pieces of furniture into it on Guy Fawkes' night. It was pouring from the heavens. There was no central heating here either, only an electric fire nailed to the wall which the nurse later took down and sold us, together with the mirrors on the back of the bathroom washbasins. She was a very mean woman. Anyway, in the kitchen was an Aga, our first Aga, and that was wonderful, as was the first knock which came to the door.'

The first knock at the front door of Loreto after they moved in 'was a doctor, whose three sons went to the grammar school. One of the boys Tom had taken under his wing and patiently prepared him, as no one else would have done, for university. There stood the man with this great hamper, holding a really hot four-course dinner. What could be a better start than that?

'But why, we asked ourselves many times after, had Miss Harrison, this woman with so much money, taken only a half acre of ground on which she built her lovely house, when all around, except for the bungalow that was on one side of us, was thick with woodland that she could have bought for next to nothing? During the years that followed we took three pieces of the woodland. They had been used as a dump during the war, and besides old beds, gas ovens and rubbish of every other description, there was a number of old trees entangled with honeysuckle, some of the branches nine or ten inches across, so strong and entwined that Tom could swing on them from one tree to another. He loved climbing.

'It took a number of years for us to buy those three pieces of land and twenty-two years to make that garden. The labour that we put into it was indescribable. How we did it I don't know: Tom would not have any assistance. I was his labourer in everything he did. This, to me, is Tom's main failing. He will not have help of any kind. He thinks he can do everything himself, and this is part of him right up to this very moment.

'I always regret one mistake I made at Loreto. There was no garage. We couldn't afford a car. All I wanted to buy was nice furniture, and although I was writing I wasn't earning as now. On a piece of land between us and the bungalow was a huge garage that would have held about four or five cars. In it was a sailing boat (the owner of the bungalow was a sailing man). It was now up for sale at £200 (remember, this was 1954). I was for buying it (I always would take a chance), but Tom was against it because it would mean another two hundred pounds on the house payments. He was always terrified about getting into debt. I never was and I never went into debt . . . Fourteen or fifteen years later, we bought that piece of land from the new owner of the bungalow and he charged us eight thousand pounds for it. All that still rankles in my businesslike mind.'

As she had been at The Hurst, Catherine was tirelessly involved in making the new house the way she wanted it. But this time it was far more rewarding. Everything came together here. In time, they even built a swimming pool. It was begun as a remedy after Catherine had damaged her back and spent three months lying in bed, but later swimming became a great source of pleasure and relaxation when the work was done.

'Looking back at the work that I did in the house . . . Tom was away at school from half past eight in the morning not only till half past four but usually eight o'clock because there were so many meetings, Scouts, parents' associations, sixth-form meetings, there was everything. I remember when his mother and father were paying their first visit, she said in amazement, "Are all your weeks like this?" I said, "Yes." She said, "I would never put up with it. You are never done from morning till night." No, I was never done from morning till night, and on looking back I am amazed how in those twenty-two years I got through the work of looking after that house, clearing it, cooking and doing the washing by hand. We had no electric appliances, no washing machine, dryer, we didn't even have a fridge until about five years before we left there, about the time we also had a beautiful indoor pool made. It was after we had paid the £8,000 for the adjoining land, but, as I said, I was a saver and a planner . . .'

At Loreto, too, Tom first had occasion to understand something of the supernatural world which Catherine encountered in the little room of her imagination. The incident occurred on Christmas Eve 1954, not long after they arrived, and it shook Tom's belief that science and mathematics could explain all. He and Catherine were busily papering a bedroom ceiling. Startled by a strange noise emanating from outside the room, Catherine dropped what she was holding and wrapped Tom in an envelope of wallpaper and glue. Venturing on to the landing, she saw their bull terrier, Bill, transfixed by something at the bottom of the stairs, the short hairs of his coat bristling with fear. She looked down the stairs but could see nothing. She then tried to coax the dog down with her, but he wouldn't budge. Then, without any prompting by her or Tom, who had by this time joined her, Bill made his own way, warily, step by step, to the bottom of the stairs, where he stood stock still, his head cocked as if someone was standing by him. Whatever was there absorbed Bill completely. Then, unaccountably, because Bill only ever sat when a hand was placed on his rear end, he first sat, then lay supine on the carpet, still looking up at whatever it was that no one could see.

A week or so later, exhausted by the decorating, Catherine was sitting downstairs alone. Resting her back against the chair, her mind in repose, she felt something, a kind of presence which she was convinced was Miss Harrison, the old lady who had built the house and died earlier that year. The following day, as she and Tom listened to the church bells ringing in the New Year, she felt it again, but this time with contentment. Whatever it was – this spirit presence – was departing through the open front door.

She and Tom deserted The Hurst on 5 November 1954. By the time they left Loreto in 1976 Catherine had published forty-one novels, her autobiography, *Our Kate* (1969), and five specially commissioned romantic novels as Catherine Marchant, a name selected by her agent, John Smith, to distinguish them from her mainstream books – and she had written many more. It was an extraordinarily productive period, which brought increasing rewards, but it changed nothing in the way she managed their lives. 'We never had separate accounts. We used to divide the money into three parts: a third would go into the bank, a third would pay for new furniture, antique furniture if possible . . .' Always there remained this care about money, born of her past. 'Since the days I put my pennies into the lavatory as a child I was a saver, a planner. I could make a sixpence go as far as a shilling.' The significance of that lavatory in the backyard at number 10, Annie Hannigan's 'little square house', Catherine's bank, her sanctuary where no one could get at her, the room in her mind in which, when she was at her lowest ebb in 1946, she felt safe to write, was such that as she began to gain popularity through her work it even influenced her dreams. When the money started to flow in, incredibly she started having dreams about lavatories. The size of her royalty cheques was presaged in the number of lavatories which appeared – 'and their condition'! Perhaps a psychologist would say that these dreams were connected with the success which she could now claim in having cleansed herself of her fears through her novels. For her recovery coincided with this period.

The mess that the Rank Organisation had made of Catherine's novel, *Rooney*, in 1958 had a knock-on effect that for a while threatened her whole development as a writer. Not only did it mean that no other production company was interested in making films out of Catherine's novels for many years, but also *Rooney*'s paperback publisher, Corgi, saw no reason to follow up their interest in Catherine with an offer to publish other of her novels in paperback. All the paperback companies had by this time rejected Catherine; they had passed up the opportunity of publishing *Kate Hannigan, The Fifteen Streets, Colour Blind, Maggie Rowan, A Grand Man* and *The Lord and Mary Ann*. Corgi had been persuaded to publish *Rooney* in paperback to coincide with the film, but then the film had failed, and the paperback had not done exceptionally well. The upshot was that it would be ten years before another Cookson novel appeared in paperback, and Corgi would not be its publisher.

Catherine need not have worried, however, nor did she, because with seven novels in hardcover on the library shelves and an increasingly faithful following, there was a solid enough platform on which to proceed, and thankfully, too, recognition by the BBC that Catherine was here to stay.

In 1958, *The Devil and Mary Ann* was the fourth of Catherine's novels to be serialised on BBC Radio, and it went out in the same year that *Rooney* flopped. Others followed: *Fanny McBride* and *Love and Mary Ann* in 1962. There had also been further interest in Catherine as broadcaster since her radio talks in the early fifties, and now, a decade later, another series went out through *Woman's Hour*, and a programme called *Home for the Day*, with titles like 'The Train to South Shields', 'Me Granda', 'Up the Creek', 'Thursday's Child Has Far to Go' and 'Playgrounds' – opportunities for Catherine to give the kind of homespun stories of the North-East that she was already giving as an invited speaker.

The next Cookson novel to find its way into paperback was one of her most unusual. It has been suggested that had Lewis Carroll been alive in the 1960s he would have written not *Alice's Adventures in Wonderland* but *Barbarella*, a science fantasy on the sexual attitudes of this permissive era, which one might assume passed Catherine by. But, in 1959, Catherine published an extraordinarily prescient image of the era in *Slinky Jane*, one of the few novels she wrote set outside the North East. In the isolated village of Battenbun, eels are known as slinky janes, their habits the secret of fishermen of the fens (Tom's favourite countryside area). The narrative turns on the appearance of a strangely alluring woman at the very moment that a slinky jane appears in a pond, where never an eel had been seen before. The novel was snapped up for paperback publication by Tandem in 1967, the very year Jane Fonda starred in *Barbarella*.

The early 1960s was a busy time for Catherine, not only writing novels, but serials for *Women's Realm* and associated romances under the pseudonym Catherine Marchant. The first of six, *Heritage of Folly*, appeared in 1962, then came *The Fen Tiger* (1963) and *House of Men* (1964). Meanwhile, *Our Kate*, her autobiography, had been in the works since 1956. In June 1962, six years after beginning it, she wrote to her friend Dr Anderson in South Shields: 'Mrs Johnson [Catherine's secretary] says she has had a bellyful of biography.' Catherine sent the manuscript to John Smith, but by 1963 she was rewriting it again.

That was the year, too, that publisher Macdonalds invited Catherine in to discuss writing children's books. *Matty Doolin*, her first book for children, would appear in 1965. Not only was she writing her mainstream novels, the autobiography, the romances, and now children's books, but she was also still busy educating herself. In October 1961, she wrote to Dr Anderson to say that every Monday night she attended lectures about literature from Chaucer through Defoe up to Henry James. Meanwhile, she was also promoting her books by giving talks to women's groups all over the country. 'This side of the business is getting out of bounds,' she wrote. 'I have now got bookings up to the end of November 1965!'

Catherine was becoming successful. Her publishing schedule was as full of reprints as of new books, 'but oh, it's tiring!' she confided. 'I went to Margate last week [to give a talk] and had to stay overnight, then to Ashford and got held up in this Go Slow. Tom was waiting on the station for me around 12 p.m.'

Although capable of amazing feats of stamina and strength – a three-day storm had her sawing fallen trees in the road outside Loreto, and now that she had a swimming pool she had become a daily swimmer – she was also still suffering from ill health, or feared she was, a symptom of the pressures under which she was putting herself and Tom, whose sympathetic tones were being tuned to concert pitch. There were the regular nosebleeds, but now also there were bouts of neuritis (pain due to inflammation of the nerves), an exploratory operation in the area of the appendix, which revealed nothing, and it was at this time, too, that Catherine developed cramps in her elbow, which led to speaking her novels into a tape recorder.

It was a difficult period for Tom for other reasons, too. Catherine was being feted by her publishers. Increasingly she was invited to functions and was the focus of attention of publicists and editors. John Smith was at ease in the publishing world. Besides being a literary agent, he was also a poet in his own right, and there was a kind of competitive literary snobbery in the air, to which Catherine of course rose, but which was anathema to Tom, who was left in his dusty old schoolmasterly world while Catherine was entering this other, more glittering sphere.

In this period, with Catherine's first flush of real success, Tom began to have serious migraines. They were so bad that he could do nothing but confine himself in a darkened room for hours and lie there waiting for the terrible pain to subside. At the same time, friends of Catherine reported that Tom had become jealous of her relationship with literary agent John Smith.

The migraines were diagnosed as the result of stress, and many a writer has blamed them on Catherine's dominating personality, but in fact there is a family susceptibility through

Tom's mother's side: 'I, Joan, Jean and Elizabeth have all suffered,' Tom's sister Edna told me. Clearly, however, Tom was at a low ebb, as I learned from an ex-grammar-school pupil, Steve Blower, who knew Tom between 1961 and 1967. 'Tom was my teacher in the A stream,' he told me. 'We had another connection: Mrs Stanbridge, who lived next door to us, was actually Mrs Cookson's cleaner. She was given a signed copy of every one of her books as they were published. I was watching a TV documentary about them recently, and I was really powerfully reminded of something that I want to share with you. It was the summer term. I had done my exams and I was just hanging around waiting for the results before I left. I was walking back along Queen's Road in Hastings and found Tom Cookson standing on the pavement almost as though he was in another world. He was completely not with it, totally distracted, focused on something that was not the world around him. I remember standing next to him for what seemed a long time and gradually his attention came back, as it were, to the present. And I just said to him, 'Are you OK, sir?' And he said, 'Hah, umm . . .' And I felt I had to say something, and so I said, 'My Mum loves your wife's books.' And he said, 'Oh . . . Good.' And that was it!'

I knew that the grammar school was originally on Nelson Road, then known as Standen's High Fields, and that in 1964 it moved to Parkstone Road. Queen's Road was where Catherine had been tempted to throw a brick through the tailor's window and close to the original site of the school. I asked Steve what he thought Tom was doing there. He said: 'I don't know. It was like he had been deposited there by some force. It certainly wasn't... we were no longer at the school site nearby. Possibly he had been drawn back there . . . he was certainly distracted, in a personal reverie.'

'But he wasn't happy?'

'Absolutely not. There was a real sadness about him, and when I was watching that programme it sort of clicked into place for me really. I just felt *desperately* sad for him. He had such skills, such talent and clearly a devotion to her. And yet it was so destructive. And she was destructive of herself and of people around her . . . Ultimately he was a free man, he had choices and that was the choice he made, not an easy one by any means.'

As is often the case when success knocks on the door, tensions took on a sexual connotation. Besides this sense her friends had that Tom was disgruntled about her relationship with John

Smith, rumours spread among relatives that Tom was also less than sanguine about her relationship with Dr Anderson, with whom she stayed when travelling alone to Shields, and who holidayed with them on their boat, the *Mary Ann Shaughnessy*. 'Kitty used to say Tom was jealous about her relationship with Manny Anderson because he used to be too attentive to her when she stayed there,' cousin Sarah told me.

When I brought this up with Dr Anderson, he laughed until tears spilled from his eyes: 'Even though she is obsessed with sex in her books, Catherine was very prudish,' he said, 'and always very proper in the confined quarters of the *Mary Ann Shaughnessy*. I remember once we came together and by mistake I put my hand on her breast. There was instant recoil. Even when you entered in upon a warm, friendly hug, she would push you away. Bodily contact was not something that Catherine found easy.'

Nevertheless, it was then that, according to agent John Smith, Catherine joked in front of Tom about taking a lover, and in the novel she was writing at this time, *The Blind Miller*, adultery drives the narrative for the first time.

Like Tom, Sarah Bradley's husband, David, is gentle, good, kind, and is better educated than she. His education is a significant element in his attraction to her, and she is 'so very grateful' to David for rescuing her from the dire circumstances of her own life, as Catherine had been to Tom. There is no avoiding Catherine's censure of all that such a man represents when David is seen not to be up to the inspirational, sensual world Sarah Bradley discovers with rough, intuitional John, David's brother.

In 1964, there was a major career development for Catherine, a move by her publisher, Macdonalds, to launch her properly in America. *Katie Mulholland* appeared in 1967, the twenty-third novel to be published under her own name. It is considered to be her breakthrough novel because it was the first to be published in America, and was tailored to that end by her publishers. It is a huge, thematically panoramic novel, and was adapted editorially to the American market.

'Everyone connected with me at this end saw the possibilities of getting into the American paperback world,' Catherine explained. 'It opened up a new era to me: I was, so some people said, discovered.'

Katie Mulholland coalesced in Catherine's mind one day in

Loreto after she and Tom had been out in the garden and come back in to the kitchen to get warm. Tom put the kettle on and they were both standing in front of the Aga waiting for it to boil when Catherine said, 'I've got this big story in my mind but I still don't know where to place it for the best.' Tom lifted the kettle off the hot plate and said, 'You're always talking about Palmer's shipyard in Jarrow. Why don't you just bring the story to the last century and set it there?' That was all it took. Suggestions had been made that she should set it in Roman times, but Palmer's was the lifeblood of Jarrow, the fount. It took Catherine back to her source environment, directly into the main imaginative artery from which all her best works flow.

Palmer's Shipyard, just a short walk west of the New Buildings, where Catherine had lived as a child, at once triggered her imagination, so often had she seen the dockers pouring out of Palmer's when the buzzers blew, floating 'like black lava' down to the mercantile dock and Jarrow High Street. And was not her childhood vision of hell sparked by the rose-tinted glow in the sky when the Palmer's blast furnaces tipped?

The shipyard had been the throbbing heart of nineteenth-century Jarrow, the steel heart. Palmer-built and Palmer-owned iron colliers would take coal from mines owned by John Bowes & Partners (of which Charles Mark Palmer was a director) to London, calling at Port Mulgrave on the way back to ship a load of iron ore for the Palmer steel furnaces. The shipbuilding Palmer's and the coal-mining Bowes enjoyed a massively successful partnership. Setting a story around this was an exciting prospect indeed, for Palmer had turned Jarrow, a village, into a town for mining gold out of steel.

Tom had provided the key to Catherine's first nineteenth-century historical novel, a genre that would produce such as *The Glass Virgin*, *The Dwelling Place*, *Feathers in the Fire*, the Mallen trilogy, *The Girl*, *The Cinder Path* and the Tilly Trotter trilogy, and lead Catherine back, ever closer to the industrial source of Kate's world, giving new depth to her mythology of the North.

This was an important turning point. *Katie Mulholland* took her back into her grandma Rose's time, to the roots of the industrial revolution, which Palmer's had fed with more than coal. The company's launching of the iron-hulled *John Bowes*, the first collier really to make money, revolutionised the shipping of coal, but it also revolutionised the shipbuilding industry. Suddenly shipyards were crowding the banks of the Tyne and by the turn of the century, Tyneside shipbuilders were responsible for a quarter of the world's tonnage.

Catherine realised that she would have to do some in-depth research and approached the grandson of Sir Charles Mark Palmer, who had built Palmer's into a worldwide force, to see whether he would agree to collaborate. The word came through that yes, he would agree to help her, but that the family was still reeling from the last time they had agreed to help an author, in the 1930s. On that occasion, the author's name had been Ellen Wilkinson, who famously led 200 unemployed workers to march from Jarrow to London in 1936; the title of her book, *A Town That Was Murdered*. Catherine's political message is less clear-cut that Wilkinson's. It was formed from personal experience and the stories her grandma told her. She actually blamed the unions for making their revolution a battleground between 'us and us' (inter-union conflict) as much as between 'them and us' (employer-worker conflict), and for all sides failing to galvanise the concept of worker/company participation.

She worked hard on the manuscript of *Katie Mulholland*, which initially ran to 300,000 words. At the end, she said that she felt she could not only speak for the working man, but 'probably make pig iron' too. But politics is not what the novel is really about. In *Katie Mulholland*, the author invests her heroine with her own energy and gumption, her own against-all-odds spirit. Catherine's theme is of endurance rewarded. And with it she was suitably rewarded with greatly enhanced royalties.

People were taking note of Catherine not only on account of her commercial success, however. In the following year, 1968, the Winifred Holtby Memorial Prize was conferred by the Royal Society of Literature on her novel, *The Round Tower*, set in the late 1960s in the village of Fellburn, the fictional environment inspired by the class boundaries evident in Hastings and St Leonards. Her protagonists, Angus and Vanessa, from different sides of the tracks, will not find happiness until they withdraw and build a house of their own within, and the walls which confine them in their separate worlds 'crumble to ruin, and moulder in dust away.' It was Catherine's first literary accolade.

She was now earning so much money that she was in the supertax bracket, which in those days meant she was paying 83p of every pound she earned to the Inland Revenue. Her accountant recommended a move to the island tax haven of Jersey. Catherine travelled there, selected a suitable house and was on the verge of buying it, but was concerned about an ugly building being erected close by. No one could, or would, tell her what it was going to be, so she stopped a passerby and asked her. The woman told her that it was the new prison. Catherine, who had in any case had misgivings about the cliquishness of an island community, left immediately and, after a contretemps with a drunk on the flight back, which seemed to take her back into her childhood rages over Kate's drinking – the man could not have known what a sensitive nerve he had pinched!) – returned thankfully to the sunken sanctuary of Loreto.

In 1969, at long last, her autobiography, *Our Kate*, was released, providing the media with plenty of new material about her childhood, and confirming to a mass audience just how autobiographical her fiction was. Over the years, the manuscript had been through eight drafts, which Catherine said had drained much of the bitterness from it, but still it made her public property in a way not experienced before. Catherine's solution to the demands upon her was to engineer Tom's early retirement. In 1969 he became, in Tony Weeks-Pearson's phrase, Catherine's 'complete factotum'.

Finally in 1969, into this environment of nerves and stress came the ultimate test – Nan Smyth, the woman who had tried her damnedest to split up Catherine and Tom before they were married. In the years since the war Nan had become a bankrupt and moved into a seedy flat on Hastings sea front. Now she had been diagnosed with lung cancer and was fading fast. Catherine stepped in to help, but was called to Newcastle and Tom took over. Nan told him that after she died he was to go to a drawer where he would find a bundle of letters that she wanted him to have. Tom was deeply disturbed by what the letters said. Whether they referred to the affairs with men Catherine had had before she met him, or to Catherine's or Nan's predilection for women rather than men is not clear. All that we know is that on her deathbed, Nan bequeathed the woman she loved and who had rejected her letters which, according to Catherine herself, destroyed her moral reputation in her husband's eyes. Nan had saved the letters all this time with one purpose in mind, finally to break Tom and Catherine's relationship. She must have gone laughing to her grave.

Thrown into confusion, Tom rang Catherine in Newcastle and ordered her, with uncharacteristic force, under no circumstances to set foot in Hastings until after Nan Smyth was buried. When, finally, Catherine walked in the front door of Loreto, saying how guilty she felt about missing the funeral, Tom told her to shut up and thrust one of the letters under her nose.

Years later, in a taped interview with literary agent John Smith, Catherine said that one of the first letters she read 'went on about all these men that I'd had'. There was then no mention as to how damning the revelations were or how true or false they were. Catherine's interest was only in Nan's hostility towards her. She reacted as if something had burst in her head. Burned up with hate, she wants to disinter Nan and choke her skeleton! John was clearly shocked at what he heard, and later shook his head and talked quietly of the 'kind of bitterness, absolute bitterness', which had become Catherine.

It was the first and last time Catherine ever spoke about the episode, except in conversation with me shortly before she died, when she seemed to try to explain her fierce reaction as part of her breakdown, never quite resolved. Nan had been unspeakably disloyal. She was the woman whom Catherine told me she never written about, but from whom she had learned that hate was more powerful than love.'

Catherine and Tom's relationship survived. And that same year, Catherine put the feeling – her fury and hate – into a novel entitled *Feathers in the Fire*. In the novel she justifies her hate as a kind of psychic scream for all humanity, empathising with Amos, the central character, inspired by Jackie Halliday, the East Jarrow coalman who lived in Bogey Hill, just west of the New Buildings, when she was a child. 'Jackie Halliday used to sell coal, tuppence a bucket,' Catherine told me, 'and as a child I thought his legs were buried in the coal. I didn't work it out that I should have seen them sticking through the cart. I very rarely went up Bogey Hill, but one day I saw this "thing" going across the back lane and I recognised his face and for the first time I realised that the man had no legs and I stopped and stared at him. Well, you know, a child's horror can affect someone, and I saw it in that man's face. It was misty; the face had gone, but the feeling remained, and I felt that I had to portray that in some way. Just imagine, in a tough area like the Tyne, where they are all he-men. Is there anything fair in Nature? Ask yourself, Piers, unfairness in Nature, when a mountain can come down and bury people in its mud. Is there anything fair? When a volcano can burst and burn people to death? Is there anything fair in Nature?'

It was at this time that, unbeknown to Catherine, John Smith, who was now in charge at Christy and Moore, had begun casting around for someone to buy the agency. Anthony Sheil, whose company Anthony Sheil Associates had big literary authors like John Fowles, author of *The Magus* and *The French Lieutenant's Woman*, explained to me how he came to take the agency over. 'The then youthful agent Gillon Aitken was with me at that time, but just then decided he wanted to leave the agency and go back into publishing as an editor for Hamish Hamilton. As it happened, the first lunch he had with a literary agent after beginning work there was with John Smith. John said to him that he was going to sell the agency to some chap who had a small agency. John had pretty well agreed to sell the agency to him, but Gillon said, "I think you could probably do better than that, John. Why don't you talk to Anthony Sheil." So, he changed his mind and sold the agency to me. Christy and Moore had had, at some time or another, most of the mainline writers you could think of, including, for example, Muriel Spark, but they had at the same time lost most of them. The two names that remained on the list were George Orwell (certain titles only; the main part of the estate had gone), Catherine Cookson, and Patrick Moore. Catherine was just coming towards her prime. So, it was an attractive package.

'I went to the house in Hastings. I remember almost the first thing she said was, "I don't know what to make of you. Here's my new agent coming, and he's got mud on his boots!" I think I must have arrived early and gone for a walk on the Downs. Anyway, she was very amused that I arrived with mud on my boots. Tom was charming. He was in a way quite forthcoming. He used to like music very much. He actually made me play the piano and not many people can do that.'

Catherine's success had seemed to occur without any great effort on the part of her first publisher, who consistently sold her to the soft market, the series romance market, and largely to libraries, even though Thompson of Macdonald, whose stock-in-trade was category romance, saw that *Kate Hannigan* had flown that pigeon-hole. It was why he hadn't wanted it.

That the novels exceeded sales expectations was largely due to a pact between the writer and her readers, made in person by Catherine talking to women's groups up and down the country, and painstakingly in person by replying to every letter she received, building a postbag that eventually reached 3,000 letters

Tom and Catherine on their boat, the *Mary Ann Shaughnessy*, named after her famous fictional character. Their boating holidays were part of Tom's efforts to restore balance to Catherine's life.

After the war, Catherine dressed the part of the wife of the Master of Norman House at the grammar school, but in her mind's eye no longer figured in the cast list of masters' wives.

Tom, Kate and Catherine with her cat, Tigger, in the garden of The Hurst.

Catherine around the time she had her first novel, *Kate Hannigan*, accepted for publication. She wasn't published then, but she had a kind of confidence. She knew things for certain, though she was far from sure that others would recognise the truth of what she knew.' (Joan Moules, a fellow student of the Hastings Writers Circle)

'Books should really be about the Tom Cooksons of this world. Because, you know, Tom is at the heart of this in relation to Kitty, not just as a husband but as a complete factotum. Everything that Tom did he did for her and I feel a little vestige of resentment that he didn't get the opportunity to express himself in the way that he could and did when I knew him.' (Tony Weeks-Pearson, a pupil of Tom after the Second World War)

Loreto, the house on St Helen's Park Road, a private road just a few minutes' walk away from The Hurst, to which Tom and Catherine moved on Guy Fawkes night, 1954. Built in 1938 in a steep hollow, which Tom turned into a maze of walks through shrubs and trees, Loreto's very topography offered greater seclusion for Catherine to concentrate on developing her life out of her fiction, both now so imaginatively intertwined.

Kate, terminally ill, dozing by the front door of Loreto. It was during this period that mother and daughter came together for the first time and understood one another. Kate died on 23 September 1956. Shortly afterwards Catherine began work on her autobiography, *Our Kate*, which would not be published for thirteen years.

Catherine returned to the North-East in 1976, and was photographed by the back door of the house where she was refused entry to a birthday party in 1915 because she 'had no da', and on the site of the kitchen of number 10 William Black Street, where so much was done and witnessed that inspired her fiction. The media had what they wanted, a myth that was true in every sense.

The demolition of the Tyne Dock arches occurred as she returned, sealing the area's history in the imaginative context of her novels.

The story of the itinerary of Catherine and Tom through the Durham and Northumberland countryside from 1976 is a story of discovery of the spirit of a place, for Catherine had never visited the countryside while a child in East Jarrow. 'Up here,' she said in 1986, 'I know that I am in my own country, not soft like the downs, nor flat like the fens.'

The back of Bristol Lodge. From a 200-year-old cottage, 'we built upwards and sidewards, and made it into a beautiful apartment. It was a wonderful place.'

Bristol Lodge across the lake at Langley. Finally, in 1981, they had found a place that met all their requirements. Here her best writing in her later period, imbued with the spirit of the Northumberland countryside, was undertaken.

Catherine receiving the MA degree awarded by Newcastle University on 3 May 1983. Two years later she received an OBE, and in 1993 was made a Dame of the British Empire.

Catherine holding a solid silver plaque in the form of an open book presented to her on 16 September 1982 for a million sales of *The Mallen Streak*. It was the first of seven million-copy celebrations that her publishers chose to mark in this way over a decade.

As the adult comes into the child's time more and more there is recognition and revelation that what we once were and what we have become are mere earthly functions of eternity, which is now.

a year. Part of Tom's job when he took early retirement from teaching was to keep the fan base carefully logged and monitored. Eventually, the success of this strategy persuaded the publishing industry to take Cookson seriously.

Catherine found it irksome that a writer who had to delve so deeply and painfully inside herself to write the novels should be labelled romantic. Sheil saw immediately that he had something quite unusual and not in any sense part of a conventional category, as he showed when I suggested that she must have been a quite intimidating author to edit. Did he think that she could have done with more editorial guidance? 'Well, that's a very difficult question. Her sort of writing is a pretty particular sort of writing. It's a classic example of something that could be *damaged* by editorial intervention. It is quite difficult to understand what is going on editorially. There is quite a lot of *spontaneity*, which gets through to the readership, and it may not get through to the editor. The editor may say, let's do it this way, and the whole thing falls apart. What the editor's probably going to do is pull it back to a more conventional sort of thing, which may take the fire out of it.'

It is the reason why Tom's scientific approach hadn't worked, his emphasis on correct grammar actually impeding the flow of Catherine's work. Anything that stood in the way of Catherine being Catherine should simply be discarded. 'She was a complete one-off in terms of her financial success, but also in terms of her quite extraordinary life, an amazing life – you know the triumph over adversity is simply astounding,' said Sheil.

Immediately, he had big plans to move Catherine from Macdonalds to William Heinemann, who would give her greater publicity, and to improve on what was going on in America, which included little of note since publication of *Katie Mulholland*.

Explained Sheil: 'She was quite a well-known novelist before she left Macdonald and the move to Heinemann was an attempt to enlarge the profile and the audience by dint of putting more money behind her. It is a much more common thing to do now than it was then. Charles Pick [Chairman of Heinemann] was one of the early, heavy, commercial, entrepreneur figures. Catherine's sales went up pretty dramatically. Pick, to give him his due, recognised her potential. He used to wave his hand at a shelf full of a uniform edition of D. H. Lawrence and say, "We'll do that for her." And then refuse to pay the money that I'd ask him for, and look out of the window with a pained expression on his face, saying, "I never thought that this would fall down over the money."

'When I first took her over, I went to New York. John Smith had an agent there and I met him, but quite early on we sold her to Dutton. They paid quite a lot of money for those days, and they sold the paperback rights to Bantam, who owned Corgi.' This looked like a neat solution, as Corgi were by now her regular paperback publishers in the UK. With Bantam and Corgi being one company, Sheil could envisage a fully coordinated English-language publication effort for Catherine's paperbacks on both sides of the Atlantic. 'Bantam paid a very, very large sum of money for eleven books. The publisher there was called Marc Jaffe. He was a very big hitter, and he decided he was going to make Catherine a huge name in America.'

All of this was merely stage one in the strategy. There would be another stage fifteen years on, to which we will come. The success of it on the English side was undeniable. By 1981 her UK paperback publishers, Corgi, had issued nearly twenty-eight million copies of her novels, which had been further popularised in book-club form by Book Club Associates, with many hundreds of thousands of hardcover books and special omnibus editions sold. Publishing rights had also been snapped up by publishers abroad, who by 1982 had made the novels available in twenty-three languages.

'Corgi certainly came to recognise the importance of her,' Sheil confirmed, 'even to the extent that at one stage they became quite worried that she was so important to them that they ought to diversify and not rely quite to the extent they were on sales of Catherine Cookson. She was selling huge amounts of copies during the 1980s.'

Instrumental in this success, which earned Catherine the attentions of coach parties of tourists, was the television adaptation of her Mallens trilogy. The first book, *The Mallen Streak*, was published by Heinemann with massive publicity in 1973. *The Mallen Girl* and *The Mallen Litter* followed in 1974. The TV adaptation followed in 1979. She claimed it gave her the unwanted title of 'romantic novelist', but it certainly brought a new respect from her publishers on both sides of the Atlantic. Oscar Dystel, President of Bantam Books (with Corgi the largest paperback publisher in the world) was so intrigued to meet Catherine that he flew the 6,000-mile round trip from New York to do so, charting a private jet for the final leg from Heathrow to Newcastle, near where she was living by then. He may have hoped to entice Catherine to America to promote her books personally, but Catherine preferred to stay home and write.

On 16 September 1982, Corgi presented Catherine with a solid-silver plaque in the form of an open book for a million sales of *The Mallen Streak*. It was the first of seven million-copy celebrations that her publishers chose to mark in this way over a decade. The others were *The Mallen Girl*, *The Mallen Litter*, *The Tide of Life*, *The Moth*, *The Black Velvet Gown* and *The Girl*. Other titles which sold a million, or close to it, in the UK in the years leading up to her death were *Katie Mulholland*, *The Fifteen Streets* and *A Dinner of Herbs*.

Under the Public Lending Right scheme details of book loans have been collected since 1982 from a sample of thirty public library authorities, and authors remunerated accordingly. From the first year (1982–3) until four years after her death, Catherine's books were borrowed more frequently than any other author's. Between 1983 and 1992 she had, on average, twenty-six of the Top 100 books. Her position in 2005 – seven years after her death – was fourth, after the children's author Jacqueline Wilson and the novelists Josephine Cox and Danielle Steel. Each year she gave her library royalties to the Royal Literary Society to help writers as yet not self-supporting.

One should perhaps pause for breath and consider what an extraordinary situation this was for the girl from Leam Lane, who every Monday morning used to take her granda's suit to the pawnshop to get the money her family would need to survive.

America was, however (despite Dystel wooing her), a different story. 'It didn't work,' said Sheil plainly. 'It was quite interesting that, for all they did for it, they couldn't bring it off. The subsequent history of Catherine in America is that she was taken over by another prominent publisher called Jim Silberman, who had a company called Summit and who was associated with Simon and Schuster. He was mad keen on Catherine. He succeeded with her quite well in hardcover and always as a main autumn selection at the Book Club. But nobody ever brought it off in paperback.

'I have always thought it was because the American popular market is much more interested at a rather rudimentary level in the psychological approach. While I am not suggesting for a

241

moment they are scholars of Freudian analysis, I think they are very aware of it. I mean, Catherine probably got the psychology of her characters right, but she didn't *refer* to anything like that. It's a different way of treating people and character in fiction.'

With this unprecedented activity on the publishing side, Catherine also had some good fortune closer to home. In 1973, she met Dr Gabb, the St Leonards doctor, who arranged for the diagnosis of her bleeding disease as hereditary haemorrhagic telangiectasia.

'I had the breakdown in 1945 and from the time I returned home to Hastings everything I had, from ingrowing toenails to psoriasis of the scalp was, so I was told, a result of nerves, and then after forty-three years of the forty-six I lived there, in desperation I changed over to this certain Dr Gabb in St Leonards. But I knew this man for only five weeks.'

Catherine first met him when he was visiting someone else who was ill at Loreto. While he was there Catherine had a bleeding. By this time she would bleed not only from the nose but from the tongue, and she told Dr Gabb that she had been bleeding since she was eighteen. 'He couldn't believe that nothing had been done for me. So, within a week, he had made arrangements for me to see a specialist in Wimpole Street by the name of Mr Ranger, who looked at my scarred nostrils and the telangiectasis covering most of my tongue. He said nothing could be done for my nose except a skin transplant and this would be touch and go, ninety-nine out of a hundred didn't take. Within another week I was in the hospital and Mr Ranger took three and half inches of skin from my hip and inserted it into the nostril, at the same time cutting a big wedge out of my tongue.

' "Eeh, my, what if I'm never able to talk again!"

' "You will talk, Mrs Cookson," Mr Ranger assured me, "Don't worry!"

'The touch and go happened that it went. The skin grafting took. It was rather a painful fortnight, but I was back home, and this dear, dear, dear Dr Gabb came to see me. He was delighted that it had been done. He also came to say goodbye. He was going to London to have an operation, he said. This was the fifth week of our acquaintance. He had heard about Tom's migraine and he had already sent to America because he had heard of some kind of treatment for migraine, and he would let me know from London. We said goodbye. I can see him holding my hand warmly. When at the end of the week I heard he was dead I just could not believe it. I could not believe that for the last five weeks he knew he was dying of cancer, that he knew he had one more operation to go through and that he would probably die. Yet he did all that for me and even from his bed in the last week he wrote to Tom and sent him the particulars for his migraine he had received from America.

'Just think, in those five weeks that he knew me, he knew his time was short and yet when he saw this woman bleeding profusely he was astonished that nothing had been done for me . . . There is a doctor, and nobody in his profession will ever come up to him.'

Chapter Ten

Return to the North

One advantage of Tom's being retired was that Catherine had a car available to her. I heard about the car from another of Tom's pupils at Hastings Grammar School. 'I attended the school from 1963 and left in 1969,' said Trevor Maxted. 'I cannot tell you very much about him, only that he always had the best car in the car park and rumour had it he also had a yacht. How true that was I don't know. I always remember he drove a huge Rover [blue], and being such a little man he could hardly see over the steering wheel.'

The boat was, of course, not a yacht but a cabin cruiser, the *Mary Ann Shaughnessy*. The blue Rover had as significant an impact on Catherine's writing. For the great development of Catherine's novels from the early 1970s – from *The Dwelling Place* and *Feathers in the Fire* on – was the charge they received from the Durham and Northumberland countryside. The best-loved novels of the 1970s and 1980s are set in and beyond a rectangle of landscape more or less demarcated by Haltwhistle (in the north west), Alston (in the south west), Haydon Bridge (in the north-east), and Allenheads (in the south east). They attest to an increasing number of trips up into the Allendale region that Catherine was making in Tom's Rover, but also to the terrifying impact this wilderness land – quite new to Catherine (neither she nor her friends ever ventured into it as children) – at first had on her.

The Mallen Streak takes a charge specifically from Shap Fell and Alston Moor, the staggeringly beautiful drive from Penrith, but also from the agoraphobia (not an unusual residual feature of nervous breakdown) which its research discovered in her. Catherine's first experience of the sublime landscape sourced two locations in *The Mallen Streak*, but at the time reduced her to a block of fear. 'We were travelling by car from Hastings. I found myself heading for what I didn't know then was the great, great expanse of Alston moors. At different times in my life I knew when I had been any place that had a deep fall to the side I had the most strange feeling, sometimes touching on terror. But what I experienced that day went past terror. Tom drove over the hills up, up, into this space that went on for eternity. The heights and everything about it found me crouched on the floor of the car beside the seat. I was shaking with terror from head to foot. All I could gasp was, "Get out of this! Get out of this!" On and on he went, aiming to get out of it, of course, by reaching the end of it. At one time he stopped the car and said, "Look, try, try to sit up and look about you. It's the most magnificent sight."

'I couldn't answer, my heart was racing so fast. My pulse was racing so fast that it is a great wonder to me now that I didn't have a heart attack then.

' "Just lift your head," he begged, "or look through the windscreen. Just lift your head."

'I managed to raise my head from my huddled, crouched position and looked through the windscreen and there I was confronted by a fly moving slowly, slowly upwards. I followed it. I followed its progress until I realised it wasn't a fly, it was a car in the far, far distance, mounting the rise, and I let out a scream and once more my head was buried.

'So on and on he drove until we ran down into some sort of a village, and he dragged me out of my cramped position and I sat on the footboard and was sick. "I'll never forgive you," I said, "for doing this to me."

'He got out the map and he said, "Well, we can't go back. We've got to go on. It isn't very far now. We've just got to go up that bank and then we'll be all right."

'We went up that bank and then I died another death because dropping straight down from the edge of the car was this great, great fall and it was studded with trees. I later used that definite part where one brother murders the other by throwing him down this hill. [Readers of *The Mallen Streak* may recognise this as the cliff where Thomas Mallen's illegitimate son, Donald, a dark, brooding character given to long silences and bursts of temper, is killed by his consumptive half-brother, Matthew.]

'All I remember next was Tom saying, "It's all right now, it's all right. We're on a flat part. There's nothing to fear at all. It's all flat." He stopped the car and I got out and again sat on the footboard. There was nothing surrounding us for miles except about twenty yards from the road there stood the wreck of an old house. I understood, after, it had once been an inn where the men driving the ponies down from Scotland to Yorkshire and Lancashire stopped and rested and had a drink. But now it only showed a broken roof, a door hanging on its hinges. The walls were standing, but the window frames and every piece of wood seemed to have been stripped from it. I stared at it and the sight of it fell into my subconscious and lay there working until I thought up the story of *The Mallen Streak* and this dirty filthy wreck of a house became the setting for the conception of a child between two of the main characters in the book [Matthew and Donald's fiancée, Constance Mallen].

'There are many characters in the book, but these two were important. They were trying to shelter from a terrible storm with their horses and it is here that they expressed their love for each other . . . I described the house, the filthy condition and their coming together, all as if I had thought it up on the day of terror on the fells of Northumberland.'

Soon after publication of *The Mallen Streak*, the Freedom of the Borough of South Shields was formally bestowed upon her. It was the first time her homeland had recognised her and it had a great impact. In 1973, she had no idea of returning to live there, but this was the first step towards it.

'I confess I never wanted to come back. It was Tom who said to me when I was seventy [in 1976] and we were still working like people in their fifties or even forties, "I think you should go back to the North and die among your ain folk." I know now, and he knew it then, he was using me as an excuse to get away. He was tired of Hastings, which was changing vastly, especially the school that he had once loved.'

I had expected her to tell me that she had at last come to terms with her early childhood and wanted to get back to her roots. But she didn't feel that. Foster Barker, husband of Rosemary (cousin Sarah's niece) and at that point the new owner of Loreto, recalls perfectly Catherine's mood after she handed over the keys and passed through the garden gate for the last time: 'I can still see her walking up the path, crying because she didn't want to leave here.'

Catherine had lived in Hastings for forty-seven years and had been happiest at Loreto. Here her imagination had been given full rein: 'Once back in the North,' she told me, 'I was terribly homesick, not for Hastings or the South of England, but for Loreto, that lovely house and garden.'

But the truth is, too, that in all the years she was away from the North (half her natural life), her early environment never left her. However hard she had tried to rub it out, she had to admit to the inevitability of her return, 'that from the wider world into which I escaped I have to return, like the eel to the Sargasso Sea, to die where I began . . .'

She explored the theme in her fiction. In *The Tide of Life*, published seven years before she left Hastings, and in the poem which gave the novel its title, she likens existence to the time it takes for a tide to flow and ebb over the seashore. At the centre of her narrative is a valuable timepiece, a fob watch, to which the fortunes and destiny of her heroine, Emily Kennedy, seem to be tied. Illness and death pervade the novel, and questions are raised about life's futility. But the form of the narrative, which begins and ends in the same location (Pilot Place in South Shields) and, as ever, concerns the resolution of strife, suggests an alternative perception of time to that implicit in the watch symbol of finite time. Finally, what she gives us is not a sense of time as a linear progression from birth to death and then nothing, but of man as his own prisoner and gaoler, of the purpose of life as release from his self-sewn strait-jacket, of time as a circular motion, of eternity as now.

A similar theme is the subject of a novel she will have been writing around the time that she returned to the North. *The Man Who Cried* (which has to be one of her best titles) was published in 1979. At the start, Abel Mason, a working man, is in his thirties and married to a nasty piece of work called Lena. They are both from the North, but are living just outside Hastings. Their son, Dick, suffers from deafness as a result of frequent slappings by his mother. The situation, which Lena has effectively created, has driven Abel into the arms of Alice Lovina, the wife of a seaman. Lena has discovered the affair and written an anonymous letter to Alice's husband, who brutally murders Alice. After her funeral, which is where the novel begins, Abel packs a rucksack and takes to the road with Dick, heading north.

Their journey, largely on foot, a gruelling odyssey via Essex, Cambridge, Leeds and Northumberland (close to Hexham), and then back to fictional Fellburn (near Gateshead on the Tyne), occupies the whole of Part I of the novel and contains some extraordinary incidents, including set-tos with a nymphomaniac called Daphne and a religious maniac called Matilda, both brilliant examples of the author's skill in handling plot. When they come upon the 'apparition' of Matilda, Catherine excels. She is indeed a character from another world, her oddness so threatening that we, like Abel, cannot help but spring back as Matilda puts out her fingers and touches his arm.

In Fellburn, Hilda and Peter Maxwell, who run a car- and bicycle-repair business, install Abel and Dick in an outhouse and offer Abel work on the cars. Abel gives them the impression that he is a widower, and when Peter dies, Hilda persuades him to marry her, an arrangement complicated by her sister Florrie, with whom Abel has an affair and who becomes pregnant.

Abel and Dick's tramp north has a strictly linear feel to it, but Abel's relationships with Hilda and Florrie, and Dick's response to what is going on, in particular his fear of a bigamy charge against his father, which brings Dick to the point of breakdown, mass into a series of busy emotional circles, which it is the author's intention to resolve.

The hero's name, the same as that of the second son of Adam and Eve, and indeed the whole epic feel of Abel's trip north, suggest that this purpose will be achieved with significance beyond the lives of Catherine's fictional characters. The author's own personal odyssey, which led her to Hastings and then, forty-six years later, back to her roots in the North, where I believe Tom did feel Catherine would find fulfilment, parallels the cyclical pattern of Abel's life on an emotional level as well as geographically. That mass of busy emotional circles reminds us of the years 1940 to 1946 in Catherine's life when she, like Dick, arrived at the point of breakdown and through a great effort of will disentangled herself from them. Abel's release, like Catherine's, is like the bursting of a great dam, the flood of his emotions ducted through his streaming eyes, and it brings, if not fulfilment, at least hope.

Catherine has written elsewhere (in an essay called 'Time and the Child') of her perception of life as a circle, the child coming to meet the adult and merging with him before 'the race is run'. As the adult comes 'into the child's time more and more', there is mutual recognition and the revelation that what we once were and what we have become are mere earthly functions of eternity, which has been with us all the time, indeed is all time. It is now.

True to the author's vision, various aspects of Abel's past reappear as active ingredients in the present. Among them is Lena, whose arrival does lead to Abel's imprisonment for bigamy. Then, with Florrie dying from injuries sustained in an air raid, Hilda takes Abel's baby in. At the end we are left with Abel and Hilda, their arms around one another, and with Abel's tears . . .

At this stage that is all. For Abel's race is not nearly run, and there is no ultimate resolution in sight. But in his tears lies hope, as his son, Dick, tells us. In shedding his tears this physically strong, stoical northerner, 'who had done nothing with his life except impinge it on four women,' shows himself capable not only of release but of transforming his agony into Hilda's joy. His tears wash the scales from his eyes and he recognises a power within him to transform. A more complete parallel with his creator would be hard to find.

Looking back, more than twenty years after returning to the North, Catherine notes an ironic twist to Tom's suggestion that she come back to die among her own folk. For her return, she considers, enabled her to live longer than she might have in Hastings.

Even after the treatment that Dr Gabb had fixed up, Catherine still bled from the nostril above where the skin graft was made, and the more critical development since Dr Gabb's passing was that she had begun to bleed internally, too. Moreover, a year or so after she returned to the North she suffered a series of heart problems, and in 1990 suffered two heart attacks. She believed that had she remained in the South, where no doctor other than Dr Gabb ever did anything for her ill-health, she would now be dead. She told me, 'From coming back to the North I know that I am only alive today because of the attention that has been paid to my blood disease. Today I have six doctors who see to different parts of me . . . finally to be kept alive by blood transfusions every three weeks. And at every turn I have endeavoured to make research possible so that some day this awful, devastating, if rare, condition will be alleviated.'

There were also clear commercial advantages to the move. 'Coming back up to the North was terribly important,' noted Anthony Sheil. The move coincided with a decision by the South Shields Borough to tear down the Tyne Dock arches around the corner from where Catherine was born. Leam Lane End went too, as did William Black Street. It was the end of an era and a coming home, all in one. The marketing filip was not lost on the local media, who pressed Catherine into service bewailing the loss of old Tyneside. Suddenly she was to be found pictured in the local paper standing on the now cleared site of number 10 William Black Street, where once she had played out so many of the dramas of her earliest books.

A year before Catherine's return, cousin Sarah had found them a bolt-hole at 39 Eslington Terrace in Newcastle – somewhere to stay when they came up for talks and research purposes – and it was initially in this house that they lived in 1976 after selling Loreto.

'We landed in Newcastle and we lived in this very nice house for about a year, but it had no garden.' Wisely, Tom nipped in the bud Catherine's protest that the Eslington Terrace town house was not a patch on Loreto with its spacious garden. He asked cousin Sarah to look for something deeper in the Northumberland countryside.

'I went round Ponteland way, towards Morpeth,' Sarah recalls, 'and came upon a converted chapel at Kirkley. They came to see it and bought it. It was lovely inside. Titled people had owned it and they were buried in the land.'

But they never lived there. Since building the swimming pool at Loreto, Catherine now longed not only for a garden but also for Loreto's lovely swimming pool. She had become a keen daily swimmer, believing that the exercise was essential for her health. 'It was the only thing that saved my back,' she said, and was determined to replace the Loreto pool in her life. 'The man who was selling her the house said he knew who to take her to, to get a swimming pool put in,' Sarah remembers. Catherine was introduced to a builder who lived close to Corbidge. His own house, complete with pool, had, until recently, been up for sale, but he'd taken it off the market. 'Now,' continued Sarah, 'this man's house was suddenly for sale again! He had taken it off the market, but when Catherine arrived he put it back on. Anyway, it was a beautiful house, Town Barns, stone built with an indoor swimming pool, which is what she wanted.'

The purchase didn't stop there. Town Barns had but a small garden, which, as Catherine explained, 'ran down the side of the house. But next to it was a great long dirty field which belonged to a farmer who only kept a sick cow in there. The only thing that grew in there was thistles. But part of the field was terribly steep. Some people said that it shouldn't be built on because it was an historical piece of land. We bought this from the farmer who said it was building land and of course charged us accordingly. I think in those days we paid about £27,000 or £28,000 for it!

'Then Tom could see it filled, because his heart was in gardens, and, well, he engaged a designer, whose men came in and Tom told him what he wanted done. He himself helped and soon there was a wonderful surrounding of trees, and one of those steep banks was covered with hundreds of beautiful crocuses. It was a wonderful sight in the spring, for he had planted thousands of daffodils around the roots of trees forming an avenue right across this field. But it didn't please all the townsfolk. Some said, "Why stick daffodils all over the place and azaleas and rhododendrons?" etc., etc. Anyway, by the time we finished, with the land, the trees, and paid the designer, it cost a straight £50,000.'

When they had first begun work on the land they had had a letter from 'one of the older residents telling us that members of the community weren't pleased that we had dug up an ancient patch of ground that went back to the building of the moat around the "town". Then I had a filthy telephone call, one of these mad sex men, and this upset me very much.' Then, at length, Catherine received a visit.

'Well,' she recalled for me. 'I hadn't been in Corbridge more than six months or so (which I spent mostly in bed because the cold weather did nothing for me and I ended up with very bad bronchitis), when a lady from the town came to tell me that people really weren't very pleased with me living here because I didn't show myself in the town. Why didn't I?

'There was also a pub on the opposite side of the road, a very old pub, where the visitors to the town used to go, and of course they were told about this Catherine Cookson and so I had people at the door at all hours wanting autographs. Then Tom was stopped in the street one day by a beaming lady who told him gleefully that she had me on the rota of the sightseeing bus in Durham. Twice before this we'd had a busload of people unload at the gate, and as I said, it wasn't a very big garden and it wasn't a very big yard leading to the garage, so they were almost on top of us. This lack of privacy did not endear Corbridge to us.'

Nor was it only fans that were the problem: 'You get an awful lot of relations and friends visiting you when you've got an indoor swimming pool. Then, after we had been there about two years, the house next to ours [Trinity Barns], came up for sale and I took this and in my glory furnished this and in fact it turned out a better house than we were in. My friends and business acquaintances went there, looked after themselves but used the swimming pool [in Town Barns], and we used it at weekends to try and get away from the constant autograph seekers. But even there without success because twice reporters came round and before knocking on the door they looked in the windows to see that we were there.'

So pressing did life become that they even bought a third house to evade media and tourists, as cousin Sarah recalls: 'The girl who had lived in Trinity Barns had a cottage in Bardon Mill near Hadrian's Wall. It was an isolated cottage. They bought that too, and used it some weekends.'

In 1977–8 the stress began to tell on Catherine's health. She suffered a series of heart attacks, two more serious than the others, all requiring hospital treatment. On the bright side, however, they registered as private patients with Dr David Harle, in whom she found someone she could depend upon in the medical department. He admired the fortitude of a woman who had suffered numerous ailments over the years, 'any one of which would have been enough for most of us to cope with,' but was less enamoured of her bad temper and knack of seeing the worst in people. Nevertheless, he became her close confidant and friend.

In 1979, public interest crescendoed yet further with *The Mallens* TV film and, in 1980, with a five-part BBC TV serial based on her children's book, *Our John Willie*. The climax came when one day Tom yelled up from the hall, "What are you doing?"

'I said, "I'm getting dressed."

' "Get away from the window," he said.

'Well, there was a high wall that divided our land from a path to the river and there, going along the wall, was a man with a cine camera. Believe me, I couldn't believe I was all that famous.'

The final straw was a burglary. No more than £450 worth of goods had been stolen, but it was enough to occasion a move ever deeper into the countryside. There was yet to be a sting in the tail of their short dalliance in Corbridge, however.

In order to justify what they had paid for the land they needed to sell to a builder. The land was only worth what they had paid for it if it was built upon and the properties sold. However, the builder they found claimed he couldn't afford both to build the properties and to pay what they wanted for the land, so they came to an arrangement whereby Catherine and Tom would receive the money for the land once the houses were built and sold. 'By the time that happened he had gone bankrupt,' Catherine told me, 'and I'm still waiting for the £50,000. Anyway, that's by the way.'

Incredibly, her work did not suffer during this period of great stress. In 1977, she published a novel which showed just how her writing was benefiting from her sorties into the Allendale area. On one such visit, she had met the granddaughter of a certain Dr Arnison, whose library had included a book on the region, published privately in 1884. She used it as inspiration for *The Girl*, which attests to the reality of living in the area in the 1850s. She set the novel in the fictitious village of Emholm. The village of Simonburn, a very similar location on the North Tyne, was chosen when the book was filmed for television.

In 1979–80, while playing musical chairs with her various houses, Catherine returned again to the coal-mining industry explored in *Maggie Rowan* in her second saga trilogy, Tilly Trotter. Setting the novels in the nineteenth century (*Tilly Trotter Wed* and *Tilly Trotter Widowed* followed in consecutive years), here was territory she knew well and she dealt with it confidently, delineating not only the spirit of the community, but also the superstitions at the root of her people's lives, and flooding the books with issues such as the way the miners' masters had kept them down by withholding education from them.

Tilly would follow the Mallen trilogy to the top of the bestseller lists and become another successful made-for-TV film. But, from 1981–2, there was something else brewing in Catherine's imagination, something that seemed to follow this thread of what it was that bound her people together ever farther back in time – the spirit of her people becoming one with the spirit of the countryside of Allendale. So it was that they came upon the village of Langley and 'our bungalow up in the hills'.

Langley grew up in the eighteenth century around a mill used for smelting lead ore, mined on Alston Moor. The stunning lake, which met the garden of a bungalow called Bristol Lodge, was originally dammed to supply water to a smelting works in nearby woodland, which, together with the disused lead-ore railway and a 30m-high chimney connected to the old mill by means of a mile-long, underground flue, all attested to the industry on which the village once subsisted. Finally, Catherine and Tom had found a place that met all their requirements. They had found what they had come North for.

Some of Catherine's best late novels take from the spirit of this place. For example, she brings the landscape alive in the main character in *A Dinner of Herbs*, the strange, witch-like herbalist, Kate Makepeace, and Bristol Lodge stands on the banks of the lake which is the moonlit setting of Robert Bradley's first meeting with Millie in *The Moth*, the goddess figure who leads Robert to his destiny.

Catherine had set earlier novels in the area, for example *The Dwelling Place*, *Feathers in the Fire*, the Mallen trilogy and *The Girl*, but only now that she was part of it could she create character as mature as Makepeace, a woman who is the personification of the land in which she dwells.

'After four and a half years we found this bungalow in Langley by the side of a lake, originally dammed to supply water to the one-time smelting works there. Today, it is probably one of the most beautiful areas in Northumberland. Tom must be tired of the times we have brought the car from Hexham to Langley from the "top" as we call it, and I have said that it is the most beautiful sight that I have ever seen. As you approach the dam you're on a hill and you look across and you see that you're surrounded by hills, and Langley seems to be in this valley. And all the way – everywhere you look – there are hills coming down, all the way round, coming down to this valley. Up here I know that I am in my country. This is my kind of country, not soft like the downs but rugged hills broken up into soft parts, an expanse of sheer mystery.'

It is indeed an exquisite location and the place where, shortly after they settled at Bristol Lodge here, I first met Catherine and Tom. I was amazed to hear her refer to it as a bungalow, until she explained that it had been yet another of their major building projects, possibly the biggest of all: 'Attached to it was a 200-year-old cottage. We gutted the old cottage, and made it into a nice apartment. We built upwards on top of the flat roof and made a forty-foot study, and we turned an awful, dirty swimming pool, which was attached to the conservatory, into a fifty-foot drawing room, and above that made a forty-foot bedroom, en suite, which was really a beautiful piece. Tom took over the garden, as always, and I the house, and there we were, and our privacy was respected, no one troubled us . . .'

Bristol Lodge was an incredible house, beautifully furnished and designed. I had had no idea that they had done it all themselves. But by this time they were well practised. The Hurst had been their apprenticeship, done on a shoestring, the hundred-pound cheques in those early days papering over the cracks of a building that needed a complete overhaul. They had loved that house and had given it their all. At Loreto, where at last their life had come together, they had been able to give the house what they had longed to give to The Hurst but had been unable to afford, a beautiful garden, with many rhododendrons and azaleas. On all their houses they lavished the love, care and inspiration of parents for their children, and with the benefit of all the lessons they had learnt since giving life to The Hurst, Bristol Lodge rewarded them most generously during the decade between 1981 and 1991.

The day I arrived, Tom met me at the front door and showed me up to the study, where Catherine was standing in the middle of the room. At the time I had read *Our Kate* and a handful of the early novels – *Kate Hannigan*, *The Fifteen Streets*, *Maggie Rowan* – and I was in the middle of *Katie Mulholland*. I had spoken with Catherine on the phone and we had corresponded, but I carried with me only a sense of her early life, of the girl from Leam Lane, and among all the interior splendour of Bristol Lodge it was this phrase that occurred to me as Catherine came towards me with her hand outstretched. Indeed, she hadn't changed. I said something about the beauty of the house, but as we sat down to talk she straightaway steered me back to the kitchen in number 10. 'Why I am sitting here today talking to you is thanks to our kitchen there,' she said. 'There have been other things bred in me and they are the niceties, but the rawness of life came from that kitchen. That's why I am able to write about the rawness of life, though there was in me, inherent, this other side, something that led me to a place like this, to a room like downstairs [she was referring to the magnificent drawing room]. And this other side of me sort of levelled off the raw experiences of when I was young. If I had just kept that side I don't know what would have happened, I may not have been a writer. It was the other side that pushed me out of that environment, that said that this is no place for you; get out of it. And yet it's always the early environment that sticks with you until you're a very old woman. But there it was, that is the hub, the kitchen . . . You see, I believe everybody is a result of their environment and no matter what was in me, what was passed on to me, it was the environment that set me on and made me what I am today. Without that kitchen you wouldn't be sitting there and I wouldn't be talking to you.'

In 1986, the South Shields Museum would open a unique replica of the William Black Street kitchen. It was a £50,000 project overseen by Catherine to ensure its authenticity. Leading visitors to the cutaway view of the kitchen was a bricks-and-mortar realisation of William Black Street and a reproduction of Cissie Affleck's corner shop on Phillipson Street. Now, in 2006, the display has been transformed in a £1-million refurbishment, part financed by the Catherine Cookson Trust, which explores the history of the locality during the time of her life.

The move to Bristol Lodge in inspirational but inaccessible Langley did not diminish the demands on her time. The more she hid herself away, the more in demand she became, and on many occasions she was happy to become involved. Before she and Tom were living full time at Bristol Lodge, in October 1981, she was asked to open a £500,000 housing project for the elderly at Simonside, close to where she had been born, and she took the opportunity to re-enact an episode of her youth which rang particularly true to her as a moral lesson in the midst of all the commercial elements attached to her life and work. She recalled the original episode as follows:

'There must have been little money in the house and Kate sent me to the pork butchers in Jarrow. It was a halfpenny tram drive and she put a shilling into my hand and told me I was to get six pennyworth of bones and three pennyworth of trotters and scramchums from bits of odds and ends of crackling, odd pieces of fat. I know that the shop sold penny dips. This was a bun with a piece of pork cracklet in it. But she didn't go in for such luxuries. I remember it was snowing and the shop was full and on this day there seemed to be a lot of commotion. I was standing near the end of the counter waiting my turn to push up to give in my order. My feet were cold and I was stamping them against the sawdust on the floor. I happened to glance down between my legs around me and saw a piece of paper sticking out. I picked up and saw that it was a ten-shilling note. Then I realised what the commotion was about further along the counter. People were looking among the sawdust, scraping their feet and a woman was crying that she'd had it, she'd had it! 'Twas then I realised that they were looking for a ten-shilling note that she had dropped. I recall that it was very dirty and crumpled because it had been trodden on and nobody had noticed that I'd picked anything up. They were all looking towards the commotion. I pushed my way through the throng and held out the now straightened but still crumpled ten-shilling note and said, 'Are you looking for this, Miss?' The commotion stopped, the woman turned to me, grabbed the money out of my hand and glared at me, then handed it over the counter and picked up her purchases and was gone. I can't recall any comment being made on what I had done, but when I got back home I put my bag on the table and said to Kate, 'I found a ten-shilling note on the butcher's floor.' I can see her now. She stopped dead in what she was doing, put her hand to her head, then made a sign of the cross and she said, 'Thanks be to God.' She held out her hand and I said, 'Well, I gave it back to the woman.' At this she just stared at me, stared and stared. Then she suddenly sat down and all I recall is that she bent her head.'

As helpless as Catherine had felt then in the matter of her mother's poverty, now she felt the need to make amends by giving every one of the state-registered residents of the Simonside home a £5 note – a symbolic gesture, but indicative of a resolution to do good by her success. A year earlier she had donated £12,800 for the purchase of equipment at the infant intensive care unit at Newcastle's General Hospital. In 1982 she gave a further £40,000 to expand the unit, and in 1983 she gave the hospital £20,000 for an ultrasonic surgical aspirator for removing tumours in the spine and brain. These were but a few of the charitable donations amounting to millions over the following years, and which she kept as silent about as she could. Her agent Anthony Sheil once questioned her about a well-thumbed, inches-thick notebook on her desk: 'I came across a notebook on the table and I think it might have been open and I said what was this and it was quite a fat notebook, page after page after page of institutions and charities and individuals to whom she had given money and went on giving money, and it really was a many-paged notebook.'

Around this time also began Catherine's extraordinarily generous gifts to medicine. She donated money to Princess Mary Hospital for research into premature birth. At her friend Dr Anderson's suggestion she funded a new Chair in Haematology at the Newcastle University Medical School, rather than fund research into her particular disease, telangiectasia. During these years of her great success, Catherine donated a vast proportion of her earnings – millions – to educational and medical establishments, as well as to all kinds of people she would encourage. She had an indifference towards money for its own sake – 'I don't think about figures,' she said. Money did not change her one iota. Tom and she looked forward only to their weekends, free of business when they could be alone, as once they always were.

In November 1983 she collaborated with Melvyn Bragg's *South Bank Show* on TV to dismantle the notion that she was a writer of romances. An eight-year-old girl, Gina Scott, was discovered by producer Jack Bond to play her in flashback scenes as a child in East Jarrow. But Catherine did not like the edited programme and felt no serious purpose had been achieved.

Another attempt to broaden and deepen the spectrum of her appeal also faltered. Composer Eric Boswell first approached Catherine in 1982 with an idea for a musical based on *Katie Mulholland*. In March 1983 he took his music to producer John Blackmore to bring it to fruition. But the script Blackmore produced with Ken Hill, director of production at the Tyne Wear Theatre Company, did not meet with Catherine's approval. He had not even read Catherine's novel. Eventually she passed a second draft, and the production went ahead, its twenty-eight performances in the 12,500-seat theatre a sell-out. Coachloads of Cookson fans travelled miles to see it. But it did not achieve critical success, which is what Catherine so very much needed, and there was to be no national tour or season in London's West End. The verdict was that without her name attached to it, the show would have been a flop.

Catherine was materially successful, but now, more than anything, she wanted to be taken seriously. In 1985 there would be another attempt by the Tyne Wear Theatre Company to adapt one of her novels. This time it was *The Gambling Man* and the script a play. It took a record 3,000 unsolicited advance bookings, and opened at the Newcastle Playhouse on 5 September, but again it was only a local success.

Then I approached Catherine to become part of a series about writers inspired by the spirit of the place and people of their upbringing. *Catherine Cookson Country* was to be the third in a series of books that included *Thomas Hardy's England* (introduced by John Fowles) and *Dickens' London* (introduced by Peter Ackroyd). She leapt at the chance, immediately seeing the benefits of an association with such literary giants. The project coincided with the announcement by South Tyneside Council of a plan to launch a worldwide Catherine Cookson Country promotion of the real-life backdrop to her life and works.

Catherine Cookson Country became a bestseller, and was later published by Headline as *My Land of the North*, but what brought Catherine honours was the sheer generosity with which she continued to pursue her charitable work. In 1984, her Charitable Trust sent cheques to 120 charities. With more public ceremony she laid the foundation stone for a sports centre for the disabled at Hexham General Hospital and launched a £140,000 appeal with a donation of £2,500, she gave £5,500 to South Shields General Hospital (the old Harton Workhouse, where she had worked) for maternity equipment. The following year she launched the Catherine Cookson Foundation with a gift to Newcastle University of £250,000, she bought a laser to treat internal bleeding for the Newcastle Royal Victoria Infirmary costing £40,000 and handed over a further £50,000 for equipment to diagnose and treat deaf children.

In 1983 she received an honorary MA from Newcastle University and a D.Litt. from Sunderland University, which thrilled her particularly. Then, in May 1985, she received a letter from Buckingham Palace asking whether she would accept an honour from the Queen in the upcoming birthday honours list. Investiture day, 7 October 1985, found her in bed at Newcastle's Royal Infirmary. She was too ill to receive her OBE at Buckingham Palace and it was not until 6 February the following year, that His Royal Highness the Prince of Wales met Catherine on Tyneside and personally bestowed the honour upon her.

Then, exactly eighty years after she had been born illegitimately in the humble, two-roomed apartment at 5 Leam Lane, Tyne Dock, Catherine's success was measured in a triumphant celebration. On 20 June 1986, her eightieth birthday, Catherine's UK publishers – William Heinemann (hardcover),

Corgi (paperback) and Book Club Associates – 'saluted,' as the official invitation read, 'Catherine Cookson OBE – Britain's most-read author' at the Ramblers Country House Restaurant in Corbridge, Northumberland.

The party also coincided with first publication of *Catherine Cookson Country*, a copy of which was presented to each guest. The invitation carried two Royal crests signifying Catherine's longevity – her birth in the reign of Edward VII and her eightieth birthday in that of Elizabeth II.

It was a swish affair. The Ramblers was anything but an ordinary restaurant. It had hosted parties for Catherine since at least as early as 1979, a lunch given on that occasion by Book Club Associates, Catherine's book club reprint publishers, who sold millions of her books.

Catherine and Tom counted the 132 guests as their friends. Many were associated with her work, but that was her life, and she specifically asked for no bigwigs from the city to be present. The party took the place over, guests arriving from all over the country at the tiny local railway station.

A marquee had been erected behind the restaurant and guests met with a line stretching from the front of the building through various ante-rooms to a position taken up by Tom and Catherine, who was wearing a cream dress, buttoned to the neck and with a bow in her hair. They greeted everyone, shaking hands with them one by one and taking time to share a personal word, while TV cameras whirred alongside.

It was, from the start, a happy as well as an extravagant affair. There were fourteen tables, tastefully clothed, thirteen of them circular and one long high table, at which Catherine, Tom, her publishers and agent sat, dominating the scene against one wall of the marquee. Off to one side stood a stage, on which played 'a distinguished octet' of oboes, clarinets, bassoons and horns from the Northern Sinfonia.

Champagne flowed, and a superb menu was served. The choice included king prawns with a delicate cucumber and wine mousse, followed by soup – carrot and coriander or wine and morello cherry (the wine a Macon Lugny A.C. Les Charmes 1984) – then 'whole prime fillet of beef baked in a puff pastry shell', served with Cote de Beaune Village Burgundy A.C. 1983.

All the courses were described on the menu in German. Guests were eating not Beef Wellington but *Gebackenes Rindsfillet in der Kruste*, the reason being, as Anthony Sheil recalled, 'It was a German-Swiss restaurant. She was mad keen on it.' The owners of The Ramblers, I discovered, were German-Swiss Heinie and Jennifer Herrmann, which may possibly explain why Catherine's hardcover editor, John Foster-White, who Catherine had insisted should continue editing her books after the move from Macdonalds to Heinemann, had failed to engineer the inclusion of Nesselrobe Pudding on the menu. The name of the dish had been included by Catherine in *Tilly Trotter*, and John had queried it, scribbling: 'I wonder just what a nesselrobe pudding is? Ee, the things you do know about!' To which Catherine had responded in pencil alongside: 'Ya wouldn't believe it, lad! It's an iced pudding made with chestnuts, sugar, cream, eggs, citron, currants, raisins, and a bit more than marron glace. Try it!' Foster-White subsequently found a more detailed recipe in *Kettner's Book of the Table* (1877), where it was called Nessel*rode* Pudding, having been created, 'by Mony, cook to the famous Count Nesselrode,' a Russian diplomat. Interestingly, John did not correct Catherine's spelling of the dish, and his efforts to get it on the menu at the Ramblers came to nought. Instead, a choice was laid before us of *Ananas mit Erdbeeren und Kirsch* (fresh pineapple and strawberries with Kirsch) and *Weinbrandkorbschen* (brandysnap basket filled with brandy cream and orange). The cheese board, black coffee with fresh cream, and chocolate mints completed the feast (in English).

Afterwards, Catherine spoke for twenty minutes, giving her audience a taste of what so many groups of her fans had enjoyed since the 1950s, when she began her trademark talks up and down the country. All of it delivered without notes. Her guests met, in particular, the three most important men in her life, her granda John McMullen, 'who had the power to put the fear of God into most people, even when he was sober,' but with whom Catherine had met in a very special place – in opposition to the rest of the inhabitants of the New Buildings; her tutor in life, Lord Chesterfield, who had taught her 'to write plainly'; and, finally, Tom Cookson, who 'has given me his life in order that I have the time to write'.

The event was covered on national television, but what the media missed was the secret shenanigans going on 'under the table'. Paying due homage to his biggest-selling author, at the top table sat Charles Pick, Chairman of Heinemann, Catherine's principal London publisher, and his managing director, Brian

Perman. Meanwhile, on her other side sat Paul Scherer, supremo at the mighty Bantam UK, which he was busy launching as the new hardcover imprint of Catherine's paperback publisher, Corgi. Alongside him sat Corgi editor, Alan Earney, and Catherine's agent, Anthony Sheil. Unbeknown to Pick and Perman, Sheil and Scherer were cooking up a bid to take away from Heinemann the right to publish her future books in hardcover, for Scherer had this powerful hardcover imprint in Bantam Books, hungry for her work.

I asked Sheil whether the deal had already been struck before the meal. 'Would Charles Pick have been sitting there beaming if it had?' he wondered. Given that Catherine was the biggest-selling author in the country at the time, this was serious business. It would impact significantly on the profit line of both publishers. Millions of pounds were at stake. The contract would be for ten new novels. Catherine may have been eighty, but Scherer had already seen ten unpublished novels sitting in her cupboard at home in Bristol Lodge.

Just four months later, after Heinemann had been given the chance to match Bantam's terms and the negotiations had been completed by Sheil, a deal was announced, its justification the improved marketing effort that could be engaged by one publisher responsible for both hardcover and paperback publishing. Heinemann were the losers. Bantam UK would be transformed by the contract, which was worth an initial £4 million to Catherine.

The mathematical logic that had won Bantam the deal was that they had their own paperback company. In those days, a hardback publisher would sell paperback reprint rights to an outside paperback publisher, and take his profit on the deal in the shape of a percentage of the author's paperback royalties. With an in-house paperback company, Bantam could pay 100 per cent of the paperback royalties to the author and still make his money on the publishing profit margin on the paperback editions. Realisation of the accountancy effect of what became known as 'vertical publishing' saw a number of big-selling authors change publishers. Heinemann were in a difficult position. They had an interest in a paperback company, Pan Books, but were not sole owners, so they didn't have the advantage Bantam had.

Bantam had another advantage in Paul Scherer, who as head of Corgi was already in touch with Catherine on a regular basis.

As Sheil noted, 'Paul certainly did work on Catherine. He did shamelessly work on her! And successfully! It was his job, of course. Bantam hardbacks was a new thing at this stage. They were looking for authors they could publish in this way.

'Catherine then went on to have some very very big contracts with Bantam. I know that I was getting, towards the end, something like a million and a quarter a book, which was stupendously big in those days, especially if you are doing two books a year and selling American rights separately. She was at a very, very high level. We sold American rights separately to Jim Silberman and later to Simon and Schuster, who stayed with her until the end.' Scherer was delighted to have all Catherine's UK publishing to himself.

Catherine was amazed by what had been done. Her publishers she saw as family. Suddenly half of them had dropped away. Later she was recorded by a local paper as saying: 'I don't think anyone is worth that sort of money. I'd write if I wasn't paid a penny.' But I remember our discussing the high level of royalty advances that first-time novelists were receiving for the so-called 'bodice-ripper romances', so popular in Britain and America in those days. She couldn't understand why she hadn't yet achieved those levels. As Anthony Sheil said, 'I don't know that she was really all that embarrassed. I think she thought these huge sums were a mark of respect for her position.'

Certainly, the beneficiaries were not complaining. Newcastle University benefited again financially at Catherine's hand when she brought the value of her Foundation to more than £1 million with an eightieth-birthday gift of £160,000. In December 1987 a seven-storey campus building was named after her, where the lectureship in molecular haematology, which she had funded, would be based. Here, in the Catherine Cookson building, Dr Peter Middleton would undertake research into the bleeding disease hereditary haemorrhagic telangiectasia, from which Catherine had suffered since eighteen years of age. The hope was that it would lead to screening for and ultimately to prevention of the disease. Catherine also gave £100,000 to the university's Hatton Gallery for the conservation of rare books.

In the late 1980s the awards continued to flood in when it became known just how successful Catherine had become. In 1988 she was included in the annual Women of Achievement Awards for the second time in six years, on this occasion alongside Prime Minister Margaret Thatcher. A year later the Royal Horticultural Society named a carnation after her. This was not a first. Five years earlier, a retired miner called George Davison successfully engineered a hybrid tea rose after seven years of trials and approached Catherine Cookson with the idea of naming it after her. Catherine agreed provided a percentage of the profits was given to charity. The rose, with light-pink blooms, strong fragrance and between twenty-six and forty petals in large, double-bloom form, repeat flowers later in the season.

Also in 1988, Rob Bettinson succeeded where others had failed when he took a stage production of *The Fifteen Streets* to London. It enjoyed a five-month run at the Playhouse Theatre. Bettinson then went on to write the first of eighteen films based on Catherine's novels that were produced for TV by Ray Marshall in just twelve years between 1989 and 2001. The film of *The Fifteen Streets* launched the careers of Sean Bean and Jane Horrocks and attracted an audience of more than ten million. Other actors, such as Robson Green (*The Gambling Man*) and Catherine Zeta-Jones (*The Cinder Path*) would also benefit from similar exposure in the early days of their careers. *The Wingless Bird* was Catherine's favourite TV adaptation of her work. The idea was seeded in Anthony Sheil's office when Marshall, who had been charged with the job of finding a programme of films for TV for World Wide International Television, caught sight of a display of Cookson titles and asked Sheil about her. A meeting was arranged with Catherine at Bristol Lodge, and Marshall also looked in at Tyne Tees Television in Newcastle and found Geraint Davies as enthusiastic as he about the idea of a TV film. Shooting of *The Fifteen Streets* began in April 1989 and it was transmitted in August. It was followed, in 1991, by *The Black Velvet Gown*, which won an Emmy for Best TV Drama.

From the start, Marshall's films used only North-East locations, and getting the environment right, he believes, was a key to their success. 'Shooting the dramas in the North East gives them a sense of place. Trying to create the atmosphere and the period detail is a challenge.' Such had been the changes in the North-East over the past decade, however, that it wasn't easy to find the cobbled terraced street he needed for his first film. In the end Richardson Street in Newcastle was chosen. One of the biggest filmic challenges came with *The Moth* which called for a major fire scene in which a country house is nearly gutted.

Eshott Hall in Northumberland was used. 'It was so realistic that the owner looked really worried!' Marshall recalled.

Success and honours undreamt of in the wildest imaginings of her ambitious nature had come to Catherine in a flood since her return to the North in 1976, but there was increasing illness, too, which threatened her living in the wilds of Langley. Bristol Lodge was thirty miles from Newcastle, where her consultant, Hugo Marshall, lived. 'It meant that I had longer distances to travel when I bled,' Catherine said. 'It was nothing for Tom to have to drive me to Hugo's private house four times a week when I'd be bleeding like a stuck pig. Then, two years before we left Bristol Lodge, I had long spells in bed.'

The bleeding disease weakened her and brought back bleak reminders of her breakdown. 'As I have said before, you never get rid of a breakdown. Well, come this day [in 1989], I was in a very, very low state. The bleedings had been bad, I had flu, and cystitis had affected my kidneys. I was taken into hospital for a time and there it was found that I was also bleeding from the stomach. Topping all this, I had what is now called M.E. This could affect me, really paralyse me, for an hour or two, when I would be unable to speak or move. I realised this state was ripe for a return of the breakdown and it came . . . the aggression . . . I couldn't walk down to the bathroom. I had to be practically lifted from the bed to the commode. And I knew now that my mind was in such a state that I couldn't fight it with my slogan "I can and I will". I would have to have help. I could not confide this to Tom. He was worried enough. But I knew that I must go away and have mental treatment. I knew this would distress him above measure, because when I went into hospital he always came with me. He would take a room so that he could be near me all the time. But on this sad day my mind became clear in a way, and I planned what I would do. On the morrow, which was the day my doctor visited me and we chatted for an hour or two (we had become friends), I would tell him to make arrangements to have a treatment. I was no longer able to right all these ills, both mental and physical.

'It was as I lay there, thinking this, that a voice from somewhere said, "Get up." I took no notice. A still small voice that speaks to me very loudly at times. Still it went on, until I cried at it, "I can't get up, you know I can hardly stand." I have written about this in *Plainer Still*, but I think it is worth telling again. The voice now said, "Put your feet out of bed." I took no notice. Again it came, "Put your feet out of bed. Sit up on the edge." Slowly I obeyed. But when the following order came, "Go into the sitting room and look at the television," I cried out at it, "Stop this! Stop this! I could never walk to the sitting room. I'm ill!"

' "Go to the sitting room and look at the television."

'I found myself staggering down a long room. When Tom opened the door, in amazement he cried, "What on earth are you doing?" And I said to him, "Take me into the sitting room to the television." Blindly he obeyed me.

'*The Railway Children* was on. I didn't mind them, but I rarely looked at television. It disturbs me. What followed next I don't remember. I only know that Tom knelt by my side, gripping my hand, and I sat dumb, really dumb, not uttering one word, not even when he said, "I'll go and make a cup of coffee, eh?"

'I was left alone and there came on to the screen the Sunday-evening religious programme. It was showing the inside of Buckfast Abbey. There were the great pillars the monks had built years ago. Tom and I had visited the Abbey . . . The camera now was moving slowly down the aisle towards the stained-glass window, which got bigger and bigger until the whole picture filled the screen with the face of Christ. It wasn't a nice face, because you can't make a nice face out of stained glass. But there it was, staring at me. What I did next I have no explanation for because, remember, I had thrown off the Catholic Church and all its man-made dogmas and doctrines. I had no belief whatever in God. Faith was the last thing I thought of. Then what prompted me to thrust out my hand until it covered his face and I cried aloud two words, "Help me"?

'Now, there's no way that I or anyone else can describe what happened because it was so swift, swifter than a flash of lightning . . . There's no way to describe it, but I only know that in that unknown instant of time I was filled with a peace that only St Paul's words can bring down to earth, "the peace that passeth all understanding". I was enveloped in it. It filled every pore in my body. In all my life I had never experienced anything like it, nor even hoped to. I turned my head and saw Tom standing at the drawing room door; his face was alight and what he said astounded me even more. "Oh," he cried, "I felt it!"

'Then Tom came up to me and held me. I said to him, "I believe in him, not in the doctrines or the religious jargon, but I believe in the man Jesus." Tom held me close. My face was wet.

So was his. I sat on in a state of wonder. There was not a fear left in me. There was not a worry left in me. There was a calmness in me that it is impossible to describe, a wonderful, wonderful peace. I had been born out of trouble. The only solace that had been given to me was the love of Tom and his help. No one else's. And now he was sharing my peace. That it was to be tested within a matter of hours I wasn't aware. I only knew that if I could live in this state for the rest of my life, all that I had gone through had been well compensated.

'It was four o'clock in the morning when I started to bleed – what I call one of my stinkers. You could hold a full pack of tissues to my nose and within minutes they would be sodden. Such was the case. Tom went through his usual routine. I would have to be got into Newcastle and to my consultant's. He rang, then dashed round seeing to the security, seeing to the dog, my beloved friend, dressing me in what I call my bloody coat because it had been sodden so much with blood over the years, wrapping around my shoulders and head a big woollen shawl. Then he went out to get the car. He got as far as the door and came back saying, "I can't see a finger before me, fog, it's as thick as ice."

'I said, "It'll be all right."

'He said, "Can't you understand, the fog, I can't see anything."

'Again I said, "It'll be all right." I wasn't worried in the least. Nothing could worry or touch me any more.

'When Tom saw that I might bleed to death he groped his way to the garage and got the car out. I have described the journey in other places. It usually took a full three-quarters of an hour from our house to the specialist's home, that is, in the night when there is very little traffic. But this journey, what with the fog, the ice and the hold-up at the entrance to Newcastle, took us nearly three hours, by which time my specialist was at work in the hospital.

'I was still calm, still at peace, but he couldn't stop the bleeding. He had to plug it temporarily before I was taken to the theatre. When I have a cauterisation or a plugging I can't have any anaesthetic, so I have to put up with it and very often it is sheer hell. This time wasn't any different, but what did it matter?'

Telling me this, Catherine was at pains to make me understand not only her exquisite feeling of peace, but precisely that this extraordinary experience had not led her back to the Church: 'I do not believe in the tenets of the Catholic Church or any other sect or religion. You understand me? I believe in him, the man, the thinker, the healer, the man who recognised the great spirit that was in him, and used it, used it to the extent of dying for his principles. He needn't have died on the cross, because he knew what that meant – the death penalty, crucifixion – and there were rows of victims hanging from trees along the road. He knew what he was doing, he was carrying out what he believed in. And so he will help me from now on. But he only. No false gods.

'I look upon him as a man born of a woman under the same circumstances as I was born, and he was a man who knew at the beginning he possessed a spiritual urge, and he used it. He was a healer, there have been many since. He was a deep thinker and knew humanity in and out, and he talked to the ignorant so that they could understand: he made his truth into stories, what are called parables. Above all, he was a magnetic character. He drew people to him. He drew the twelve followers to him. There have been many such since. There have been men in history for whom a friend or a person would die, give their last breath, follow them to the ends of the earth. Some people are born with this magnetism. And above all this man was a rebel. And as such he died for his own opinions. That is what I admire about him. And in my childhood every Good Friday, about three o'clock, I used to cry about him. Well, whatever he had is in more or less degrees in all of us. It is a spirit, and if I believe in nothing else I believe in that, or it, or whatever you would like to call it – this power that can sometimes create what you can term a miracle.

'I did not return home from hospital until two days later. I was still in the after-effect state, but I felt I must tell someone, and who but my dear friend, Father Tom Power. I have a number of friends who are priests. One is dear Father Tom of Haydon Bridge. Poor Tom, he did his best to get me back [to Catholicism], until I had to emphasise that he was flogging a dead horse. Twice he has written to the Pope about me, and the Pope has signed plaques, one for my eightieth birthday and one for my ninetieth. But Tom maintained that I was more with God and more religious than anyone he knew.

'Well, I told Father Tom. Was he ecstatic? He said he knew that God would work his way in the end. But it was from this time that the peace faded, and you can say that I returned to ordinary humanity, but with a difference. I have with me now the knowledge of a spirit, a great spirit belonging to perhaps the greatest man who ever lived. This great healer, this man who understood human nature so well, and, so that his wisdom would reach the minds of the fearful and the ignorant, he turned it into parables.'

The ferrying of Catherine from Bristol Lodge to Newcastle and back again became such a frequent occurrence that it was clear something had to be done. May 1990 saw her fighting for her life in hospital, having suffered a severe heart attack. Tom was by her bed of course. Catherine said that her heart specialist told her that the only reason she survived was that she was a cantankerous old woman. Admitting to the cantankerous but not to the old she was back in Bristol Lodge in time to celebrate her golden wedding anniversary in June. That was followed by her eighty-fourth birthday and in July she began writing once more. The strain proved too much. In August she suffered a second coronary.

Again she would recover, but she must have known that it was a deteriorating picture. Even as she achieved stability in her heart, her bleeding disease worsened and in February 1991 she was back in hospital. 'It couldn't go on. My specialist advised that I must get into the city or somewhere near him and the hospital. It was either I die there [in Langley] or get attention to my bleeding. So in we came. Five and a half years ago, my specialist's wife, Ann, found us a lovely little house in Jesmond, so secluded in the centre of the city that no one would believe that it wasn't in the depths of the country. It broke my heart to have to assent to a sale. Most of the beautiful things I had collected since 1930 had to go. But as Tom said, they would be of little use to us if I was dead.

'I wouldn't buy this house till I'd seen it, so one day they carted me here from the hospital, and the poor woman who lived there couldn't believe it when three times I asked for a bowl and vomited blood. I tried not to spoil her carpets, but she had been a midwife and she understood.

'As soon as I walked in I saw it was open plan and knew what I wanted done. Inside there were, altogether, only eight rooms and I realised I would only be able to get one-third of my furniture, the good pieces, in. The kitchen had to be gutted, and there was no en-suite bedroom. There was, however, a garage big enough for four cars.'

Catherine drew up a plan and acted swiftly. 'Eighteen Geordies worked for a fortnight, close on three weeks – "Wor Kate" is what they called me – and I had the garage cut into two and one part turned into a utility room. Outside, where they kept the dustbins and the oil tank and coal-houses, I had another room built on . . . So now here we are in this transformed, beautiful little house.'

Chapter Eleven

White Lodge

When Tom and Catherine arrived in leafy Jesmond, *The Black Velvet Gown* was the number one TV drama, her novel, *My Beloved Son*, was the number one novel, and incredibly there were still twenty-three more novels yet to be published. In 1993, Catherine was made a Dame of the British Empire for her writing and her charity work. It was the ultimate accolade for the girl from Leam Lane, and when she received the news she fell into Tom's arms and they both cried.

Even as she reaped the rewards of her determined ambition, however, in her personal life there still raged undimmed the pyrotechnics of her restless psyche – battles that would never be won, their effects felt in the strange savagery of her fiction and by one in his quieter suffering, her husband Tom, who had come to believe that he was born to the task of supporting his beloved wife in her endless struggles.

Cousin Sarah, who, after Catherine and Tom returned to the North in 1976, typed all her manuscripts and acted as her secretary, realised long ago how devoted he was to her, but how controlling this made her of him, and it was doing him no good. 'Tom nearly left once,' she told me. 'I was upstairs in the office in Bristol Lodge and Kitty was downstairs in the bedroom with Tom. I heard this rumbling going on, but you couldn't make out what was happening between them. And when I went down she said, "Did you hear what was going on?" I said, "No," and she said, "He's got his case out, you know." I said, "His case, whatever for?" She said, "He wants a divorce." He had a real up-and-downer with her. Whatever it was about I don't know, but whatever happened between them in their life, Tom was always the one who had to say sorry. He always had to go and kneel by her bed.'

I think that we have seen that Catherine was not made to be happy. Because of her breakdown, she saw too far into things. She knew firsthand things about herself that most people never face. Her hate and aggression emanated from deep inside, mostly when she was awake in the small hours speaking her novels into the Grundig Dictator. 'I'm a nasty individual,' Catherine laughed in interview with Granada TV towards the end of her life. 'Really horrible in some parts of me. Because we have always got our thoughts, you know, we have always got our deeper instincts, and mine come out at two o'clock in the morning when I am lying here awake, and thinking.'

In *My Beloved Son* (1991) a mother veers maniacally between deep smothering love and chilling violence towards her son: 'As I opened the door I saw her take her hand and swipe the lad across the room . . . but then she got down on her knees and started to howl over him.' Similarly *The Maltese Angel* (1992) opens savagely with evidence of terrible brutality, the chaining and whipping of a young boy. The charge of womanly cruelty seems to spring from self-hate, and it is almost impossible not to think of Catherine and Tom when reading about Fanny's relationship with her husband Ward Gibson, whose love is 'overpowering. Her returning love, measured against it, was as something minute; and she knew it wasn't good or healthy to be held in such high esteem and made to feel she was incapable of any mean thought or action. To be put on such a plane caused her to feel less than human. However, she knew she could never make her husband understand this, for he saw her as being apart from all others.'

Some of the novels were a channel to drain the hate, 'the aggression, deep aggression, against my early suffering, against my mother . . .' but time and again they returned Catherine to the source of her problems – both *The Gillyvors* (1990) and *The House of Women* (1992) examine what it meant to her to be an illegitimate child. It was a loop out of which Catherine could not escape. As she put it, it is 'a treadmill that we are on. The only thing I get satisfaction from is the urgent desire to write and write. I see my brain as an old machine that requires daily oiling and the only way I can keep it going is to oil it with words.'

But it was also true that Catherine's sense of humour raised her emotional repertoire to heroic levels, as Sarah, who never liked the aggressive hate in the novels and told Catherine so, is quick to point out. Once, Sarah protested about having to type up a character in *The Parson's Daughter* (1987), who was too raw for her taste: 'I couldn't take the horrific parts she put in her books. There was one part when this character, the gentry bloke, who I hated, he took this girl down . . . and Catherine *knew* what I would think and said, "What do you think of him?" and I said, "He is terrible!" And she killed him off! Then she said, "What did you think of that?" I said I was delighted. And she said, "Have you no compassion?" You had to laugh; I said, "Not a bit." '

But then, suddenly, something from outside would get confused and caught up with some complex element that so completely absorbed her psyche, and her aggression would pour out onto the scene. People had begun to have to watch very carefully what they said in her company. 'I used to ring her every week' recalled Foster Barker, 'and I had to write things down that I mustn't say, because if I let slip, bang! She'd be at me! She used to get inside you. She loved to have a hold over people, and if you ever went against anything then she could be threatening.' Foster then told me a story about a son of theirs, which is vintage Cookson material; anyone who knew her well would recognise Catherine's part in it immediately. 'I've got ten grandchildren, she always used to send them money – birthdays, Christmas – except to my son Ross's children. Then one time in Jesmond she said to me, 'I'll never forgive Ross.' Now, years earlier Ross had jilted a girl. It wasn't an altar situation, he had a long-term relationship with a girl and he had packed her in. But she broke her heart, this girl. Catherine said, "I know what it's like to feel jilted." She was talking about this love affair when she was jilted [Jim Dailey]. So I just turned round and said, "Aren't you pleased that you were jilted, otherwise you would never have met the marvellous man that you married?" And she went very quiet. And I came back to Hastings the following day and she actually apologised – I'd never known that before. She said she was sorry and she put a cheque in the post for £500 to Ross for the two children because she had never sent his children any money.'

To Catherine, Ross's jilting of his girlfriend *was* Jim Dailey's jilting of her fifty years earlier. At no point in the story did she change her mind about that. The change of heart came because Foster allowed her the indulgence of believing that, but guided her along a new line of consequences flowing *from* believing it. Had he said that likening Ross's action to Dailey's was preposterous, different circumstances, etc., there would not have been a happy ending.

The problem that people had with Catherine was avoiding being caught on one of those negative hooks, and, once caught, making the fatal mistake of trying to shake free. She knew about these hooks and wrote about them in 1995 in *Plainer Still* (after the 1988 memoir, *Let Me Make Myself Plain*), admitting that however hard she tried she couldn't help seeing the negative side of things. Foster helped her along positive lines in this instance, and his grandchildren reaped the reward.

Her formidable, testing nature made relationships into a tricky but potentially rewarding game of 'Diplomacy', in which there was the possibility of ambush or reward around every corner. For cousin Sarah, who was the only family member other than Tom to be directly involved in the minutiae of Catherine's professional life, the potential for getting caught on a negative hook was far greater.

On the professional level she met Catherine's expectations for seventeen years. The work rate was extraordinary, answering fan letters and typing some thirty-five manuscripts at least twice: the first draft plus the one that followed Tom's editing; more when a mistake occasioned the re-typing of a page, for there were no word processors in those days and Tippex wasn't allowed because of the carbon copies required. Things could get fraught. 'When she was ill once,' Sarah told me, 'she was going into hospital and she asked me to look for a manuscript upstairs. When she went into hospital all the work went in, you know, all the post. I couldn't find this manuscript anywhere and I came down and she really went to town on me, and I came out of the bedroom and I started to cry, and Tom said, "Don't take any notice of her." I knew she was ill but she didn't have to be so nasty. [My husband] Jack went to the hospital with the car to bring Tom back and Tom came back with a message from Kitty, "Tell Sarah I am sorry."'

'That was something. She never forgave. Twice she apologised to me. That time from hospital, and before she died we had an up-and-downer and she rang me up and said, "I would like to thank you for all the love you have given me over the years." Now that was an admission!'

Catherine said she envied Sarah's peace of mind, but there was one – a namesake – who recognised Catherine's brokenness as the very source of her achievement. For years Catherine corresponded with an American nun, Sister Catherine of the Dominican Sisters of Mission San José in California. In a letter to Tom, written after our Catherine died, she spelled out what she thought her namesake's purpose was: 'She was willing to share her brokenness with the world and as a result became a giant, cosmic fountain from which all others could drink . . . Catherine nourished and strengthened hundreds of thousands of people and gave them courage and purpose just by announcing who she was. This is, in actuality, the only purpose for our existence. If we do not connect with others and affirm them in their struggles, we miss the whole point.'

Catherine received thousands of letters each year claiming an affinity with her, feeling her pain as if it were their own. Others, among them Catherine's publishing associates, locked onto a quite different persona. On a professional level there was no room for weakness. I worked with Catherine on five books. She was an absolute stickler, but that had to be a good thing. I remember an error cropping up in *Catherine Cookson Country*. Both she and I had missed it in the proofs, but when it appeared in the finished book her searing response took more than ninety minutes to deliver on the telephone. Some have complained in interview that she was demanding, but her agent Anthony Sheil said, 'My recollection of her was that she expected the highest possible performance, but not that she was unreasonable.' For Sarah, I believe it was different because she was family, and so was involved at emotional as well as professional levels.

In 1994, a fortnight after a trip with husband Jack, ironically to Lourdes, Sarah suffered a heart attack, and decided it was time to stop working for Catherine. Hugo Marshall's wife, Ann, took over. Ann Marshall is also a doctor, so there were obvious advantages in the arrangement now that Catherine was becoming weaker.

At White Lodge, Catherine had fast become bedridden and isolated from the outside world. 'Since we arrived here,' she told me in 1996, 'I have been out of the house on only three occasions, special events, other than to go to the hospital; and in the past three years not at all. I have only been out in the garden twice this year, and had to be carried out. But my corner, where the bedroom is, is really beautiful and likely I shall have to pass the rest of my days here.'

One who was with Catherine practically every weekday during this final period was the next-longest-serving member of Catherine's staff after cousin Sarah. Hannorah (known as Noreen) White worked for them as housekeeper for eighteen years altogether. 'They bought Bristol Lodge in Langley from Derek and Nancy Robb, and I came with the house. That was 1980, 1981. In 1991, when Catherine and Tom moved to White Lodge in Jesmond, I went with them. By then we lived at Fell End, a farm on the military road near Greenhead [near Carlisle in Cumbria]. It was forty-six miles one way to Jesmond, from my door to her door.

'I was driving nearly 100 miles every day, often in bad weather. I'm not great in snowy weather, and there were some days I didn't get there, but they were few. My position was housekeeper, which involved normal, general cleaning, cooking meals for them, shopping, washing, and quite a lot of confidential stuff they used to tell me. I felt they trusted me. As Mrs Cookson became more ill in later life, I was looking after her more than after the house in a way. I was at her beck and call, but not in a nasty sense. When she was mostly in bed, I used to sit by the bed and just have a chat about things and massage her feet sometimes. Stuff like that, you know. Just having someone she could talk to would help.'

I asked Noreen about the bleeding disease that had brought Catherine back to Newcastle, to be near her consultant, Hugo Marshall. 'You'd just be having a laugh, you know, and she would suddenly spurt this blood, and it was like all hands on deck, panic! The doctor would come and he would plug it or cauterise it. You could hear her making a noise that was obviously painful. And Mr Cookson would be outside screwing his face up and wishing it was him not her. It was quite frightening at times, with the volume of blood that come out. You couldn't believe a person had that much sometimes.

'She was still recording her books more or less right to the end. She had a lot of charity work, which she kept going, and all the letters she had to answer. Mr Cookson used to read the letters to her in the morning, and she would tell him what she wanted written in reply, and he would write them down. Then Ann [Hugo's wife] would do them up. Then, when it got to when Mr Cookson wasn't well, Ann used to write what the answers were.

'I enjoyed working for them, I had a lot of fun with them. She had a great sense of humour and we used to have a great laugh, me and Mrs Cookson, and Mr Cookson too, because Mr Cookson was from Grays in Essex, and I was from London, from Bethnal Green, and we moved to Dagenham when we were kids, so I kind of knew Grays and that, so we had something in common.'

Then, about two years before Catherine died, a new employee, Patricia Madin, came in because by then Catherine was having twenty-four-hour nursing care and she needed somebody to do the evening meal. Patricia would arrive about two o'clock in the afternoon when Noreen left, and by all accounts came to regard herself more as Catherine's friend than her employee. This didn't seem to bother Noreen, who saw her only briefly each day, when she handed over to her, but clearly there was no love lost between the woman and Tom. 'I don't think there was any mutual feeling towards each other,' was the way Noreen put it.

Towards the end, Sarah and Jack had again been away in France, this time visiting family. 'When we returned, we heard that Kitty had been asking Noreen when we were coming back. We were going to leave our visit to the afternoon, but Kitty wanted us to come "now". I am sure she thought she didn't have long. She wanted to see me before she died. Tom took me in to where she was lying in that conservatory room. Tom was standing there, and of course she couldn't see me [by this time Catherine was blind]. Tom said, "It is Sarah and Jack." It wasn't a long time with her,' said Sarah, 'and of course she was bent right over by then. I expect we went into the kitchen and talked to Ann and Noreen. Tom was very fragile. It was two days afterwards when Kitty died.'

Visiting Catherine in bed in 1994, in this self-same 'conservatory room' (it had french windows that opened out to the garden), her vision already limited to sight of shapes, it was her strength of will that struck me, and this continued to the end. Nothing could keep her down. When her spirit was low, her WP as she called it – her will power – came into play. In 1996, as we worked on the first edition of *The Girl From Leam Lane*, she was completing her latest novel, *The Silent Lady*, and she continued to record tape after tape for me during this period.

Often she would make these tapes early in the morning, her most creative time, and sometimes I could hear the venom with which she still held her past. Each tape delivered not only answers to my questions, but a symphony of feelings ranging over the near century of her life. The final tape was long in the making. Catherine had been very ill, she hadn't even the strength to pick up the microphone. Yet when it came through, that resolving note of humour which rings out and triumphs over suffering in so many of her best works, can be heard right through it: 'It has been some days since I have talked to you... It is six o'clock in the morning. I have been awake for the past two hours, as usual thinking back, and I ask, Piers, why are some people born to fight? It's been a tough life. But the last stage has been more than trying. In 1977 and 1978 my timekeeper played up five times and the only way I won, my heart specialist said, was because I was a cantankerous old woman. I admitted to the cantankerous, oh yes! – but not to the old. Anyway, it's at it again, not only threatening to go on strike, but it's got its associates in all my other departments to back it up, and they will unless I raise their wages by giving them two pints of blood every two or three weeks. And so I am faced with an ultimatum. But I've still got one ace up my sleeve, and that's my WP, so we'll only have to wait and see who wins . . .

'Well, there goes the buzzer, and this is the end of these reels of rigmarole, and I doubt that you'll get a lot out of them. But nevertheless I hope you'll learn more about this old girl.'

Dame Catherine passed away peacefully at her home in Jesmond, Newcastle, on Thursday 11 June 1998, eight months after first publication of my biography and just nine days before her ninety-second birthday. Tom was with her, holding her hand. Always Tom was there when Catherine needed him; his devotion was absolute.

Immediately the news broke, the media circus began and Ann Marshall, her closest aide, was swamped with condolences and, of course, birthday cards from those who hadn't heard. It was a testing time. Tributes were legion. Catherine had been an inspiration to many – actors, writers, friends and readers.

In *The Girl From Leam Lane* she had been so frank that on sending her the manuscript I was worried less about mistakes than that she would want to backtrack or tone down some parts of it. But she didn't. 'I think it is splendid,' she wrote to me in March 1997, 'and Tom cannot speak too highly of it,' adding more darkly, 'He has made remarks here and there. There are one or two points I may want to discuss with you later.' Remembering the ticking-off I received over an error in *Catherine Cookson Country*, and preparing my defence like a guilty schoolboy, I anticipated that these 'points' might have to do with my cutting a sliver more deeply under the skin than she had expected, as when marking her out as capable of all that even her cruellest characters do. I was wrong. She had enjoyed the analysis.

Now she was gone and there would be no more banter over the phone, which she loved so well. Had it been possible, I know what would have been on the agenda. Before her death she had been given the last rites, even though only two years previously she had told her dear friend Father Tom Power that he 'was flogging a dead horse' trying to save her soul. Her life-long battle with the Roman Catholic Church had been about its dogma, which she felt concealed rather than revealed the naked truth. I believe that this arch-storyteller, understanding the manner in which her own stories dispensed truths about the human condition – we spoke about this a lot – found a way to accept the Christian story as a vehicle, its purpose to awaken a response to the truths that inspired it. From this position, intellectually, it was but a short passage to accepting her anointment as the symbolic affirmation of these truths, the challenge of which she had long met. Given the ferocity of her own struggle to arrest truth it would be a harsh judge who saw her acceptance of the last rites as an example of the hypocrisies she had spent a lifetime rejecting.

The sequence of events was as follows. Catherine died on Thursday 11 June 1998. Her funeral was held on Tuesday 16 June. Tom was admitted to hospital on Tuesday 23 June. Tom died on Sunday 28 June.

Dr Brantingham, Catherine and Tom's GP, had been called to Catherine's bedside on 11 June and realising immediately that the end was near had made her as comfortable as possible and turned his attention to Tom. He told me, 'Tom had been in hospital with heart problems, and I had delayed going on holiday because I suspected that he would take Catherine's death badly.'

'When she died,' said Sarah, 'Ann rang me, and we went over to see what we could do. It was then that Tom said to me, "Would you help me?" I said, "Yes what can we do? Would you like us to stay?" And he said, "Yes," and we stayed eleven days. Jack went back for our things. After Catherine's death Tom was eating and kept up very well. We got in touch with Edna, his sister.'

'I was with my sister-in-law in Fern Dale in Wales,' Edna told me. 'I spoke to Tom on the phone and said, "Do you want me to come?" He said, "No." So I said, "I'll come up after I get home." He said, "All right." ' Usually we were in touch only at Christmas. I was sorry that we hadn't been in touch. My husband, Bill, didn't want to seem scrounging. It was one of those things. Bill had died in June 1996.'

A close friend of Tom told me that in the period leading up to Catherine's funeral, he had not seemed unwell, but one can imagine his state of mind. It was the first time for many decades that Catherine and Tom had been apart. Catherine's funeral followed on the Tuesday and was deliberately low key and private. Afterwards, Tom sat in Catherine's chair and welcomed a small circle of friends.

On more than one occasion, Catherine had said to me that she hoped Tom would go first because she knew that when one of them died, the other would follow and she wanted to spare Tom those few, painful, intervening days. I took this as a statement of their devotion to one another rather than as a prediction, although Tom himself had been quoted as saying, 'Life without Kitty would be no life at all,' which was why one journalist asked me if his death less than two weeks after Catherine's funeral had been suicide. It was not. But Catherine's death did bring with it a new responsibility for Tom.

Prior to the funeral, Hugo Marshall, her consultant for the previous twenty-five years, took Tom out for a haircut. Apparently the gardener usually cut his hair. I can easily imagine Catherine insisting on it: he keeps the grass well enough, why shouldn't he cut Tom's hair? It was the first time for many a year that Tom had left the house, other than to go to hospital, and the trip, which also included choosing and ordering flowers, was a poignant reminder of how isolated from the world both he and Catherine had become.

When Tom came to pay he discovered that he had no money. Neither he nor Catherine carried any; they had no need to, they never went out. Money simply didn't figure in their lives, except as a happy opportunity to encourage others.

Like it or not, money was going to figure in Tom's life now, as people began to wonder what Catherine's will would reveal, who would get what. On account of her illness and demanding needs over many years, people were bound to wonder how the money would be apportioned. This was never something Catherine used to her advantage. Money was not power to her in that way. She knew about power and she knew about greed, she knew about everything that characterised the fictional people in her books. Human nature was an open book to her. But people's attitude to money was far less interesting or important to her than, say, their faithfulness to husband or wife.

Her generosity goes unquestioned. More than a million pounds would be left to her closest relations, friends, employees and business associates, but the will had yet to be read, and Catherine had been busy sponsoring projects almost up to her death, and some were nervous as to whether that sponsorship would continue. With this, Tom, in his saddest hour, now had to deal, and there is no doubt that he felt the stress of it. Catherine had always made the decisions about what and who to encourage with her money. Tom will not have been at ease taking that responsibility while devastated at the loss of his wife of nearly sixty years, nor should he have had to, given that Catherine's will was clear and had been drawn up and signed, except that most of Catherine's estate now passed to Tom, and with it the responsibility of managing it. In this unhappy situation, suddenly without Catherine, the woman he loved, and at the same time feeling vulnerable in the position, wholly new to him, of having to command Catherine's millions, Tom took ill.

Philip Brantingham agreed that there was a general expectation that after Catherine died, Tom would soon follow, but played down the effect on Tom of those jostling to secure the patronage of the estate, even if the emotional temperature was heightened by the supposed imminence of Tom's demise.

'The position was, *nobody gets access*,' he told me. 'Tom was closed off from visitors at that point.' I know this to be true, and that Dr Brantingham and Tom's solicitor ordered his isolation, but the policy was executed only after the problem first raised its head, when Tom would have suddenly seen what a responsibility had now fallen to him, and that he wanted none of it.

Tom will have wanted very few aspects of the life that he now saw unfolding for him. As Dr Brantingham said, 'He realised he had nothing to live for any more. Whatever Catherine did, he was always a foot behind her . . . He realised now he was on his own, and it wasn't for him. He became depressed. He just had nothing to live for.

'He managed well until after Catherine's funeral was over. It was then that I realised he had not come to terms with her death. He looked at the flowers, I remember, and said something like, "Someone has died." And I said, "Yes, Tom, and you know who that is, don't you?" And of course he did. He was just shutting it out of his mind.'

'I went in one morning,' said Sarah's husband, Jack, 'and he was just lying there. I asked him if he wanted a shave, and he said, "That would be nice." So, I got his electric shaver and shaved him. He went down and down after that.'

Meanwhile, Tom's sister, Edna, had returned from Wales to her home in Grays. She had then telephoned Tom. 'I said, could I come up? When I arrived, the doctor was waiting for me and Tom was already in bed. I hadn't known he was ill even. They said, "You've arrived just at the right time. He's not well. He's going to hospital. Would you go and stay with him." '

There was, however, time for a reunion between brother and sister, who hadn't seen each other for years. 'Edna and Tom were laughing and talking about old times and how they had missed twenty-odd years,' said Sarah. 'And we all thought, Oh he's going to have a new lease of life, do the things he wanted to do. Because they sounded so happy.' It was one of several moments after Catherine was gone when Tom nearly returned to himself. Earlier, an invitation by a friend, Alex Morris, to visit his home had been met with almost boyish enthusiasm.

But it was not to happen. The day after Edna arrived, on Tuesday 23 June, Tom was admitted to the Royal Victoria Infirmary in Newcastle. 'I was asked to go and stay at the hospital with him,' Edna recalled. 'I went up on the Monday, and he died on the Sunday morning. He gradually went down in the course of the week. He was coherent at the beginning. He was telling me about when he was in the RAF, how he had gone up for commissions, and Kitty managed to put the kibosh on it each time. She hadn't wanted him to fly. She hadn't wanted him to go anywhere else. I don't know how she did it, but some people could. It's been done. She managed to put a block on it each time. He didn't actually say he regretted it. But come the end of the week, no; I think he couldn't say anything.

'The first room they gave him was all right. I had a bed next door. Then they shifted him out. I'd been out and when I came back he wasn't there. "Oh," someone said, "he's down at the end." And he was on an airbed. He couldn't move, because every time he moved the whole bed collapsed on him. Well, I said, "That won't do." And then they shifted him further up and that wasn't a nice room at all. The corner was taken off with the bathroom, which he couldn't use.

'I was in the hospital all the time,' continued Edna, 'apart from when Hugo came and took me out. Hugo was wonderful with me. He eased me through the week when Tom was in hospital. Sarah and Jack took me back one afternoon with them, for tea, so that I could get out. No one else came to see him. I think they tried to keep people away.' No one, except, incredibly, one of the people Catherine had sponsored who found a way to him.

'I was with him when he died,' Edna told me. 'They called me. I was in the shower. A nurse came into the room and said, "Will you come as quickly as possible!" So I came out and got dressed and went up to him. I stayed there until he died. There were two nurses. They sat one side of him, one had her hand on his pulse and I was sat the other side. I said my goodbye. Hugo and Ann then took me back and I stayed with them. I think Sarah took me to the train next morning. I then went back up again for the funeral.'

Tom's funeral proved to be an enlightening experience. He had always refused to discuss his life before he met Catherine. Frantic sleuth work by Tom's friend Alex Morris and Canon Frank Dexter faced with the difficult task of delivering Tom's funeral address with precious little to go on, revealed some interesting facts hitherto unrecorded. At that time, we knew nothing beyond the fact that he was the son of a parish verger in Essex and had attended grammar school and Oxford University. I hadn't been aware that Tom's father had died early and that his mother had married again, this time to a plumber's mate.

Because of his Oxford education, I had, at that time, not fully appreciated that Tom, like Catherine, had come from a poor background. When they met, he was a man who had overleaped as enormous social barriers as she, but had none of the upstart pretensions that Catherine had in her rise, and which so primed her for breakdown. I had never before considered the impact of this successful but classless young man on Catherine. After meeting Tom, she had to face her true self in the mirror of her breakdown and the pseudo-lady was cast aside, she became free to be herself and write about her people. It seems likely that Tom was her educator in more than English grammar, therefore, and that the integrity of his aspirations, otherwise so similar to hers, lay at the bottom of Catherine's enervating dependence on him. At his funeral I was moved by fresh evidence of Tom's ability to get through to people as an educator. When Catherine died he received letters of condolence addressed to 'Dear Cookie' from pupils he had taught nearly half a century earlier.

Catherine and Tom's was an all-consuming relationship. They had friends and numerous acquaintances, they had publishers, agents and doctors by the score, but since their first meeting in 1936 until the end of it all, sixty-two years later, there was only really the two of them against the world – only 'thee and me', which was how Catherine described it in a poem read at the funeral.

Working with Catherine I had a glimpse into how mesmerisingly inspirational, how compelling and demanding she was. Her relationship with Tom may have deprived him of a 'normal' life, but on the plus side, life with Catherine was more electric than he can ever have imagined it could be. The point is that Tom revered (as strongly as Catherine did) the nature of what inspired her to create characters as diverse as Fanny McBride, Mary Walton, Mary Ann Shaughnessy, Anna Brigmore, Kate Makepeace, Alice Walton. He was always the champion of the projects I undertook with her because he understood that I was as fascinated as he about the nature of her inspiration.

'Do you know, really I am a frustrated actress,' she once said. Then, eighteen months before she died, when she was completing her final novel and I asked whether the actress in her was still working, she replied rather irritably, 'I *am* the part!' Her kind of acting was of the Method school. She became her characters wholeheartedly, the warm, humorous Fanny McBride, the spiritually true Mary Walton, the cheeky innocent Mary Ann Shaughnessy, the sensual, highly self-disciplined Anna Brigmore, the strange, wise, bewitched Kate Makepeace, the ruthless Alice Walton. Or rather, she didn't become them, she *was* them, each was a part of her. Tom helped Catherine bring all of these alive within her. No wonder she said he met her 'searches'.

Noreen expressed the feelings of many when she said: 'I am just pleased that they both went together, because whichever one went, I think the other would have been very lonely. They were truly devoted to each other, and it wasn't a show. It was a definite devotion. Many people might think, having seen them on the telly, that it was just for the cameras, but it wasn't, it was a true devotion.

'I have no idea where her ashes were finally placed. Tom was cremated as well, and they put the ashes together. Catherine wanted them to be scattered over Tyne Dock, so whether that was carried out I have no idea. That's as far as I know.' Nobody seems to know when or if or by whom their ashes were given to the winds at Tyne Dock. No ceremony was ever reported. It is perhaps the final mystery in the life of an enigmatic woman, which leaves no shrine or final resting place for people to visit.

The question of Catherine's future is in the hands of the Catherine Cookson Trust, whose trustees include Hugo Marshall. Catherine's and Tom's wills worked in such a way that whoever died first, the other would inherit all the deceased person's estate after any personal bequests had been paid. In the event, Catherine made thirty-four bequests in excess of one million pounds, including £250,000 to the Medical School of Newcastle University. Two trustees, John Ravenscroft and William O'Brien, from the Catherine Cookson Trust were appointed by Tom as executors of his will.

On 21 October 1998, following the disbursement of Catherine's will, the District Registrar valued Tom's Estate at £20,222,381 net. Out of that, Tom made two bequests, one (as Catherine had done) of £250,000 to the Medical School at Newcastle University, and the other of White Lodge to Hugo Marshall in a codicil signed by Tom and John Ravenscroft, and witnessed by Ravenscroft's wife, on 17 June 1998. The rest of the Estate was bequeathed to the Catherine Cookson Trust.

Substantially less than £20 million appeared in the Trust accounts, however: £15,070,928 was transferred from Tom's Estate in the 1999 accounts, with £2,542,086 showing as 'due', of which £570,778 only was transferred by 2001 and nothing since, up to 2004. The total transferred from Tom's Estate according to these accounts, which are in the public domain, is thus £4,580,675 less than the net valuation of the Estate by the District Registrar.

I am advised that as the two bequests account for a relatively small proportion of this, that inheritance tax would have been minimal (payable on the amount by which the combined value of Tom's personal chattels and house exceeded the inheritance tax threshold, which in June 1998 was £223,000), and that probate fees and expenses would not have been excessive either, one must assume some large fall in the value of Tom's assets between death and realisation, or extra liabilities overlooked when the probate papers were prepared, or a change in the direction of benefits, i.e. by a deed of Variation, away from the Charity. The Estate accounts, which would explain the dramatic shortfall, are of course private to the executors and trustees of the Catherine Cookson Trust as residuary beneficiary.

The Trust, which passed on the opportunity to comment on its work when I approached them, was set up by Catherine to support 'a wide range of activities including education and training, environment and conservation, arts and culture as well as general charitable purposes. The Trust's principal aim is to identify and meet the local needs of the area in which Dame Catherine was brought up and resided. In particular the Trust supports work with young or disadvantaged people.'

Charitable donations (grants) of between £250 and £100,000 are awarded annually. No grants are listed in the year ending April 1999. In 2000 the figure was £737,245, five to the maximum value of £100,000, two for £50,000 and 137 much smaller grants averaging around £1,000 each, many of a few hundred pounds. The Hastings Writers' Group got £250, which is nice, but mainly the grants are made in the North East. In more recent years, grants have been far less – £459,350 in 2003 and only £284,750 in 2004 – before a sudden increase in 2005 to £779,259, while the fund balance has increased, due to investment, incoming royalties, etc, to £20,167,207 in 2005.

Some of the Trust's larger grants have helped build the Newcastle-based Percy Hedley Sports Academy for disability sports, and the Beamish Museum's Regional Resource Centre, which houses thousands of North-East heritage items and a Collectors Study Room with industrial, agricultural and domestic collections. One of the most moving letters I received was from the Royal Grammar School in Newcastle, of which one of the Trust's trustees is an old boy. RGS Newcastle have so far received £105,000 for their quite amazing bursary campaign to give a privileged education to children from challenging backgrounds such as the notorious Hendon area of Sunderland. They have eighty-three pupils on bursaries, more than half of them on 95 per cent. One boy, who suffers from Asperger's Syndrome and has a 100 per cent bursary, just attained straight A stars at GCSE. As the headmaster said: 'The future of the North-East is going to depend on able people [such as these], and people like that are going to achieve here in a way, most unfortunately, they are most unlikely to do elsewhere.' Catherine would indeed have been proud to make this kind of difference.

Catherine's future as an author is also in the hands of the Trust. Royalties continue to trickle in from Festival Film & Television, who made her TV films, and her popularity in libraries, the traditional Cookson stronghold, remains high. As I said, from 1982–3 until four years after her death, Catherine's books were borrowed more frequently than any other author's, and her position in 2005 – seven years after her death – was fourth, after the children's author Jacqueline Wilson and the novelists Josephine Cox and Danielle Steel.

Income from royalties on book sales, the bedrock of the Cookson industry, is another story, however. Royalties to the Trust in 2000 were £836,970. In 2003 the figure was down to £531,101. In 2004, the figure was £671,883, a large part of which was due to an enterprising partwork based on Catherine's life, which came unbidden from a publisher who had already enjoyed success in the same way with Agatha Christie and shows the hidden potential of the Cookson portfolio, while the contribution from her mainstream UK publisher, ultimately responsible for keeping the 'brand name' visible, actually contributed less. In 2005, the Trust accounts show a mere £170,258 royalties received.

It is not easy to maintain the momentum of so large an oeuvre as Catherine's, particularly as there are no new novels to galvanise the market, her agent has changed, her long-term editors have died, and there are few people, if anyone, left in the publishing business who have actually read her works, which means that strategies for reissue and exploitation in publishing and other media tend not to be built along editorial lines. Catherine wrote many different sorts of fiction – humorous, historical, violent, psychological, romantic, fantasy, autobiographical, regional, some adult, some for children – which, now that there are no new titles to help publicise her as a 'brand', would benefit from very individual marketing approaches.

Most damaging of all is that less than good new novels, published after Catherine's death, now block up the publishing system and bog down her publishers in a mire of hefty unearned advances. The temptation, after she died, was to publish anything as yet unpublished. A stream of novels that had been consigned to her attic as less good suddenly appeared in the bookshops, with the result that one reader wrote accusing her publishers of finding someone else to write under Catherine's name to continue the literary dynasty. This was not the case.

If Catherine Cookson is to live on into the future there will have to be a fresh start, a concerted effort to manage the portfolio with insight into what is there and with imagination as to how and in what form to bring it to the attention of a twenty-first-century public.

Index